F.M. HALFORD

AND THE

DRY-FLY REVOLUTION

F.M. HALFORD
AND THE
DRY-FLY REVOLUTION

TONY HAYTER

ROBERT HALE · LONDON

First published in Great Britain 2002

ISBN 0 7090 6762 3
ISBN 0 7090 6773 9 (*leather edition*)

Robert Hale Limited
Clerkenwell House
Clerkenwell Green
London EC1R 0HT

A catalogue record for this book is available from the British Library

2 4 6 8 10 9 7 5 3 1

Set in Sabon by
Derek Doyle & Associates, Liverpool.
Printed in Great Britain by
St Edmundsbury Press Ltd, Bury St Edmunds
and bound by
Woolnough Bookbinding Limited, Irthlingborough

Contents

FOR

Φ

Acknowledgements

Writing a book of this sort would not have been possible without the assistance, advice and encouragement of a number of people and institutions. First of all, I gratefully acknowledge the kind help of John Halford, and the access he gave me to the papers and documents of his great grandfather. Without the use of this valuable primary source, the project would not have been worth doing at all, for it provided the structure upon which everything else depended.

My thanks are also due to the staffs of the British Library and its newspaper branch at Colindale, the Public Record Office, the National Army Museum, the Principal Probate Office, the Record Offices of Hampshire and Wiltshire, the City of Westminster Archives Centre, the Brighton Local Studies Library, the Winchester Registry Office, University College School, the National Museum of Photography, Film and Television at Bradford, and the Family History Centre; to Meryl Beament and Raya McGeorge of the Fishmongers' Hall, Simon Ball, David Beazley, Heather Birch, Richard Bland of Clifton College, Geoffrey Bucknall, Fred Buller, Kenneth Callahan, Robin Calvert, Peter Calvocoressi, Anna Charin of *The Jewish Chronicle*, Brian Clarke, David Coke-Steel, Ralph Collins, Tom Corrie, Andrew Crookstone, William Daniel, John Drewett, Suzanne Eward, Beverly Fairey, John Francis, Nick Giles, Michael Gray of the Fox-Talbot Museum of Photography at Lacock, Judith Gregory, Marian Griggs, Christina Grindon, James Hardy, Peter Hayes, Ray Hill, Simon Houfe, David Howard, Arthur Humbert, Martin Kendall, Ruth Kitchen, John Knott, David Le Cren, George Lehmann, David and Gina Livermore, Christopher Lloyd, Nan Mantle, Patricia Marston-Walker, Jim Merritt of

Princeton, John Morgan and Tim Boycott of the Fly Fishers' Club, Cath Pettyfer and Christine Humphrey of the Fly Fishers' Classic Library, John Pury-Cust, Charles Rangeley-Wilson, Mrs Stuart Rose (Dodo), Gerald Sanctuary, Valerie Sanders, Jenny Tanfield, Bernard Venables, Simon Ward, Glynne Wickham, Helen Werly, Renée Wilson, Jonathan Young, Marcella Bingley and all at *The Field*. Finally my gratitude is due to my wife, who has done some of the photography and provided some secretarial help as well as constant encouragement, and who has endured without complaint the frequent and unsolicited intrusion of Halfordian topics into domestic conversation.

I also acknowledge permission to reproduce material from *The Field*, *The Fishing Gazette*, and *The Journal of The Fly Fishers' Club*, and from C.F. Walker (ed), *The Angling Letters of G.E.M. Skues* (1956) published by A. & C. Black, and from P.M. Smythe, *The Diary of an All-Round Angler* (1956) published by Faber and Faber.

Author's Note

To avoid confusion, I have had to find a method to distinguish between the two Houghton Clubs. What is generally known as the Houghton Club was formed in 1822 and has had a continuous existence to the present day. The Houghton Club to which Halford belonged, and which in *An Angler's Autobiography* he calls 'our Houghton Club', was quite different; it began in 1875 and lasted until 1892. There was no connection between the two clubs, and for this period of nearly two decades Halford's club fished the lower or Houghton water after the older club had lost control of it. I have referred to the first (or original) club as the Houghton Club, and to the second as the Houghton Fly Fishing Club.

Throughout the book (except within some quotations) artificial flies have capitals, e.g. Blue Winged Olive, and natural flies take lower case, e.g. pale watery dun.

I have not attempted to burden the book with footnote references, which would have been numerous, after the manner of an academic work. In fact most of the quotations come from *The Field* and *The Fishing Gazette*.

Illustrations

Between pages 96 and 97

Colour

Between pages 192 and 193

Black & white

Credits

John Halford: 1, 10, 11, 16. Philippa Hayter: 2, 3, 4, 5, 12, 13, 14, 15. Charles Rangeley-Wilson: 6, 7, 8, 9. Geoffrey Bucknall: 17. David Beazley: 19, 29. Philippa Hayter & Heather Birch: 18. David & Gina Livermore: 20. Kenneth Robson: 23, 24, 25, 36. John Halford: 21, 26, 27, 35, 37. Patricia Marston-Walker: 22. Robin Calvert: 28. Christopher Lloyd: 30, 31, 32, 33a&b. John Morgan: 34.

Introduction

In the last quarter of the nineteenth century a great and radical change took place in fly-fishing in the south of England. In former times the interesting developments had for the most part been associated with areas further north and with Scotland. Chalk-stream fishing seemed to have little to offer that was interesting. In 1854 'Hampshire Fisherman' (Richard Clarke Sewell) wrote in *The Field*: 'There is very little *new* to be said on the subject of fly fishing.' In fact the dry-fly method was just beginning to be practised in 1854, and the pronouncement of 'Hampshire Fisherman' was soon to become strikingly inappropriate, for, after some years of incubation, the new technique leapt forward in such a dramatic way as to justify the word revolution. It was to take about thirty years to run its course. By 1900 the dry-fly revolution was accomplished, and its dynamic began to run down a little. But in those thirty years great alterations had taken place in the technology of tackle, in the dressing of flies and in the scientific study of their natural counterparts. Men who were old enough to remember looked back to the primitive notions and practices of the 1860s with wry amusement. Side by side with these material advances had arisen an entirely new method of attacking chalk-stream trout with floating flies. It was to spread to many other parts of the globe, where, as a general rule, it was practised in a rather more relaxed and pragmatic fashion. But on the chalk streams the new rules of engagement congealed into a curious pattern that was to last for decades (traces of it still exist in the twenty-first century). A new vocabulary of terms came into being to describe this code and its devotees, many with a theological flavour, such as cult, rite, sacred mystery, ritual, creed, prophet or disciple. In many cases these terms were not intended to be complimentary.

Nothing quite so odd had ever occurred in the world of fishing before.

The man who presided over this revolution, and to a great extent decided its direction, was F.M. Halford (1844–1914). He came to the River Test in 1877, and was therefore a comparative newcomer to the scene. Subsequent writers have pointed out that Halford did not exactly invent the new method of fishing. Signs of the revolution were already noticeable, and the technology that made it possible was maturing. Also, at least two other anglers were to play an important part in the process of change; to be fair, Halford always acknowledged as much. He may not have made the system, but he certainly marketed it very effectively. The angling world regarded him as the authority, but this was because it was, after all, he who had taken the trouble to write the books.

Halford's great achievement mainly resides in the effect of his first two books: *Floating Flies and How to Dress Them* (1886) and *Dry-Fly Fishing in Theory and Practice* (1889). On the basis of these alone he is entitled to be regarded as one of those important figures who change the way men think (in the opinion of G.E.M. Skues, he would be a great man if he had written nothing else). However the legacy he left was not of unmixed benefit. On the one hand, he had played a crucial part in angling history as a teacher, and by demonstrating how fly-fishing could be made much more interesting. What before had been local and haphazard had been systematized. But there was a drawback to this. By 1900 many anglers in the south were coming to feel that what should be a liberating movement had in fact become oppressive and dictatorial. They were being told that the dry fly was more than just another technique: it was the *only* technique. Nothing else worked in Hampshire, and certainly not the sunk fly.

Part of the explanation lies in the millenarian nature of the dry-fly movement. It was so new and intoxicating that Halford and his followers rather lost their sense of proportion over it, and treated it as having banished all former practice. Also, he had somehow succeeded in investing the whole business with a daunting air of mystery and difficulty. Perhaps he did not intend this. His habit was to follow each branch of the subject through ever increasing complexity, and his powerful, if somewhat myopic, intellect revelled in points of detail. He could have admitted to his public that much of that detail was for him a pleasure and an entertainment, and was not strictly necessary for the business of catching fish. But he never gave that reassurance, and the result has been to frighten generations of beginners. Many writers since Halford, such as Ray Bergman (1932), Terence Horsley (1944), T.A. Powell (1947), and W.F.R. Reynolds (1947), have tried to put this right, bidding newcomers to be of good cheer and not take alarm: they are not required to pass an examination in the Linnaean classification of all water-born flies, or to be able to put a fly on the proverbial sixpence at fifteen yards, or to know the ultimate secrets of the onion dye.

Halford's own career as a writer and law-giver is a good example of the rise and fall of reputations. For most of his life his stock stood very high indeed. William Senior wrote in 1903: 'The Halford series [of books] embodies all that can be told at present of the mysteries of fly-fishing.' And John Waller Hills wrote in his last book in 1936: 'No fisherman of this age can realize the effect that Halford's books had upon our generation.' But a new theory will often follow a predictable path: at first there is a rocketing rise in general opinion; then follows a period of acceptance, as if that theory had become part of natural law; then an eroding decline until it has been supplanted and cast into the lumber room of history. In the 1920s Halford's reputation began to falter, partly at least due to the writings of the other great authority on chalk-stream fishing, G.E.M. Skues. In the period after the Second World War his great services to angling seemed to have been forgotten. Once influential, he was now yesterday's man. Much of his doctrine had by then been absorbed into the general practice on chalk-streams, and it was easy to ignore the fact that it had once been novel and audacious. The only thing that seemed to remain in the general mind was his Canute-like stand against the use of the sunk fly. Open season was now declared on Halford, and he was extensively misrepresented and cried down in books and journals. C.F. Walker referred in 1960 to 'the fashionable pastime of denigrating Halford'.

The reprinting of some of his works in the 1970s gave a new generation a chance to make a fairer assessment. In 1989 *Dry-Fly Fishing in Theory and Practice* was reissued, with a sympathetic introduction by Dermot Wilson, who pointed out how relevant was much of Halford's advice one hundred years after it had been given. The chance of a balanced judgement now seems within reach. Writing this book is my attempt to seek one.

1 Early Days

The man known to generations of anglers as F.M. Halford, the High Priest of the Dry Fly, was born Frederic Michael Hyam on 13 April 1844, at Spring Hill, Birmingham. It was to be many years before he changed his name to Halford. The Hyams were a Jewish family, originally from Germany. For the most influential writer on fly fishing of his time it was perhaps a slightly unusual background.

At this date the Jewish community was fairly small (in 1831 there were only 30,000 Jews in Britain). In the latter part of the century much larger migrations took place as a result of persecutions in eastern Europe, and large numbers of unfortunate and often extremely poor people moved westwards in search of safety; between 1881 and 1914 150,000 came to Britain alone. But the Hyams, like the Montefiores, the Goldsmids, the Franklins and other well-known families, had arrived much earlier. By the time Frederic was born the family's wealth and status in England was assured, and it had attained the sort of position where the term 'dynasty' becomes appropriate.

The Hyams' success story in manufacture and commerce, like those of many other Anglo-Jewish families, was one of boldness, tenacity, and excellent business acumen. The founder of the family in England, Simon or Simcha Hyam (also known as Simon Ipswich) was born in Hamburg about 1740 and came to Ipswich about 1790. His son Hyam Hyam, married Hannah, the daughter of Moses Lazarus of Rochford, who had come originally from Worms in the Rhineland. From these two families derived a spreading network of descendants, all more or less successful in the world. At Ipswich, and later at Colchester, the Hyams built up a considerable manufacturing and distributing business in clothes, giving employment to increasing numbers of people. The local population must have realized the economic importance of the family, for the customary market day in Ipswich was changed from Saturday for their convenience – for that date a rather surprising mark of respect.

The family business, or rather businesses, began to move forward at a great rate in the 1830s and 1840s as the Hyams perceived the new market trend towards ready-made clothes. At the beginning of the nineteenth century such clothes were almost non-existent, apart from slop clothes for the poor. By 1860, though, bespoke garment-making had declined considerably, and 60% of people in Britain were wearing ready-made clothing; by the end of the century ready-made and convenient garments were a commonplace of life. The Hyams and their commercial rivals the Moses family were the leaders in this process.

The children of Hyam Hyam went off to found their own business empires, and as a boy Frederic would have become aware that the name of Hyam was widely known in Victorian Britain and throughout the empire. Benjamin Hyam ruled in Manchester, creating mass tailoring there. The firm of L. Hyam, founded by Lawrence Hyam – probably the largest, employing 8,000 people – had eleven branches in leading provincial cities, and advertised themselves as 'the best, the cheapest and most extensive Clothiers in the world'. From their shop in Gracechurch Street in the City, known as the 'Mart for the Million', poured forth a torrent of shirts and other ready-made clothes. Samuel Hyam, Frederic's father (1813–1891), set up business in Birmingham in 1836, when he was in his early twenties, and married in 1838. A few years later he moved to Leeds, then came to London when Frederic was still a young boy, and opened a large shop in Oxford Street to sell the produce of his Leeds works. By this date the Hyam dynasty were employing many thousands of people in their factories, crouched for long hours over Singer sewing-machines adapted to run from steam engines. Many more people were involved beyond the factory gates, for clothes often had to be finished by the 'putting-out' system, whereby agents of the firms went round the neighbourhood dropping off garments (a few at a time only, lest some desperate outworker might abscond with stock) and collecting them a few days later. If the Hyams got into difficulties, then it is clear that large numbers of dependent people would do so too. But – apart from temporary troubles, such as the cotton famine during the American Civil War – the story was one of expansion. The secret of their success was the well-tried formula of large production, fast turnover and competitively low margins.

In time (although this is to anticipate), Frederic became a director and shareholder in the same trade, and made enough money from it to be able to retire in 1889 at the comparatively early age of forty-five and spend the rest of his life sorting out fly-fishing problems. In later life he was always inclined to be a little reticent about his career in commerce. His friends at the Fly Fishers' Club knew that he had an office in Cannon Street; most of them probably thought he was a financier of some sort, and he may have preferred it that way. In the first place, there was a prejudice against 'being in trade' in Victorian England, and this was particularly strong among the gentry and leisured class, with which, as a leading fly-fisherman, he consorted. This prejudice seems to us now a historical curiosity, and an excellent example of Victorian hypocrisy: commerce after all was one of the factors responsible for building up the national prosperity and extending British influence abroad. But there was also another, and older, notion: that of the gentleman – chivalrous, perhaps of ancient lineage, magnanimous, and more likely to follow field sports and the outdoor life than intellectual pursuits, despising what was perceived as the grabbing and grubbing after money of a latter-day commercial age. Those with a military background, in particular, were likely to feel uneasy with bourgeois entrepreneurs on the way up. There have been many examples in the last three centuries of families who have risen through trade, only to withdraw from the counting house to acquire a country estate and perhaps a coat of arms. After another generation such families would have taken on the attributes of an entirely different class culture, and often preferred to forget the origin of their new status.

Frederic may also have had a more particular reason for being sensitive about the Hyam connection. The clothes trade was always likely to be suspected of sweating its workers, and in the mid-nineteenth century it had come under considerable scrutiny. Thomas Hood's famous poem 'The Song of the Shirt' (1843) played its part, with its doleful refrain 'Stitch! Stitch! Stitch! In poverty, hunger, and dirt', and shortly afterwards, in the year of Frederic's birth, the Chartist paper *The Northern Star* attacked his grandfather's firm for the treatment of its tailors in Colchester, 'who eke out a miserable subsistence at slop work for the "respectable" Messrs Hyam & Co.' A few years later Charles Kingsley delivered a bitter attack on the trade in his tract 'Cheap Clothes and Nasty'. He was followed by the pioneer investigative journalist Henry Mayhew, whose letters in the *Morning Chronicle* in 1849–50, totalling a million words, on the desperate plight of the submerged classes of London aroused great public interest. In fact conditions in the clothing industry were hard for everyone, and the Hyam works were no worse than anywhere else. Pressure from philanthropists at this time was gradually gaining ground, and hours and conditions of work slowly improved, although the sweated-labour stigma stuck for decades.

For several years the young Frederic, the third of five children, lived with his parents Samuel and Phoebe (née Levy) in a substantial house in a semi-rural retreat not far from Birmingham. *An Angler's Autobiography* (1903) describes the attempts of the three elder children to fish in a pond in a nearby meadow, Frederic being at that time only six years old. As far as is known, for two of the three children this was merely a passing fancy, but the delight and enchantment of angling invaded the soul of the youngest and made a permanent conquest. Perhaps this lends support to the theory that the true angler is born so, and it is merely a question of time and occasion before the fact is found out.

When the family moved to London young Frederic's expeditions were to the Serpentine in Hyde Park, and, when he was a little older, to the Thames and elsewhere. But he had less time for these visits, for in 1851, at the tender age of seven, he started to attend University College School. He was fortunate in his school; UCS was something quite novel at that date, and refreshingly different from the rather alarming public schools of the time. Nowadays in Hampstead, in the 1850s it was adjacent to University College, famously described by Dr Arnold as the 'Godless institution on Gower Street'. Both the college and the school had been founded by Benthamite Utilitarians, and their plan for young people was a little different from the complacent norms of the time. Latin and Greek, it is true, were still thought important at the school, but Mathematics, English, French, German, Drawing, Chemistry and Physics were also in the curriculum. Most unusual of all, there was no corporal punishment. Neither was there any programme of religious teaching or worship in the school: matters of that sort, it was felt, were best left to parents. Indeed it would not have been an easy thing to manage, with such an interesting mix of Anglicans, Catholics, Jews, Baptists, Unitarians and other categories from middle-class families in London. This means that Frederic went to what was to present-day ideas a very modern sort of school, in strong contrast to G.E.M. Skues, his dialectical rival in angling history, who was at Winchester College in the 1870s.

In a kindly way, his parents encouraged him to take school seriously, and, in spite of his humorously self-deprecating remarks in the *Autobiography* he did well enough. As in many Jewish families there was an emphasis at home on scholastic progress, on music and on cultural development in general. For his mother's thirty-ninth birthday the young Frederic laboriously copied out the first thirty-nine stanzas of Tasso's *Jerusalem Liberated*, employing an artistic script, illuminating the capitals and having it professionally bound in green morocco (no doubt his father and the school drawing master were drawn into the scheme).

The only drawback to UCS was that the pupils had to leave at the age of sixteen. It was years before the school decided that, in order to compete with others for university places it had to create a sixth form. As Frederic was destined for the world of business, however, this was less important for him. On leaving school in 1860 he went into one of the Hyam businesses. Very little evidence survives of his life in commerce, but, from what we know of his personality in other contexts, his energy and his ability to focus powerfully on a subject must have been important. In his spare time he continued to fish on the Thames, and in the mid-1860s involved himself in the Volunteer movement, a popular thing with young men at the time. His school had been keen on the Volunteers and had started its own cadet force, and this may have encouraged his patriotic feelings. (The original stimulus to the movement had been the apparent threat of invasion posed by Napoleon III, who was enlarging his army after its successes in Italy in 1859, building coastal defences and constructing new warships of a power previously unknown.) Frederic became an officer in the 36th Middlesex Volunteers in February 1866, by which time the French scare was over. As they had to pay for their own equipment the officers tended to come from the more substantial part of the middle class. Much of Frederic's time must have been spent in the routine of the drill hall and the parade ground – volunteers were expected to do twenty-four drills a year – but he became adept at rifle shooting. The *Autobiography* refers in passing to this part of his life, but modestly refrains from mentioning the silver cup which he won in a shooting competition.

Fishing was, however, never far from his mind. When his *Autobiography* was published in 1903, many of his readers were astonished to learn what a varied angling career had been Halford's when he was a young man. The purist who appeared only to deal in the driest of dry flies had in fact passed through many of the stages of freshwater fishing – long-corking for bream and barbel on the Thames, paternostering for perch and spinning for pike. It was even more surprising to learn that he had done a good deal of sea fishing, and had persuaded the local experts at Eastbourne to fish from a boat with a rod and reel instead of the customary clumsy hand line. All this provided a different view of the austere and dedicated scientist of the chalk stream, and helped to make him more sympathetic and human to an angling public which by 1903 was rather in awe of him. Even his introduction into the world of the brown trout had been by way of spinning and live-baiting in the weir pools of the Thames.

For several years his constant attendant on the Thames had been George Rosewell, a professional fisherman on the reaches at Shepperton and Halliford, and it was Rosewell who moved him on to the trout and who provided that most useful of all services, watching the river for his patron. To have your 'man' on the spot was a great point, for a particular trout would have a feeding routine which could be learned. The sudden dramatic explosion of small fry into the air or the pursuit-wave on the surface right across the river would usually occur at much the same place and time each day, perhaps on the edge of darkness or at first light on a summer morning. Professionals were well paid to pass on this sort of information to their 'gentlemen' and to keep it from competitors. Thames trout were not caught in numbers, and there might be many days of fruitless pursuit, but each fish was a prize, especially if it was an eight-pounder or larger. Fish up to sixteen pounds had been known, and there were old stories of much bigger fish: a trout weighing twenty-two pounds was said to have been caught near Windsor in the 1830s. The Thames anglers were fascinated by these large fish-eating trout, and many dreamed of seeing a specimen on the wall handsomely mounted in a glass case by Cooper or Rowland Ward. Francis Francis, Angling Editor of *The Field*, caught the largest trout of his angling life, a fish of twelve pounds, in the weir pool at Hampton in 1850, and this portly fish, finely set up, still exists today – a trout whose perfect proportions could not be improved upon. The columns of *The Field* and from 1877 *The Fishing Gazette* would carry the latest reports about catches each season soon after April 1, and taxidermists braced themselves to receive the familiar parcels and notes of commission. Frederic caught several of these interesting fish in the late 1860s. At last in 1870, with Rosewell's expert advice and help, he secured a trout of 9lb 12oz, and therefore worthy to be dispatched to Cooper of Radnor Street in the City for the glass-case treatment. It was captured by the conventional Thames method used at that time (and indeed for a long time afterwards), with a dead bleak on a spinning flight. Even here his ingenuity and desire to improve on an existing practice can be noticed, for he added to the otherwise conventional flight three flying trebles in tandem tied in reverse. And it was one of these trebles that secured a fast hold on the trout. This fish also has survived, with the adapted flight beside it in the glass case.

It might be supposed that capturing such a fish would be enough to fire the angler to greater efforts in the weir pools. But this was Frederic's last Thames trout, and soon afterwards he ceased to fish the Thames at all. He retained feelings of gratitude and affection for the river and those men of slender means who lived from it, and for years after he had quitted the river he would remember to contribute towards the cost of the annual dinner of the Thames professionals. He was now moving into his next phase, that of fly-fishing, which for him had been steadily overhauling other forms of angling for several years, and which in the end was to occupy his entire attention.

In the season of 1868 a family friend made him free of a stretch of the River Wandle, one of the most prized fisheries near London. It is impossible to think without heartache of the tragic but inevitable fate of this lovely stream, long ago engulfed by Greater London's ever-spreading tide of bricks and mortar. Even in 1868 the capital was a vast sprawl of over three million people, but there were still a number of streams within easy reach. It was quite feasible to leave one's home or club in central London, take a cab, then a railway ticket, and alight soon afterwards at a station in one of the Home Counties, clamber into a trap waiting by arrangement and be carried off through a quiet rural landscape to a fair stream full of clear water. The bedlam of the town might be only ten miles away. Frederic could easily get to the Wandle by way of London Bridge Station: the journey would take about half an hour, and his first-class ticket would cost two shillings and threepence.

From its origin near Carshalton in Surrey, the stream ran down towards London through farm land, private parkland and several villages, which are now well within the urban envelope. The valley was a place of great beauty; Sir Humphrey Davy called it 'the best and clearest stream near London', and Ruskin wrote admiringly of it in *The Crown of Wild Olive*. Lord Nelson fished here: he is not recorded as having achieved much with a fishing rod, but the abiding charm of the valley, especially around Merton, was sometimes in his conversation during the wearisome blockade of the French fleet. Courtney Williams records that in the early part of the nineteenth century there were a number of small industrial concerns along the valley, including a copper works, a brewery, twelve calico works and several snuff mills and flour mills – in fact along the stream's course of less than eight miles there were forty-two different plants. But they seem to have been on a small scale, and the purity of the water remained unaffected until about 1880. There was mayfly here, and the rapid and prodigious growth of the Wandle trout was probably due to shrimp and snail. Large natural trout of two and three pounds were common in the first half of the nineteenth century: near Hackbridge an angler called Lemann captured three trout weighing sixteen pounds in one afternoon, and another, Charles Hudson (after whom a killing Wandle fly was named), caught four hundred brace of trout in a period of four months. The well-known Victorian angler Alfred Jardine – chiefly remembered for his exploits with pike – once had eighteen trout weighing thirty-two pounds in one day on the Wandle. Not surprisingly the riparian owners were fully aware that this was a rare and choice stream, and the fishing was not cheap: in 1857 Francis Francis wrote that 'the rents upon some parts of the Wandle almost amount to £1 a yard'.

Other streams near London have been similarly affected: the celebrated Cray; the Darenth, where Alfred Jardine once caught a trout of 6lb 8oz in the era before it was poisoned by paper works; even the

Ravensbourne, which Frederic tried one afternoon in the 1880s, only to find that its life as a trout stream was already over. Many London rivers have literally disappeared underground, like the Effra, the Tyburn and the Holbourne. We may dream of it, but we cannot any more catch trout in Lewisham, or fish the Fleet from Hampstead down through the meadows to King's Cross – or for that matter flush a woodcock at Marble Arch. All these experiences were common enough once. But for fishing the little Wandle was the best of them all.

Frederic began his fly-fishing career at the age of twenty-four with almost ludicrous disadvantages. He tells us in his autobiography that a friend who professed to know something of fly-fishing undertook to furnish him with the right equipment and accompany him on his visits to the river. It seems doubtful if the friend knew much more than he did. Together they provided themselves with a great deal of tackle, most of it unsuitable even by the standards of the 1860s (he was later to write in scathing terms of the know-all shop assistant who served the two young beginners). The rod was an invertebrate affair, the line was of plaited silk and horsehair and the flies were much too large. These items were discarded as his education progressed. The Wandle put him on his mettle, and at first there must have been some spectacular humiliations which he chose not to describe. Things improved when he got hold of one of the new lines of braided silk. This line, however imperfect it may have been compared to later ones, was an obvious advantage on the Wandle, where creeping and crawling and a quick accurate cast were all necessary. Henry Bohn wrote in 1861: 'No sport need be expected in the Wandle unless the fishing is fine in the extreme:- a single hair should be used for the foot length, or at least gut as fine as hair, and small blue and yellow-bodied duns.'

An interesting point about the Wandle in the 1860s was that the dry fly was widely practised. Flinging a team of wet flies downstream in a small clear stream would not have been very effective. By the middle of the nineteenth century dry-fly fishing was being practised in a more or less haphazard way in several parts of England, but it had been a local rather than a general development. The practice was still in its infancy, and the design of the flies, invariably tied to gut, was defective. When Halford and Marryat eventually came to the task of redesigning a whole range of dry flies there was a good deal for them to do.

The proto-dry flies available at this date may have left much to be desired in construction and floatability, but they were good enough to catch fish, and by using small patterns Frederic began to have some success. He never encountered any of the enormous fish mentioned in the Wandle annals, but the Halford family still has two fine trout in glass cases as evidence of his progress there. One was caught at Carshalton on May 20 1869, and its capture is described in the *Autobiography*. Frederic had long had an eye on this fish, which had taken up a position made impregnable by a bankside tree. He marked the offending branch with white paint, got leave of the owner to remove it in the winter, and was able to resume his debate with the trout on better terms the following spring. This extraordinary fish, although only fifteen inches long, was also fifteen and a half inches in girth, and weighed 3lb 2oz, and its plump form, lying in its eternal rest in a handsome Cooper case, is testimony to the rich feeding in the Wandle. Some weeks later Frederic captured another trout of the same weight but rather more conventional shape: seventeen inches in length. Trout caught here at this date were frequently well over the usual weight for length: twelve-inch Wandle fish were said frequently to have weighed 1lb 2oz. They were also excellent to eat, and had always been admired: as long ago as 1630 a writer called Folkingham wrote in *The Art of Survey* 'The Wandall Trout is held in high esteeme'.

Frederic continued to fish the Wandle for several years, and at one time rented a short stretch with five other anglers, paying five guineas a year for his rod, which, he wrote in 1898, 'in those days was considered rather a fancy price'. But all the time suburbia was advancing. His last day on the stream was at McRae's fishery at Mitcham in August 1881, by which time the writing on the wall was clear. In his booklet *Where to Fish Round London* (1880) Samuel Highley wrote ominously that it was little use now fishing the Wandle below Merton. William Senior complained in 1889 of numerous pollution incidents, and of the sad changes taking place in the neighbourhood, with historic houses and parks disappearing, railways and roads multiplying, and the antics of the modern builder, 'the gerrymandering fiend who runs up cockney villas supreme in their scamped workmanship'. The long-running case of *Selous* v. *The Wimbledon and Croydon Local Boards and Others* in 1884 and 1885, with its mountain of appalling evidence about crude sewage and noxious odours in the area, was not enough to delay the inevitable. Neither was the formation of the Wandle Fishery Protection Society, rather late in the day in 1890.

The Wandle experience was clearly a milestone in Frederic's life. Many anglers can look back to certain times when their education accelerates under a new stimulus and makes them in a short time into much better performers. His next challenge, which was to require another leap forward, was to be in Hampshire.

In the 1870s Frederic was still working hard and could get only odd fishing days, mainly on rivers near London. In 1873 he moved from his parents' home at 109 Westbourne Terrace to his own place at 62 Inverness Terrace near Lancaster Gate, within a short walk of Hyde Park. Other Hyam relatives lived near at hand: Lawrence in Leinster Gardens, Montagu in Kensington Gardens and his elder brother Arthur in Gloucester Gardens – all in solid, respectable upper-bourgeois districts, the London of the Forsytes rather than of the Pooters.

In 1872 Frederic married Florence, the only daughter of Samuel St Losky, and granddaughter of Kershel Shen Kolowsky, a rabbi; this family had originally come from Poland. Their son Ernest was born later the same year. On the marriage certificate Frederic Hyam is described as 'ship builder', an indication of the diversity of his business activities at this date. One of the witnesses was his wife's uncle, Samuel Montagu the banker, later Lord Swaythling, and once described as 'the fastest calculator in the City'. In 1877 Frederic, Florence and their young son moved from 62 to 35 Inverness Terrace, where they were to live until 1892. With them lived his mother-in-law, Hannah St Losky, until her death in 1883, and several servants.

The various businesses of the Hyam empire continued to flourish, and at first Frederic's share from the profits of the firm of M. Hyam were between £10,000 and £12,000 a year, even though he was by a long way the smallest shareholder. In the 1880s his income from this source rose considerably: in 1888, the last year before he left the business, it was nearly £22,000. In 1875 all the partners in the firm, including Frederic, changed their name to Halford. It is not clear why they did this. Name-changing was always fairly common in the Jewish community, but was usually done when the original names were somewhat outlandish or unpronounceable to English tongues, which was not the case here. He certainly was not about to repudiate his faith and his race. His private accounts show that he gave generously to Jewish charitable causes, such as hospitals, orphanages, schools and care for the elderly, following the ancient tradition of more fortunate Jews of giving generously to the poor and helpless. Later he served as honorary secretary to the Building Committee of the New West End Synagogue, and for five years was one of the treasurers of the United Synagogue.

In politics the Jews of Victorian Britain, like the Protestant nonconformists, tended towards Gladstonian liberalism, and Frederic was no exception. He supported the Marylebone Liberal Association and the National Liberal Club, and some years later his accounts show a subscription of two guineas towards a statue of Gladstone. I find no evidence that he ever encountered anything overt in the way of anti-Jewish prejudice. Anti-Semitism existed in an ugly and dangerous form in Russia at this date, and some years later it was virulent in France at the time of the Dreyfus Case. But England did not have the problem on this scale; if it was never entirely absent, it usually spent itself in hurtful remarks to individuals. The records of Frederic Halford's life show that he was unreservedly accepted into an angling fellowship composed of men from a quite different background.

It was in 1877, when he first began to fish the River Test at Houghton, that the next great change in Frederic's life was to take place. He was now on the eve of his chalk-stream career, and the new world he was about to enter needs to be examined in detail.

2 The Chalk-stream World

By the 1870s fishing and managing English chalk streams had developed a great deal since the beginning of the century, and much of the detail would be familiar to us today. There were far more anglers, rents were rising, and river-management techniques were improving. Changes were also taking place in tackle technology, and a new style built round the dry fly was emerging. This rapidly changing world upon which Halford was entering in 1877 contained much that was complex and difficult to learn. But he had an enormous appetite for learning. Years later William Senior was to apply one defining word for Halford and his way of doing things – he was *thorough*. Skimming would not do: he must plunge into the heart of a subject. Hampshire presented him with a challenge. His powerful and dogged intellect was brought to bear first on learning and catching up, then on recording and tabulating everything to do with chalk-stream fishing, then interpreting and imparting his findings to the world. Only after years of study and practice would he feel confident about making pronouncements. His first article of any length in *The Field* did not appear until 1885, nine years after his arrival at Houghton, and his first book in 1886.

The modern impression of the chalk-stream world of Victorian times often tends to be that of an idyll – of unsurpassable fishing, carried on (generally by rather privileged people) in a pastoral paradise. No ugly sights and sounds of the machine age, apart from a picturesque steam train that decants the lucky angler onto a small station platform in the depths of rural Wessex. Then there is the waiting pony trap, the drive by hedgerow and park land, a respectful keeper in attendance, and a pleasant fishing hut to which one can resort after a three-brace forenoon, there to meet two other agreeable fellow rods. All around is unspoilt countryside, with mills and water meadows, and the seasonal work of village and farm proceeding picturesquely as it has for generations. And the sun shines benignly, but not too brightly, upon streams filled with natural fish on a scale unimaginable to us in our sad latter days.

Pictures like this have passed into folk memory. The above version might be a little idealized, for the distance of the years can lend a rosy enchantment, though some of it at least would be true enough. It must have been a wonderful time in which to fish. All the same, the picture deserves a critical look.

Take the level of stock in the river. We have to go back to an even earlier generation to find records of really heavy bags of trout – at least if we are thinking of genuine wild trout. It seems likely that many of the dubious triumphs at the end of the nineteenth century, such as those recorded by Lord Granby and F.G. Aflalo, were based on heavy stocking with hatchery trout. The enormous catches of the Regency period were at least of wild fish. Wordsworth wrote to his sister Mary in June 1812 regretting that he had been prevented by an engagement from going with Humphrey Davy to fish 'some little stream about ten miles from London', (probably the Colne or the Misbourne). He adds: 'Davy appears to have attained a wonderful skill in Angling. . . . he says that the finest fishing is the preserved Brooks near London, that there are many spots of this kind where he can pull as many trout as he likes from 3–5 pounds weight, and that they make a point of throwing back into the stream every fish under two pounds and a half.' Catches of this sort, and those of Durnford and Hawker in Hampshire, seem to us nowadays to belong to the Stone Age. The Rev. Richard Durnford, fishing the Test around Chilbolton and Newton Stacey between 1809 and 1819, recorded bags of twenty or thirty fish a day. On 17 June 1809 he and his friend Penrose, using the crazy tackle of that age, caught eighty-eight fish ('Began at the carriage at the Turnpike Road and fished to Dodmore. . . . N.B. – Penrose fished only from 11 till ½ past 2'). And here is the noisy and eccentric Colonel Peter Hawker, veteran of the Peninsular War, writing on 10 April 1833: 'Longparish. Engaged with a party of fishing gentlemen who unexpectedly popped in on me. Three of us killed 50 brace of trout in a little more than four hours.' And some time in the 1850s an angler called Harris killed forty brace at Longparish in one afternoon. All these great killings took place on the Test, but early accounts show that the Itchen and other chalk streams teemed with fish in the years after Waterloo. In addition to the natural fecundity of these streams, there was another factor: they were only fished by a small number of people, who generally left soon after the mayfly time; after this the rivers became heavily-weeded sanctuaries. (Hawker was the exception, prepared to fish in July and August, or indeed January if the humour took him.)

The natural stock of the Test and Itchen began to decline about the middle of the century. For example, the records of the Longstock Club, where a great weight of trout was expected each mayfly season, recorded a steady falling off in catches between 1850 and 1870. By the time Halford appeared in Hampshire, fishing had become slower. Great draughts of fishes could still be made, and keepers were sometimes sent for the handcart, though this was usually on fisheries liberally stocked from the hatchery. But such was not the policy at Houghton, or at least not at first.

Other factors combined to make the chalk-stream experience in the last quarter of the nineteenth century rather different from the commonly-held ideal. Some have a sadly modern ring about them. There was the matter of the weather, always something of anxious interest to the fisherman. In 1889 Halford rather scornfully rejected the idea of the older anglers that the weather had been better in their youth: 'Do you honestly think that the prevailing wind and weather during the successive seasons have not as nearly as possible followed the same immutable law of average?' In fact he was wrong: there are cycles in weather history and, as it happened, he was to struggle through season after season of harsh springs at Houghton, followed by wet, cool summers (see Chapter 5).

The bad weather contributed to a much bigger problem in the countryside, for these were the years when British agriculture was sliding into a catastrophe. The middle part of the century had been fairly prosperous, with corn prices – regarded as the main index of success – at a fairly high level year by year. This did not of course bring any great comfort or benefit to the ordinary workers in the fields (in 1850 the wages of the Hampshire labourer averaged about nine shillings and sixpence a week). Prosperity was more likely to be found in the farmhouse than in the worker's cottage. But this prosperity, which for years had seemed so secure, was about to be eroded by cheap imports from abroad. The first signs of foreign competition appeared in 1875, and by 1878 farming in Britain was sinking into a depression that was to last for a generation. An immense flood of prairie grain, at first from the United States, then from India, Australia, Canada and Argentina, was the main threat. Stock farming held up for a while, but the development of refrigeration ships in the 1880s enabled foreign beef and lamb to be brought from great distances. Only milk was immune from competition, although Danish butter was well established in the grocer's shop before the end of the century. By this date a pound of New Zealand wool could be brought to Britain for one penny, and a quarter of prairie wheat* for three shillings. When Henry Rider Haggard was journeying around the countryside gathering material for his alarming book *Rural England* (1903) he noticed that the catering at the hotels where he lodged relied almost entirely on foreign produce. A good deal of migration to the cities or to British colonies took place at this time, and politicians talked earnestly of 'the flight from the land'. One curious result was that labourers in many parts of Britain became thin on the ground, and so at least could bargain for a better wage.

So the simple view of the English village before the Great War as unchanging and snugly feudal is not tenable: traditional society had already been breaking up for decades. Throughout the greater part of Halford's fishing life the countryside in which he carried on his pursuit was not a happy place. No doubt many anglers took little heed of this: they merely came, fished and went away again. Others saw more deeply into things. In the autumn of 1879, as the rain fell, the sheep died, and the price of wheat sank to that of barley (an unheard-of thing) kindly Major Carlisle, in the middle of a fishing report to *The Field*, wrote 'I am glad I am not a farmer'. As I shall show, Halford became keenly aware of the conditions in the villages along the Test valley, and did what he could to give help in hard cases.

The sad plight of British farming had a considerable effect on the anglers, whether they were sympathetic or not. In earlier times fishing had been the poor relation among field sports, and landowners had not troubled to develop its potential on their estates. Local enthusiasts could often get fishing for the asking, and a gentleman

* A quarter was a measure of eight bushels, or sixty-four gallons.

visiting a district and putting up at the village inn would seldom be disappointed if he sent a note with his card up to the big house. But, with the great surge in popularity of fly-fishing and the landowners' need for alternative income in the latter part of the century, this easy-going attitude began to change. All over the chalk country, as elsewhere in Britain, returns on land declined. In the Whitchurch area rents fell by 50 per cent between 1875 and 1912. Some great landlords, such as the Duke of Bedford and the Earl of Pembroke, were benevolent enough (and perhaps had sufficient cash reserves) to listen to the complaints of desperate farmers and to forgive rents. But most magnates had their own problems, with their properties burdened with awkward marriage settlements and other charges. Evictions for non-payment did not help either; times were so bad that some farms stood empty for years – better a struggling tenant than none at all. And so, on many a noble property up and down the land, Agent would be advising Lordship to look to sporting resources as yet untapped. Stretches of less-obviously good fishing were taken in hand about this time, or let to newly-formed syndicates. Often an immense amount of work was found to be necessary to make such fisheries useful. When T.J. Mann the brewer came to the Horsebridge reach of the Test near Bossington it was a wilderness, needing a considerable capital injection. His excellent keeper Penton, who had learned his trade on the Anton, set to work to make war on the pike, and in two years removed many hundreds up to 25lb in weight. In 1891 the Wilton Club took over a stretch of the Wylye that for years had only been fished on a casual basis – amongst others by Marryat, H.S. Hall and Dr Tom Sanctuary – or simply poached. The local people, regarding it almost as a matter of common right, had got used to helping themselves to Lord Pembroke's trout, and it was several years before the resentment against the club of newcomers had died away. But there was no lack of willing members for the new syndicates, waiting lists soon developed, and local money was generated, both for the riparian owners and in the neighbouring villages. Major Carlisle, writing in *The Field* in 1891 reckoned that the fishing rights on the lower Test were worth double the value of the surrounding water meadows.

The lamentations of our own age about too many fisherman and not enough fish were already familiar in the last years of Queen Victoria. Contributors to *The Field* and *The Fishing Gazette* frequently complained that there were now ten fly-fishermen for every one thirty years ago, and the new craze for the dry fly, by adding so much interest to the sport, was sometimes blamed. This new situation involved other drawbacks besides rising costs. There were fewer fish to catch, and those that remained were more difficult to deceive. Carlisle wrote in *The Field* in July 1885: 'It must be remembered that on those English rivers producing trout of 3lb. and 4lb. weight there is now a tremendous run by anglers, and that almost every bit of such water is now scientifically fished.' The chief advantage of the Halford doctrine, once it had been fully developed, was alleged to be that it was more delicate and skilful than the old-fashioned downstream raking with two or more flies, often large. The effect of this crude method was often merely to scare fish, it was claimed: the new method enabled the enterprising modern angler to keep ahead in a world of fewer and cleverer trout. As I shall show below (see Chapter 10), the new purists were rather too eager to condemn the old ways root and branch. The wet fly on the chalk stream could be as lazy and haphazard as Halford and his followers claimed, but, in the right hands, it could be subtle and effective. How otherwise could trout have been caught at all before the dry-fly revolution? In 1900 William Senior wrote in ironical wonderment: 'Wonderful trout, those, in the early years of the century, which knew not the distinction between shades of hackles, dry-fly and wet, and cared not for the exact length of wing or the material of which the whisks were composed.'

Pollution was not absent from these apparently crystalline streams. On the chalk streams it was at least present in the most familiar and ancient form of all, rather than the poisoned effluent of industry common in the Midlands and the North. The nuisance was widespread and varied from the cottage drain to the effluent of whole villages or towns. Martin Ridley Smith, one of the elders of the original Houghton Club, wrote in 1904: 'Look at this glass of Test water, clear as crystal; looks fit to drink, does it not? But I would not advise you to, for all the Stockbridge sewage is in it!' Winchester's sewage seeped into the Itchen until 1879, although the river had a greater volume in those days, and contemporary anglers do not seem to have noticed (though Francis Francis thought that it made the weeds too prolific). A serious pollution incident on the River Anton in 1896 gave rise to a lawsuit in which, relying on the Rivers Pollution Act of

1876 the plaintiffs were able to defeat the Andover Corporation, a rare triumph. Other and more serious pollutions went unchecked for years. The most striking instance in the chalk country was at Dorchester, where the sewage was allowed to escape into the Frome, Dorset's premier chalk stream. Trout of enormous size fattening on the refuse of the town could be caught here by anyone prepared to approach this particular stretch – which is said to have required some courage. In the early years of the twentieth century the scandal and danger to public health became impossible to ignore, and a proper sewage system was constructed for Dorchester. For a while the monster trout remained, losing condition and puzzled at the cutting off of their bounty, then they faded away out of history.

The problem of weeds in rivers occupied the columns of *The Field* every year. Weeds grow rapidly in chalk streams and can render fishing impossible. Cutting them was, or at least should have been, an artistic technique; some keepers understood it, others did not. T.J. Mann of Horsebridge complained that not one in fifty knew the way of it: the average keeper 'mows all away as if he were in a cornfield at so much an acre'. The real difficulty lay in achieving an agreed programme of dates for weed cutting for the whole course of the river. From time to time *The Field* would optimistically announce that the thing was all settled, but another wave of complaints would soon follow. On 21 May 1881 a *Field* bulletin (by electric telegraph, of which they were very proud) reported quantities of weed coming down the Test 'just as the trout season is reaching its height'. Unanimity among keepers was not enough. Millers, who often disliked anglers anyway, would cut weeds at will as the fancy took them. And the drowners who floated the water meadows would often cut weeds just before turning out the water. If they managed to confine this, as they were asked to do, between 5 and 15 May, the river should then have been clear of masses of floating weed by the expected arrival of the mayfly about 22 May. But in many seasons their programme seems to have slipped. It was during these years that many owners and lessees went to the considerable trouble of having weed racks made.

The intricate water-meadow system, which seems to us another picturesque part of the nineteenth-century Never-Never Land, was not looked upon as an unmixed blessing at the time, because it could produce a surprising and unpredictable change in the river level in the middle of an angling day. Francis Francis wrote in 1883, after a day of low water on the Itchen: 'That is the way of these Hampshire water meadows. The drowners are always humbugging the water about, turning it off the meadows or on, and you never know how it will be.'

Weed-cutting may have had an important bearing on the decline of the grannom in the 1880s. Formerly the rise of the grannom was a phenomenon to behold, a great mass of fly swirling into the air and, like the mayfly at Hungerford, making it difficult to distinguish objects on the far bank. It provided the first big orgy of the season for the trout and, as the *Chronicles of the Houghton Club* records, it brought a stampede of anglers into the Test valley every year. Halford was fascinated by this fly; indeed it was his interest in the grannom which impelled him towards his first experiments as a fly-dresser. By 1884 he had got to the stage of developing a pattern for the pupa, but that seems to have been the last year in which the fly hatched in any quantity at Houghton. It never quite disappeared, but by 1890 the big grannom blizzards were seen no more. Even more alarmingly the Test mayfly declined as well. When Halford came to Houghton its appearance had become patchy and unreliable. It increased about 1890, then tantalizingly declined again, and J.W. Hills said that by 1906 it had vanished altogether, and that no trout at all were killed with the artificial at Stockbridge. If one wanted to see mayfly in quantity one had to go to the Kennet.

Poaching was prevalent everywhere. In the early years of the nineteenth century the attitude towards the poacher was harsh and unrelenting. Fears of popular disturbances that might lead to revolution on the French model may have accounted for this. The poacher was seen as a rural threat, like the machine-breaker or the rick-burner. But as fear of revolution receded a certain tolerance grew up, at least in some areas. This tolerance declined again in the last quarter of the century, when fish preservation and syndicating increased, although some magistrates could see the difference between the poor man out of work with a family to feed and the menacing gangs who netted fish in quantities to sell. Francis Francis said little about the first, reserving his scorn and disgust for the second. He reported at length on the Rooksbury poaching case in 1876, venting his anger as much on the local receivers of trout and pheasants as upon the poachers. There was little sweetness or light with some of the poaching gangs and violence was never far off. Francis Francis reported in July of that year:

> I am sorry to say that an attempt to poach the water belonging to the Andover Club was made on Sunday night last, and on the keepers making their appearance, one of them, H. Penton, was struck on the head with a hedge stake, and knocked senseless into the water, where he would certainly have been drowned had not the other keeper contrived to pull him out on the bank. The poachers took to their heels, leaving a bag with several brace of trout in it, and their net in the water. Many of the trout, being still alive, were returned to the water, about a dozen brace (mostly small) being past recovery, and but for the promptitude of the keepers a sackful of fish would probably have been sacrificed. . . . Poor Penton was insensible from the blow on the head for many hours, and he is still in a serious condition. Two men have been captured, and are in custody.

This sort of incident was fairly common, and serves to temper the romantic image of the poacher. In February 1877 one of the most dangerous poachers in the Andover area was sentenced to a term of hard labour – he had only just emerged from prison for similar offences.

The Itchen at Winchester was also much poached. In 1879 Francis reported that 'a fellow named Jefferies, a regular practitioner' was fined for snatching fish on the stretch known as the Weirs, and that a gang of boys had also been in court:

> A Master Winkworth, said to be the leader of all the young ruffians in Winchester, and who has been convicted for various matters about ten times before, with two companions was summoned for beating the water and snaring, they having fish in possession. Master W. was cheeky, and his friends also; so he got £5 or two months, and his friends 10s. or a fortnight, with hard labour.

The unofficial capital of the chalk-stream country was Winchester. Stockbridge might claim to lie astride a more prestigious fishery, but there was no water here open to the public, and the casual visitor seeking fishing would be speedily sent on his way. Around Winchester, however, there was a surprising amount of ticket water.

Here beginners could cut their teeth on the ways of the chalk stream. But the quality of the fishing was so good that many eminent fly fishers would also be found at work here, often fishing quite close to anglers in the early stages of blundering apprenticeship, and mixing with them after hours in the George or the Royal in the town. In this way Winchester became not only an encouraging place for beginners, but also a forum and a forcing house for new ideas about tackle and technique. As early as 1874 H.S. Hall was discovering how valuable waterside conferences with the local regulars could be. The fact that this was one of the places in Britain where the dry fly developed is not surprising.

The boys at Winchester College were particularly fortunate. Other public schools, such as Marlborough and Bradfield, are by chalk streams, but none had Winchester's advantages for the young entry into the world of fly-fishing, and a number of well-known anglers started their career here. Edward Grey is the best known: in his book *Fly Fishing* he mentions the kind helpfulness of George Selwyn Marryat, who was often to be found lounging about the stream and helping the unskilled, as if conducting a sort of unofficial seminar in the open air. Marryat had formerly been at the College, as also had Dr Wickham (the inventor of the Wickham's Fancy), Dr Tom Sanctuary, E. Valentine Corrie (who owned the hatchery at Chilland on the Itchen), and his brother A. Wynne Corrie, Graham Clarke (who wrote in *The Field* as 'Glanrhos'), and many others. The conditions under which Winchester boys fished, as Grey remarked sadly, were not ideal. The school authorities, in setting up the timetable of the average day, had quite unreasonably taken no account of the hatch of fly, and the boys could only get to the river at certain set and rather short times. Neither could they normally come out in the evening. On most days they missed the best of things. Perhaps in the long run this made better fishermen of them. The unfortunate Skues – a scholarship boy, mad keen but short of funds and good tackle – was not able to make much of the fishing while at school. Some boys did well (see Chapter 10). Grey's largest fish was 3lb 8oz, but his total of seventy-six trout in his last season as a schoolboy, on a difficult, hard-fished water, was impressive.

The ancient town of Winchester, with its massive cathedral, old hostelries, and the branches of clear Itchen water at the end of cobbled streets had a compelling atmosphere, which drew men to it year after year. H.S. Hall wrote: 'The place and its surroundings possess a strange fascination for me – infatuation, some of my friends call it.' No one responded to this charm more than the redoubtable Francis Francis, Angling Editor of *The Field* from 1856 to 1883. This journal had a paramount influence in the sporting world of the nineteenth century – a research project into the history of almost any sport in Britain would have to begin with *The Field*. For anglers it played an important role in pulling together numerous angling practices and attitudes, and assisting them towards becoming developed schools or doctrines. And for nearly thirty years the writing was mainly done by Francis (F.F. to his friends). *The Field* paid him an honorarium of £200 a year, for which they got good value.* He was an all-round angler, who ranged far and wide in the British Isles and parts of Europe in search of fishing and copy. He happily fished for salmon with the fly, pike with the spoon, perch with the paternoster, and barbel with the trotted worm from a punt. But the trout were his great love, and every spring his readers would know that his weekly column would plunge into fly-fishing, and that mention of Winchester would soon occur. Then, for several weeks, his writing would treat of the ticket waters there – of Winnal above the city, where he fished with Marryat and E.R.J. Nicolls, of the Old Barge and College Meadow, and further downstream of Shawford and Bishopstoke, where he once had seventeen trout weighing forty pounds. And there would be visits to the Andover Club run by Mr Fowle on the Anton, and to the Houghton Fly-Fishing Club, of both of which he was an honorary member and unofficial adviser. In early June he would shift his quarters to the Kennet, where after 1877 he was also free of the waters of the Hungerford Club, to take advantage of the later appearance of the mayfly there. His descriptions of his mayfly expeditions have all the zest of a schoolboy released for the holidays. There is still a tradition handed down in the Francis family that the arrival of the mayfly telegram would galvanize the household at his home in Twickenham: womenfolk and servants flew about gathering belongings in a sort of domestic maelstrom, with F.F. stamping and roaring at its centre. Eventually to everyone's great relief he was stuffed into a cab and dispatched to Waterloo. He wrote in 1882:

* Francis had a reasonable private income, largely from some property in Southampton.

> The prognostications that 'the fly' would be up early this year were not without confirmation; for fully a week earlier than usual I heard of it being seen, and then on Derby day, the 24th, I had a letter from friend L., who makes the Royal his headquarters for three months in the year, inclosing me a couple of specimens, and M. confirmed its advent, which was conclusive. I never as a rule think of moving before the 1st, as that is about the usual time. However, down I went, and found grand doings at the Royal. . . . The yeomanry were out, and made our hotel their headquarters, bugles were blowing, sabres clanking, and silver lace was flashing galore, and we were tremendously military. Their band played in the garden to assembled multitudes outside our window every evening while we were at dinner, and a capital band it was too.

The annual gathering at the Royal was always referred to by Francis as 'the Mayfly Mess', and was presided over by George Ledger ('friend L' in the quotation above; 'M' was of course Marryat). Something similar to this gathering existed for years at the Bear in Hungerford and at the Lion in Farningham on the Darenth. We may imagine F.F. emerging from the down train, picking out the likeliest porter and barrow to take his formidable load of strapped trunks and rods round to St Peter's Street. Then there would be the arrival at the Royal, the roar of applause at his entry, the excited meeting with old friends, the vast meals, the whisky and tobacco, and the good talk far into the night.

Even his tackle resembled himself – it was larger than life. There were giant fly boxes for dry Mayflies and carry-all fly books for other flies, all to fit (with his lunch: a cold chop and a thick slice of buttered bread) into a large basket designed by himself and strong enough to bear his weight. At a time when many anglers were using single-handed rods he remained faithful to the two-handed weapons of his younger days. Some of his tackle has survived, including several of his immense rods: placed beside one of the toy wands of the twenty-first century they appear rather to belong to the medieval jousting tournament than to the gentle art.

His affection for Winchester shines out of his columns. Here he is again writing in 1877:

> Is there a pleasanter town of its kind in England than Winchester? I think not; if there is, I have not yet discovered it. It is so venerable,

> yet so sturdy, in strong, quiet, enduring vitality. . . . As you walk down the handsome streets, the fresh breeze comes off the hills opposite, and fills your lungs with good healthy oxygen; the shops look clean, fresh, and solid, the public buildings and monuments as if they had been there 500 years, and meant to be so for 500 more. There is a real worthy John Bullishness in its best aspect about Winchester which makes one love and feel proud of it. It is all old, even to its chief tackle maker, old John Hammond. He is terrifically old, excessively high-dried; he is the oldest inhabitant, and his birthday is said to be lost in the mist of ages. If you want to fish at Winchester, you must go to him.

This last jocular reference was to the man who ruled the angling world around Winchester. There was enough angling going on hereabouts to support several angling shops, but John Hammond dominated. He first set up in Winchester in the early 1850s. His rival H. Pottle, who already had a shop in Great Minster Street, must have been one of the first fly-dressers in the area to respond to the local demand for the new dry flies. In *The Field* of 12 December 1857 we find Francis praising Pottle's floating flies. However in that year Pottle retired and Hammond took the premises in Minster Street. He at first described himself as a 'working cutler and fishing tackle manufacturer'. But the opportunities in Winchester for the second line overshadowed the first, and 'working cutler' was soon dropped from his trade card. By 1871 he had moved to Jewry Street, and soon afterwards migrated to the Square, where his shop became the local emporium for guns and fishing tackle, and a clearing house for news.

A number of useful things could be found here, apart from the usual run of rods and tackle. Hammond's flies, derided by Skues years later for their old-fashioned construction, were at any rate good enough to compass the destruction of untold numbers of Itchen trout. Four of the patterns in his stock carried his own name: Hammond's Adopted, a sedge fly with a wing of woodcock, very effective on the edge of darkness; Hammond's Champion, a pattern for the green drake; Hammond's Favourite, a blue dun with starling wing and a flat silver body ribbed with gold wire; and Hammond's Little Tempter. Hammond's Patent Landing Net with its bow of ash was popular, and continued to be made by Chalkley after Hammond's death. He also invented a cork hat band to carry flies, and a number of other gadgets.

Anglers often dropped into the shop in the Square to learn about the state of the water, or sometimes just to talk. As a hard-up schoolboy, Skues was allowed to sit and read from the selection of sporting books, with no pressure to buy; and it was here that the momentous meeting between Halford and Marryat took place in 1879, as described in Chapter 4. Conversation with Hammond was likely to be interesting. George Currell recorded that Hammond once showed him how to use a decanter of water in which to float a dry fly so as to observe its colours from below. Francis wrote in *The Field* in June 1878: 'I met Old John Hammond going down to the Old Barge, with a thousand or so of flies [i.e. mayflies], which he had procured up above to turn down; and I hope his attempt may succeed, for on the lower part of his water about Shawford there have been a good show, and a lot of nice fish have been killed there in consequence.'

However the most significant thing about the shop was that it was the centre of a complicated fishing empire, with a range of ticket options according to venue or period of time. Over the years Hammond had acquired more and more parcels of fishing on lease. By 1875 Francis was able to tell his readers:

> John Hammond has now about seven miles of water above and below Winchester. His charge for the whole is, I believe, £10 per season; but portions of it can be fished by the month, week, or day. Though I do not fancy that day tickets are granted on the best water, I can safely say that, if the angler is up to his work and the weather is suitable, he will get as good spring fishing here as in any part of the kingdom.

A visiting angler making his arrangements with Hammond could therefore get access to St Cross, the Old Barge, the College Meadow, the Mill pond, to the part of Winnal later acquired by Irwin Cox and more familiar to us nowadays as Abbots Barton, or even to far-away Worthy, afterwards in the hands of the Corrie brothers. In fact there was probably even more fishing available in the 1860s, for in the easy-going times before the depression in farming several riparian owners below Winchester had not troubled to assert their rights, and anglers had enjoyed what they believed was free fishing. In 1913 Major Carlisle, in an article in *The Field* entitled 'The Itchen Fifty Years Ago' looked back to the halcyon days when life was less complicated, and one could fish all the way down to Shawford with no one to say you nay.

All this made Winchester a unique place. Francis wrote in November 1879: 'The great charm of Winchester fishing, to my mind, is that it is not a close borough, but that one meets fishermen from all parts of the kingdom, and of all degrees of skill, with whom you can compare notes and exchange experiences. Had it been a mere club, I should have been tired of it long ago.' In 1885 Dr Tom Sanctuary wrote enviously that he wished his home town of Salisbury would develop its fishings in like manner: 'Winchester has long been a fishing centre and the trade of the city has profited by many hundreds of pounds. Why should not Salisbury, with its railway facilities and its unrivalled advantages of water, profit in the same way?'

The best known of Hammond's waters was the eastern branch of the Itchen below the city, developed as a canal in the seventeenth century to bring coal and corn up from Southampton. This was known as the Itchen Navigation, or more familiarly as the Old Barge. Its commercial usefulness had always been doubtful – Defoe was scornful of it as far back as 1724 – and its days were numbered once the railway came to Winchester in 1839; the last barge came up in 1869. But for anglers it was a paradise. Francis wrote in 1879: 'There is a great stock of fish in Old John's water, and they are not to be caught by muffs.' The supply seemed inexhaustible. Francis continued: 'Half a score of people fish this bit of water every day through the season, and . . . one of them last year took 400 fish out of it.' Edward Grey in his book refers to one of these local rods – it may have been a man called Marshall – who came and went silently and was the most effective fisherman in the district. It is a pity not to know more about these quiet, scarcely visible anglers of the Old Barge. Some of them were poor men, who were selling their fish in Winchester; for them the river was a resource in the anxious business of making a living, along with guiding the moneyed visiting anglers and picking up other casual work (rivers, like the ancient forests, have always provided opportunities to get by for folk on the margin of rural society). No doubt they were not above poaching at times. But on the Old Barge they seem to have fished fair, and with great skill. For these fish were not to be caught easily. They were case-hardened by the constant casting, and by seeing strollers and dog-walkers always on the tow path. Anglers had to get used to passers-by walking just behind them (and sometimes absent-mindedly in front of them). Consequently fish did not take alarm and fade away from view, but continued to rise. Experienced hands on the Old Barge knew that the usual rule of attack had to be inverted: instead of resting a trout the successful policy was to cover it frequently and rapidly in order to catch it off guard.

'Old John' was accused by Major Turle of cramming too many people onto this stretch, and sometimes it was difficult to find a place to fish in a line of anglers. But year after year this 'much-enduring stream', as H.S. Hall called it, produced literally thousands of trout. They were usually not large. The limit was twelve inches, and the average in most years was probably sixteen or eighteen ounces. But there was an ebb and flow, and some seasons produced bigger fish. In June 1879 Francis reported:

> I never saw such fine baskets of fish as have been taken out of Old John's water. The numbers have not been remarkable, but the size and quality have, from two to four brace being about the ordinary take of any decent fisherman; but from 1½lb to 2½lb has been a common size of something like a half of very many of the takes; and for condition they are perfection, being as red as cherries inside, and as round as little pigs.

Much larger trout were caught in the city waters, but under conditions that were somewhat artificial. One favoured place was by a fish smokery that operated near Child's Yard in Eastgate Street. Here the trout appreciated the heads and guts of fish, which, after the cheerful custom of the age, were thrown into the water. Over the years a number of unnatural monsters of eight pounds and upwards were caught, invariably with bait. The largest, caught in September 1888 at Water Lane, weighed 16lb 2oz. This trout had been well-known to local anglers and was said to have been fond of bloaters. It was set up in a case and in June 1891 was sold at auction to Chalkley, the Winchester tackle-maker, for the high price of twenty guineas.

Hammond presided over this crowded and exciting angling scene for many years. Francis wrote in 1879: 'A good many people grumble at Old John, who no doubt, like the rest of us has his faults, but I don't know what they would do without him.' He was well aware of the value of advertising and kept in close contact with Francis at the offices of *The Field*, who passed on his remarks to the readers. In early April 1875 he reported poor sport, perhaps with tongue in cheek – few anglers, it seemed, were able to exceed five brace – and in May 1877 he mentioned a catch of four trout weighing fourteen pounds. At the end of February 1879 Francis was able to report excellent stocks in all Hammond's waters around Winchester: 'A good many of his old patrons will be going to the Cape, so that he has plenty of vacancies' (a reminder of the Zulu War, at that point not going very well after the disaster at Isandlwana).

Hammond gave up his shop and some of his waters at the end of 1879, but kept the Mill Pond and part of the College Meadow. St Cross passed to Cox the gunmaker of Parchment Street, and Chalkley acquired the lower College Meadow. Visitors wanting fishing could therefore still get access, but they now had three people to choose between.

Hammond seems latterly to have been in poor health. A taste for drink may have been a factor in his decline (descriptions of him often refer to his 'rubicund countenance'). Eventually this unusual man, who had given so much delight to so many people, and who had coached so many beginners, including generations of Winchester boys, died rather suddenly in December 1882, perhaps unsurprisingly, from liver disease. Although known to all for a quarter of a century as Old John, he was in fact only fifty-three.

Three months later Francis reported in *The Field* that Hammond's widow had been left rather badly provided for – 'During the last year or two of his life things went wrong with him somehow' – and with characteristic generosity launched a subscription for her: H.S. Hall, Halford, Dr Wickham, and others all contributed. Some customers wrote to say that they owed money to Hammond but had never been able to get proper accounts from him. Francis wrote: 'I am afraid poor Old John was not a top sawyer at business, and kept his accounts rather loosely, or he would have been much better off.' The remainder of his empire, except for a small stretch run by George Currell, passed into the hands of Chalkley, where it remained for many years.

In later years sad things were to happen to the Itchen at Winchester. The fishing in the Old Barge deteriorated towards the end of the century, and many local anglers took to fishing with large flies at night. A villainous scheme of gravel extraction to make up the

Hyde Abbey road ruined part of the river, and at about the same time the mayfly also disappeared. Skues thought that the two things were connected, but it seems more likely the mayfly was declining as a result of some little-understood natural cycle. Even worse was the tar poisoning which killed many trout in the early years of the twentieth century. The Itchen survived these events, but the fishing around the city became much more of a closed shop in 1910, when Chalkley's interest was given up, and the College, which had formed a fishing club with the encouragement of Sir Edward Grey, acquired a lease. Apart from the free water at the Weirs, always regarded by Francis as a great school for poachers, Winchester thereafter ceased to be the welcoming haven it had once been for the wandering angler in search of chalk-stream fishing. But it had served its turn in providing a chance for anglers of slender means who might otherwise not have got on to a chalk stream. To outsiders the sister river, the Test, must have appeared an impregnable fortress. The main trouble about chalk-stream fishing has always been that there is not enough of it.

3 Chalk-stream Tackle and Technique

When Halford came to Houghton the technology of angling had already begun to improve in many ways, bringing significant changes in doctrine and practice. And practice increasingly came to be regulated by a complex protocol. It had not always been so. The fishing atmosphere of earlier times had been casual and rackety: a man pleased himself. If he angled for coarse fish he used any method he liked. The fish on the bank was the test. The gorge bait and other methods nowadays banned were in use, and in Norfolk Parson Woodforde used to send for a man to pull a net through his lake after an unsuccessful morning with rod and line. A trout fisherman might use flies if he was an artist, but if things were slow he would change to the blow line or the cross line or to bait fishing. Here is an angler whose diary has come to rest in the Wiltshire Record Office, fishing at Stockbridge in May 1798: 'Weather cold and stormy – Fish rose badly, little brown dun Fly the best – and another Dun fly, with yellow body – was told by experienced fishermen that the season was too far advanced for the common fly, that they rose best in warm weather in March and April – the Minnow now preferable to the Fly.' During the Regency period the hunting and shooting scene was full of combative and larger-than-life individuals – such as Thomas Assheton Smith, Squire Osbaldeston, John Mytton and many a colourful other – and to some extent the anglers shared in the breezy anarchic approach of the age.

Things began to change in Queen Victoria's reign. The rise of the middle class, the decline in public disorder, the influence of the Arnoldian public school and of evangelical religion, and many other factors in society worked together to create a very different culture. Merrie England was being shut down and dismantled, to be replaced by respectable society, and all change was regarded as Progress. By mid-Victorian times writers were looking back with some embarrassment to the raffish days of fifty years before. The new age was more organized, more formal, more regulated, and field sports shared in this tendency. There grew up an accepted notion of how each sport was to be carried on. It was not just a matter of efficiency but also one of good behaviour in the field and of the courtesy of gentlemen towards gentlemen. The influence of the sporting papers, and in particular of *The Field*, in pulling together these unwritten rules was crucial to the development of the sportsman – unselfish, keen to do well, but as anxious about 'good form' as about success. Fly-fishing shared in this formalizing process, and Halford through his frequent contributions to *The Field*, was to play a bigger part than anyone. Starting with straightforward advice about the tackle and method most likely to succeed, he moved on to questions of what was permissible behaviour on the river, until in the end his teaching was felt by many, even in that formal age, to have become rather too dictatorial and oppressive. The way in which a practical programme of advice about fishing techniques could turn into a matter of ethics and even of social class is one of the most curious and fascinating developments in fly-fishing history. It could probably not have come about in any other place or time, and perhaps tells us something about the odder side of Victorian England. However, these abstract ideas came later, and as a result of the changes in tackle and knowledge, to which we must now turn.

In the pre-Halford period the great leap forward in entomology, as far as anglers were concerned, was the appearance in 1836 of Alfred Ronalds' book *The Fly-Fisher's Entomology*. In earlier times attempts had been made to introduce some organizing principles: this fly was good in March, that one in April; use this colour on a dark day, that one in sunshine. But these were rules of thumb, little better than mnemonic devices, and took little account of the intrinsic natures of fly and fish. Natural flies had been discussed, but not very successfully, and books with plates of artificials were not new. All this changed when Ronalds, whom Hills called 'the father of the modern angler-naturalist', produced what became one of the most useful fishing books of the nineteenth century. The beautiful coloured plates, with natural and artificial flies in the same picture for comparison, were such an obvious step in the right direction that one wonders why it was not more imitated. John Jackson of Tanfield Mill did in fact do this in *The Practical Fly Fisher* (1854), but he was unusual, and Halford never followed this excellent plan. If he had done so, four of his books, perhaps five, would have benefited greatly.

Altogether Ronalds' book described forty-seven natural flies and their artificial counterparts. Twenty-one were ephemeropteran flies; seven were diptera, or two-winged flies; four were trichoptera, or sedges; and four plecoptera, or stoneflies. Beetles, hopperbugs and representatives of other orders of insects make up the remainder, including the ant and the alder. This valuable work was reprinted many times (Sheringham considered it still valuable and interesting enough to bring out another edition in 1921). But there was still a good deal of ignorance in this area after 1836. Perhaps this need not surprise us. It is one thing to produce a book, but for a wide public to read it is another, and many anglers never consulted Ronalds or any other book. The author of *Fly Fishing in Salt and Fresh Water* (1851) had no idea if duns derived from water or land, and Cholmondeley-Pennell, in *The Modern Practical Angler* (1870) thought that the willow fly and the stone fly were part of the *Phryganeidae*. Major Carlisle referred to the ignorance of anglers at Houghton and Stockbridge in the 1870s. They made no attempt to distinguish between the smaller up-winged flies, lumping them all together under the term 'pickked wing' (i.e., peaked wing). 'The Mayfly they knew, the alder, and perhaps the sedge, but their entomology ceased at that.' *The Field* did its valiant best, and from time to time published pieces urging anglers to go to nature rather than accepting the traditional shibboleths of the past. In 1854 'Hampshire Fly-Fisher' published several articles on entomology, in particular on sedge flies, suggesting among other things that the Welshman's button was a caddis not a beetle. This would have gladdened the heart of Halford had he ever lighted upon this back number of *The Field* (see p.226). The curious habit of calling natural flies by their artificial analogues was also widespread, and authors would write lyrically of a dance of quill gnats over the water, or of a drift of hare's ears coming down the stream. The practice to which I have referred of publishing handy lists of 'flies by the month' in books continued well into the Halford era. Francis Francis was guilty of this, but by 1882 was having second thoughts, after noticing that natural flies had an unnerving habit of altering their seasons.

Sound, reliable knowledge was therefore hard to come by. Perhaps this made things more interesting: there was a field for learning, speculation and experiment. Some observers, such as David Foster of Ashbourne, were inclined to believe that all the olives were really one species, merely varying because of changes in season or temperature – and this in the teeth of Ronalds, who had a much more accurate idea about up-winged species. What is still more surprising is that it was possible for Halford to incline towards this entirely erroneous view in *Floating Flies and How to Dress Them*. But in 1886 Halford had not yet read Pictet.

Francis Francis was deeply interested in the problem of natural flies, particularly the olives, and wished for 'a regularly established society which can investigate these matters accurately'. In *A Book on Angling* (1867) he wrote in rather mystified vein: 'I am almost inclined to think that the yellow dun is but a modification or sort of second crop of the blue dun.' A later passage is also delightfully vague: 'Several duns find their way to the surface during this month [July]. I think they are but repetitions, or, at any rate, very near relations, of earlier flies, as they very closely resemble them.' These remarks from the leading angler of the day are enough to indicate the sketchy state of knowledge in 1867 (and Francis saw no occasion to revise them in the otherwise much-altered sixth edition of 1885). In 1878 he became interested in the blue-winged olive (was it the same, he wondered, as the old whirling blue dun?) with wings as dark as the iron blue. He wrote in 1882: 'I have known that "blue-winged olive", as we call it now, for about four years. I noticed it with friend M. first in Hampshire, and we saw it subsequently in Derbyshire. . . . Some people confound it with a little fly called the apple-green, but I doubt if it is the same fly at all.' H.S. Hall wrote in September 1882 of a mad rise on the Itchen at 'the big dark-winged apple green'. In fact by 1882 Marryat and Hall had already made several attempts at designing a pattern for this baffling fly. By September 1882 it was beginning to dawn on Francis that the 'gold spinner with a ball of green eggs rolled up under its tail' was the imago of the blue-winged olive. But, side by side with these gropings towards the light there were large areas of ignorance. Francis was convinced, for example, that the nymphs of the mayfly were ferocious carnivores – no doubt by analogy with the larvae of dragonflies, which they superficially resemble – and therefore should not be allowed in an artificial pond with trout fry. But at least he was not guilty of the bizarre belief, expressed in 1876 by 'Old Log' (Colonel Tickell, a frequent contributor to *The Field*), that the mayfly hatched on the bed of the stream and floated up to the surface in a winged state. In 1882 H.S. Hall bewailed the confusion and chaos of entomological knowledge ('Ephemerids make us all puzzled'). To study water flies carefully and systematically, he wrote, however interesting, would involve too much time and trouble for most men. 'Is there not some enthusiast with plenty of leisure who will come to the rescue, and help his enquiring brethren?' In January 1888 in *The Fishing Gazette* the well-known naturalist Dr Edward Hamilton made a brave attempt to sort out the scientific names of the July dun, the yellow dun and others, in a piece in which the names of natural and artificial flies got hopelessly entangled – e.g. 'The Hare's Ear is the subimago of Baetis bioculata [sic].' Hamilton's difficulty was that he was relying on Stephens (1833), Ronalds (1836), Pictet (1843) and Eaton (1883), all of whom had different views about scientific nomenclature, and his flies wandered about between Chloeon, Baetis and Potomanthus until his readers must have become more confused, rather than less. He did however conclude on a hopeful note: 'Mr F.M. Halford has been steadily working for the last two years in making and carefully recording a great number of observations on the ephemeridae.' Halford was responding both to the chaos of knowledge and belief and to the appeals of a number of writers to produce a system of nomenclature and recognition. He was not going to be ready to publish for a long time, but this was the genesis of his *Dry-Fly Entomology* of 1897.

The chaos of entomology was paralleled by that of the artificial trout fly. The average beginner in 1870 must have been perplexed. Authors from the time of Venables and Cotton had advised that nature should be studied in order to design flies, but they had given very little direction as to how this might be done. In any case, many anglers were too busy, or too indifferent, to trouble to study the natural fly. For many the artificial was not an attempt to imitate nature but purely and simply a device for catching fish. The tackle shops stocked a confusing medley of patterns, all said to be killers.

Some tackle merchants sought to provide a thread through this labyrinth by producing small booklets with coloured pictures of artificials. The enterprising G. Little of Fetter Lane sold fly books with a picture opposite each parchment pocket, so that the flies, if not lost, could be returned to the correct place. The list was graded by season in the traditional way, and each picture was accompanied by an encouraging if somewhat vague description, e.g. 'No. 6 – Gold Eyed Gauze Wing. This is a good fly on the Colne and Coquet; in season from July till August.' Another and much better known authority was H.C. Cholmondeley-Pennell, already a prolific writer when Halford was entering upon his fly-fishing career. He was an all-round angler, editor of the short-lived *Fisherman's Magazine* in the 1860s and a great improver of all forms of fishing tackle. His views on flies were set out in *The Modern Practical Angler* in 1870. He dismissed the theories of Ronalds, and indeed of anyone else who believed that nature could be imitated. His argument was that flies were generally fished sunk, and under-water drag would render them unnatural anyway. Minute attention to detail was therefore hardly necessary. He proposed, probably with Stewart's plan in mind, that anglers should only carry three general patterns in green, brown and yellow, and in various sizes. Significantly he thought that the exception to his plan would be with dry-fly fishing, where close imitation should be attempted. But at this date Cholmondeley-Pennell knew little of the new and not yet commonly practised dry fly, which he thought usually meant mayfly fishing.

The above advice at least made life a little simpler, even though it ran counter to the advice of most other contemporary writers. The three-pattern plan must have come as a great relief to the young angler finding the going a little hard. The average beginner would have been presented with a vast array of patterns in the tackle shop. As I have indicated above, the names had little connection with those of natural flies. Many were brand names, as inventors made a bid for immortality, or referred to the killing qualities of the lure. This was of little help to the beginner, peering into the boxes on the counter labelled Drake's Extractor, Deller's Little Wonder, Artful Dodger, Jerry's Favourite, Flight's Fancy, the Carter, the Hudson, and many another. The charming and mysterious names of an earlier age, such as the Moorish Fly, the Shell Fly and the Dun Cut, had all gone, and the new, sometimes brash names, often devised more to catch angler than trout, fitted in well with an era in which advertising and the hard sell had come of age. So powerfully established had this system, or rather guessing game, become that Halford used it as the basis of the list in his first book *Floating Flies and How to Dress Them* (1886), and made no attempt to reject it until 1903 (see Chapter 8). It is still with us today, and the beginner has to learn that a Little Marryat is intended to imitate a pale watery dun and that a Kite's Imperial is for the dun of the large dark olive.

Shop flies for chalk streams were improving however. For one thing, they were becoming smaller, a natural response to the increasing shyness of trout. Granby (1898) tells us that it was the custom at Longstock on the Test to use large flies, i.e. size 8 (Pennell) or 7 (Redditch), in the earlier part of the century, but that this began to change from about 1860, when anglers began to use tiny dry 'gnats' (not literally gnats; this is a term of art for small flies). Many of the older die-hards continued to use flies that were both large and wet for many years (Major Carlisle records them doing so at Houghton in the 1870s), and this may be one explanation why some anglers caught little after the mayfly, unless they were fishing after dark.

The growing sophistication of fly patterns was partly due to the existence of a number of skilful fly-dressers, who were prepared to give time to the suggestions of the best anglers. In Crooked Lane in the City of London the firm of Eaton & Deller, who had been commissioned by Ronalds decades earlier to sell his patterns, were still making much-admired flies. Other anglers in London were faithful to Mrs Letitia Brocas of Rochester Row, Victoria, who also gave lessons in fly-tying. Probably the best known professional was Mrs Ogden Smith, the daughter of James Ogden of Cheltenham. She had married his employee Smith and set up business in Lordship Terrace in Battersea. Her flies were said to have been immediately recognizable because of her distinct way of tying in the wings. Her daughter Mrs Richardson of Kingston upon Thames also made flies for years in the last part of the nineteenth century. In Winchester, as well as Hammond, there was George Currell, who sold exquisite small patterns for the fastidious trout of the Itchen, many of them worked out by his father Lloyd Currell in the 1850s. In Parchment Street reigned Mrs Cox, with a back room full of girls turning out excellent flies, many of them to the prescriptions of clients. W.H. Aldam recommended a correspondent to go to Mrs Cox, 'for she is the most painstaking Person I know to carry out the views of her customers'.* Francis Francis regarded his visit to her, when he would collect his previously arranged order, as an important and pleasing part of his annual mayfly pilgrimage to Winchester. She was still working for him as he approached the sadly premature end of his career. During his last full season before his stroke, he wrote:

> The next day [i.e. towards the end of May 1882] I went to see Mrs Cox about my Mayflies, as she has taken so much trouble to get the proper colours and patterns, that I have had my entire stock of her this season; and I usually require about eight or ten dozen. . . . She has as fine a lot of flies as ever I saw turned out, and they were much admired by all beholders. All the wood ducks, florican, and bustard hackles, &c., I had to send myself, as they are not easy to procure.

This interesting passage shows that some nineteenth-century anglers regarded the artificial Mayfly as not likely to endure beyond the catching of one trout before having to be discarded. The fact that Francis was well known for his frequent smashes may also have a bearing.

Several writers at this time, observing that many of the professionals were female, wrote pieces in *The Field* and elsewhere urging more women to take up this sort of employment. A correspondent wrote in 1877:

> The acknowledged dearth of employment for ladies, who from various causes generally quite beyond their own control, are thrown on the world with insufficient means, and in some cases utterly destitute, induces me to make, or rather to renew, the suggestion – for I am quite aware it is not an original idea – that the tying of flies is an employment which might be adopted by necessitous ladies with advantage, and without involving any sacrifice of their dignity.

He added that professional fly tiers could make from £4 to £6 a week, sometimes £7 or £8. The editor added cautiously that there were in fact a good many people in the business, and that it was a competitive one. Major Carlisle added his opinion some years later:

* Irwin Cox termed Mrs Brocas and Mrs Cox 'The Queens of tiers'.

'There must be hundreds of young ladies who are condemned to lead a life of drudgery on a mere pittance as governesses, who would find tying flies not only a pleasant but a very profitable undertaking.' Perhaps he was right: although there were exceptions, being a governess in the Victorian age, seems from most accounts to have been not very enjoyable.

By the 1870s dry-fly fishing was in a transitional stage, and was in use in a more or less haphazard way on the Wandle, in Derbyshire, on the Itchen and Test, and probably in several other areas. Letters in *The Field* in May 1857 show that by that date it had reached the Wylye in Wiltshire and the Coln in Gloucestershire. Some modern writers have stated that it appeared on the Test a good deal later than on the Itchen, and J.W. Hills' discussion of this question in *A History of Fly Fishing for Trout* (1921) may have been responsible for this. Hills only mentions the testimony of Froude and Charles Kingsley, who were wet-fly fishermen, and Herbert Maxwell's book *The Chronicles of the Houghton Club* (1908). Maxwell made no mention at all of the dry fly at Stockbridge, 'which is truly amazing', comments Hills. I doubt if it is amazing at all. The impression handed down to us of the original Houghton Club is one of a cheerful, convivial group of friends: a country version of one of the more relaxed West End clubs of the time, where the social side was as important as the fishing. Members were there to enjoy themselves, and used fairly simple and traditional methods, such as blow-lining, cross-lining, spinning and baiting with live minnows. Members, such as Francis Popham (d. 1859), who stuck exclusively to the use of the artificial wet fly were unusual. This was hardly a powerhouse seething with the latest ideas, and when the dry fly began to come into the Test valley it was some time before it found favour on the waters of the Houghton Club. But we cannot speak of the Test in general from a particular fishery. In 1905 Henry G. Green, a veteran of the Fly Fishers' Club, wrote that he first saw the dry fly used in 1854 on a reach of the Test just above Romsey; and, as I have shown above, it was known and used from 1860 at Longstock. Besides, with so many anglers fishing both streams, it would be quite inconceivable for practice on the Itchen to have been so far in advance of that on the Test (as has been often suggested).

The question of the antiquity of the dry fly has been discussed a good deal, and I do not enter into it here, except to say that it has always seemed to me that something more or less like the dry fly may have been used for hundreds of years. Old-time anglers cannot have failed to observe fish feeding at the surface. On many fishing days they would float their flies if they could and for as long as they could – when they sank they became wet flies. In 1845 a well-known angler in Exeter was making his own floating flies, using cork for the bodies. There may have been many such examples. If anglers were not practising dry-fly fishing in a fully-developed sense as we know it, it was because the right technology was not yet available to them. In 1886 the veteran angler H.R. Francis, remembering his youth in the 1840s, wrote: 'Every fly-fisher must have occasionally seen a fly, which he had just bent on, taken by a fish before it had ceased to float.' The well-known passage from Pulman (1851) is often quoted as if it was a milestone in practice. Literary evidence can be useful, but the fact that the dry-fly technique was not unambiguously described in earlier books need not be conclusive. What might be called inherent probability can sometimes be a useful starting point.

However it may have originated, by 1870 it was an established practice on several streams. The flies were not well designed, they were whipped onto gut (and usually whipped off again fairly quickly at the river side), and did not float well. And the rods and lines required to deliver the small dry fly accurately at a particular rising fish were only just becoming available. There was little guidance in print, and anglers were more likely to learn the technique by watching and talking to their more experienced brethren.

The two great steps forward were firstly better fly construction, and secondly the development of a waterproofing agent. As to the first, Halford played his part, but only after Ogden, David Foster, and, some years later, Marryat and H.S. Hall had all worked in the field. By 1886 a well-made dry fly would have a substantial hackle, perhaps two, for good floatation (something David Foster insisted upon) a body probably made with stripped peacock quill, whisks from long fibres from a spade cock feather, and split wings of doubled fibre, for durability, taken from opposite wings of a bird, probably a starling. This last feature, mentioned by Ogden and developed by Marryat and Hall, produced an outward-curving flare in each wing, so that (it was hoped) the fly would alight as if by parachute on the water in a cocked up position like the natural dun.

The use of floatant, was also a great advance. It reduced the amount of false casting required to keep the fly dry and buoyant – always a wearisome activity with the heavy rods of that time. It also extended the range of materials that could be used in fly dressing. In pre-floatant times Francis, Marryat and other experienced chalk-stream hands were convinced of the value of quill. It is less popular nowadays, due to its opacity from most angles, but it has a good snappy appearance on the fly-tying table, can be dyed to any colour and, best of all, is impervious to moisture. With the advent of paraffin, fur dubbing could now be used, as Halford pointed out, although rather oddly he failed to take his own advice (see Chapter 8). Skues became an ardent convert to the use of sparkling furs for dry flies, in order to produce a transparent halo around the body silhouette, although he was aware that the trout's perception is likely to vary a good deal according to the relative position of fish, fly and light source.

Hills, writing in *River Keeper* (1934), thought that the use of paraffin arose at Stockbridge in 1895, adding: 'The Houghton Club has always been prudently conservative: but it has always led the way in fishing reforms, and so paraffin or one of its many offspring soon became the common practice.' Apart from the rather misleading suggestion that the Houghton Club led the way in new thinking in the nineteenth century, his notions about the first use of paraffin are not borne out by the evidence: Major Carlisle was using it in 1892, with no suggestion that it was new in that year. The practice began some time in the late 1880s – probably after 1887, the year in which George Bankart was calling for the invention of a 'delicate, greasy solution into which floating flies could be occasionally dipped and then whipped dry'. Halford credits Thomas Andrews of Guildford with popularizing (though not inventing) it, but without giving a date. In earlier years there were several experiments in this direction, all more or less futile. A curious plan of varnishing flies, tried by several anglers, failed to work because wings and hackles became brittle. In 1874 one enthusiast sent *The Field* some flies in which the wings of natural mayflies had been varnished and attached to the artificial; Francis Francis admired the appearance of the result but was understandably dubious about its durability. Some anglers may have used grease; the use of Eaton & Deller's famed deer fat (at 9d a tin) for greasing lines was widespread, and on a hot day in mayfly time it is easy to imagine a fisherman, with the grease in a state of liquefaction, realizing that he could also anoint his fly with it. Some professional fly-tiers were trying to find ways of waterproofing flies tied to gut as early as 1880, but whatever the substance may have been, there were complaints that it caused the wax to dissolve and the gut to draw. (George Holland of Failsworth reminded the public that his waterproofing produced flies that would not come apart, a method for which he had been awarded a silver medal at the Norwich Fisheries Exhibition.)

Perhaps the most interesting attempt to deal with the problem was that of Dr Tom Sanctuary, recorded by him in a letter to *The Fishing Gazette* in 1924:

> It was in April, 1867. I was enjoying an Easter holiday, fishing the late Mr. R.B. Sheridan's water on the Dorsetshire Frome, and was accompanied by a very intelligent lad, who carried the impedimenta. A few weeks earlier, John Hammond, the well-known Winchester fisherman, had initiated me into the art and mystery of making my fly float on the crystal waters of the Itchen, after I had completely failed to entice those wary trout by the usual two or three wet-fly means. No lubricant then, only continual whipping to get the fly dry enough to float, and, I'm afraid, it never occurred to me to grease it. Anyhow, that day subsequently on the Frome my lad, in answer to my complaint, that after a few throws the fly would persist in sinking, remarked, 'Pity, zur, that you can't oil the fly like a duck oils his feathers, then her wud float surely.' This set me thinking. The next duck that was killed at home had his oil gland carefully extracted, and I carried it about wrapped in a piece of chamois leather, and greased my flies with it successfully, till, after many days, it became somewhat 'whiffy', and I was obliged to discard it.

For most Hampshire anglers in the transitional period between 1860 and 1880 there was no conflict between the dry fly and the wet fly. Some inclined to one style or the other: others were proud of their mastery of both. It would have been quite common to arrive on the river at Houghton in the late 1870s and to find two or more different styles of angling being practised on the same day. Devotees of the new art would be propelling small dry flies into the teeth of a north wind with rods of ten or eleven feet, while traditionalists with long wands trailed a large wet fly (perhaps two) across and down. The notion that the former was in some way morally superior, or that the latter was a nuisance on the river, had not yet arisen, but it was only a few years away. It was beginning to be felt by some, however, that the wet fly was a more crude method, with less intrinsic interest. In 1876 one of Major Carlisle's early contributions to *The Field* referred to the approach of the new season, and advised, in view of the bad weather, that 'the only chance would be to use two flies, an olive dun for tail and Wickham's Fancy for dropper, casting them anywhere and everywhere, even downstream, letting the flies sink . . . but this is to my mind, bungling horrid work, and not worth the trouble.' Francis Francis was less fastidious, beginning his season on Anton or Itchen with the sunk fly, then, as weather and water moderated and trout became more cautious, changing to the floating fly. On dark, windy or rainy days in the summer he would change back to wet fly. It was left to Skues years later to point out that, although the downstream method was often crude and primitive, it could be rewarding. A skilled and subtle performer would fish in short drifts over the tail of weed beds or other likely spots, and without letting rapid and unnatural drag develop before lifting and casting again.

Also, early wet flies were not all dressed on clumsy meat-hooks; Durnford is known to have used quite small patterns, and the Kienbusch collection at the Princeton Library includes some flies which date from the late eighteenth century on hooks equivalent to the modern size 18. Wet flies used by Francis Francis were small in size and used in a discreet manner, so as not to disturb the water. Towards the end of his life he was saddened to find that the rules of engagement on chalk streams were beginning to change and harden in favour of the exclusive use of the dry fly. If he had lived on until 1900 he would have been even more dismayed.

Angling authors were critical of the usually available hooks of commerce. Stewart was devoted to the round-bend hooks of Bartleet and Adlington, and recommended Charles Kingsley to take them up and to abandon using Kirby snecks, square snecks and other undesirable products. Francis Francis, well known for his dramatic and extensive disasters in playing fish, blamed hooks and gut impartially. Hammond was wont to say that he never knew anyone rise so many fish as Francis, or lose so many. One day at Winchester Francis lost a well-known fish he described as

> the king of the district, a huge fellow of quite 6lb, who took a small quill gnat and some 20 yards of line upstream with it. Hooks are not what they used to be, however, that is quite certain; and he broke it when there was but a moderate pull on him, for I know too much of my fish to haul on a big 'un. If I could but have got him on a mayfly! Jeerusalem!

These earlier flies were all tied to gut. When Halford came to the Test in 1877 there would not have been any eyed flies amongst his equipment. The story of the development of the eyed hook has been dealt with elsewhere by Courtney Williams in *Angling Diversions* and in David Beazley's interesting articles in *The Journal of the Fly Fisher's Club* in 1995, to which the reader is referred for more detail. Attempts had been made in the past to develop the eyed hook, but most examples were clumsy and more useful for bait fishing. The perfecting of a light, strong, well-profiled hook for flies, and in particular for floating flies, was a difficult achievement and had to wait until the late 1870s, when Henry Sinclair Hall and George Bankart co-operated, to the lasting benefit of fly fishermen. They had been inspired to think about the idea after seeing W.H. Aldam's book *A Quaint Treatise on "Flees, and the Art a Artyfichall Flee Making"* (1876). This magnificent work, its text taken from a manuscript of around 1800 in the vernacular of Derbyshire, is today one of the treasures of angling book collectors. Its important feature lay in the twenty-five artificial flies included as examples in sunk mounts. They were all dressed on gut in the usual manner except for two Mayflies with detached bodies in the final mount, which were tied on eyed limericks specially made by Bartleet of Redditch. Hall and Bankart went about the task of designing a small, neat, eyed hook with great thoroughness (Bankart later said that he had received 240 letters from Hall on the subject) and of finding a suitable manufacturer. Eventually, after several false starts, they secured a batch of which they approved from Hutchinson of Kendal (successors to Adlingtons) in March 1879.

The advantages were obvious. Any reasonable combination of hook size and gut diameter could now be used, and the angler had the option of deciding the combination, rather than having to rely on the opinion of the fly-dresser. For example Francis Francis complained in 1876 that his entire consignment of Mayflies had been tied on gut that was much too fine. Also, and equally important, the fly could be retied whenever it seemed as if the fatigued gut was about to part through energetic false casting. In 1889, just before paraffin came into general use Halford was advising the angler to false-cast up to *thirty* times when the fly had become waterlogged. Moreover, a fly on an eyed hook will last for years in a fly box, long after the gut of a blind-eyed fly will have perished.

Eyed hooks were not entirely new: Marryat had been using them in the early 1870s, and Farlows claimed to have been supplying them for twenty years. But no one had been able to make the excellent practical product that Hall and Bankart had brought into being in 1879. Soon afterwards Hall gave parcels of the new hooks to a number of chalk-stream anglers – Major Turle, Henry Collins of the Hungerford Club, Marryat, Marston, Francis and Halford. Francis, writing to *The Field* in 1880, called it 'the hook of the future'. Marryat became an instant convert and began to use them from August 1879. He wrote to Hall in 1880:

> I consider you and Messrs H. *have created the eyed hook for trout flies*. I wandered east and west for years hankering after a right hook; then I spotted some in ——, heavy and bad; then I bought grosses of Mr Aldam; then I bought of you, and having at last got *the* thing, I have some stacked away in case of accidents. I have always insisted that Adlingtons and Hutchinson were the only makers. The fault they had has been too deep barbs; this is remedied in the present hooks, and they are as good as can be. I shall never use any but H. and Sons eyed hooks till I get to flies too small to tie on them.

In 1900 a correspondent in *The Field* called the eyed hook and the dry fly the two biggest advances of the nineteenth century in trout fishing. The development of the second could not have made much progress without the first. It seems all the more surprising, therefore, that this excellent idea was slow to catch on. In 1886 Halford devoted the first chapter of *Floating Flies and How to Dress Them* entirely to the eyed hook and its obvious advantages, but at this date many people were still using flies to gut. In particular, wet-fly anglers in the north, such as E.M. Tod and Henry Cadman, stuck to the old ways. Tod said bluntly 'I do not like eyed hooks'. They thought sunk flies on blind hooks 'swam' better in the water (a belief shared by G.E.M. Skues), but of course they did not have the problem of false casting. The men in the south were slow to change too. T.J. Mann never took to the eyed hook; his heavy catches of Test trout were caught on flies to gut, which he continued to use to the end of his life. Edgar Shrubsole the tackle dealer believed that eyed hooks led to false rises and scratched fish. A lengthy and at times short-tempered correspondence on the subject arose in the *Fishing Gazette* in 1886 and lasted for weeks, and it is interesting to find R.B. Marston, the editor, siding against the eyed hook. It was some time before he was converted. In spite of setbacks the trade, with Hall's help and guidance, continued to develop eyed hooks in several shapes, and in sizes down to 000 (or 17), then regarded as being as small as was safe for trout fishing.

If hooks were a problem gut was much more so. At that date it was the least reliable item in the angler's equipment. For many years, right up to the age of nylon, books of general advice on fishing continued to contain advice (often running to several pages), about the use and numerous drawbacks of gut. Because it was a naturally produced substance the only thing about it that could be relied upon was its variability. In the 1870s nearly all the silkworm gut available in Britain was imported from the province of Murcia in Spain, where a large number of villages were involved in its production, at least when not interrupted by appalling visitations of cholera. The unfortunate caterpillars were raised to maturity, then steeped for several hours in vinegar; skilled women then drew out the entrails and washed and dried them. A certain amount of rough sorting took place in Murcia, and the lengths were then tied up in hanks and sent away. Further sorting by length and diameter would take place on arrival in Britain. From time to time representatives of British firms would travel out to Valencia to try and influence the mode of production. In 1886 Marston wrote:

> The thanks of all anglers are due to Mr. Samuel Allcock for the great efforts he makes to put the best procurable gut into the market. He goes to Spain, where the house has a manufactory, every year, and we

> believe he is having experiments made with a view to getting longer and finer undrawn gut than is possible at present. May he succeed!

It was not common to get more than sixteen or seventeen inches of gut from each silkworm. In February 1886 Hardy Brothers proudly announced that they had just received from Spain a good stock of 15,000 lengths of 'beautifully fine gut', calling attention to the unusual fact that they averaged nineteen inches in length.

Making up a tapered cast involved much selecting and rejecting of samples and tying of connecting knots. Each piece of gut was often not of regular diameter throughout, but tended to tail off for an inch or two at each end, and these extremities needed first to be cut off. Flat or 'tawsy' gut was rejected. For colour, a neutral pearly hue was most admired. The gut lengths then had to be soaked in water before being knotted up into a cast. The best advice was to keep gut in soft wash-leather, and not to allow it to get too dry or damp or expose it to direct sunlight. Even with all this care, it was a treacherous substance, and had a low level of breaking strain. Gut of seven-thousands of an inch was usually rated as 4x (though even here there were different views), and would break at about a pound and a half dead weight. One wonders how large chalk-stream trout in weedy rivers could ever have been landed at all in the reign of Queen Victoria. (Modern standard nylon of equivalent diameter would break at three to three-and-a-half pounds, and double-strength at about six pounds.) Furthermore, gut was more subject to damage in use, and soon lost its first strength. The practice of 'drawing' some gut samples between steel plates to make its diameter more regular made things worse: it may have improved its appearance, but it had the effect of removing the outer skin. Drawn gut soon began to fray with casting and collision with bankside vegetation, and some experienced anglers avoided it. C.H. Cook ('John Bickerdyke') wrote in 1889: 'My advice is never to use it if trout can be caught without it. More than one of my angling friends will never use it under any circumstances whatever.' On the other hand, it was becoming an article of faith in the south of England that educated trout in clear streams needed delicate tackle. Francis wrote in 1882: 'Fine gut and small flies form the whole back-bone and mystery of our Hampshire fishing', but he continued every year ruefully to record a wave of disasters with lost fish. 'Finest undrawn' was frequently recommended, and many chalk-stream anglers preferred to fish with heavier points and land more fish, even if it meant rising less. Tom Sanctuary throughout his life never used finer than 2x undrawn, or indeed flies smaller than 0 (or 15). Halford's policy, after many bitter experiences, was to fish with heavier gut. The tale of breakages in his diary went on for years. With the advent of the eyed hook things took a slight turn for the better, but his diary continues to record sad events – 'Broken five times this evening' is typical. This may have caused him in 1889 to advise the angler to keep his hand off the line as the fish rose, and to 'strike from the reel', in order to avoid a smash. Skues was disapproving of Halford's tackle when he first met him in 1891, writing, 'I took a look at his fly and was not a little shocked to see how coarse was the gut'. On the other hand Skues was to receive a sharp lesson a few years later when he was invited to Halford's fishery at Ramsbury, where 'I found my Itchen points over fine for the powerful fish of the Kennett [sic], for they smashed me again and again'.

It is likely that at this date gut was less reliable than it became fifty years later. Hills was quite sure of it; in *My Sporting Life* (1936) he wrote: 'Gut is stronger than it was. There is a story of Marryat fishing up the Black Ditch and being broken time after time by the mighty fellows which it harboured. That could not happen today to a novice, still less to a Marryat.' (It might be added that Marryat on that occasion lost *nine* fish.) But Marryat and Halford, although very subtle in all that led up to the deception of trout, were exceedingly rough and bullying when they had hooked them.

In the matter of the quality of gut Halford had no influence at all on any improvement. When we come to the development of lines and rods it is quite different, for this was an area where he was to become very active. In his Wandle days he began, as we have seen, with the traditional line composed of horsehair and silk. Some anglers stuck with the old type of line for years after it had become obsolete, and as late as 1914 William Senior confessed to a sentimental and illogical love for it. The modern angler might wonder wherein lay the charm. A major drawback was that it was too light for effective casting until it became waterlogged, after which it became sagging and unmanageable. Another was that the hair component would soon start to break, and a number of points or prickles of hair would protrude and prevent the free running of the line in the rings. Shooting the line was not to be thought of. By the 1870s the more advanced lines made all of silk had been available for some time. In *The Practical Angler* (1857) Stewart wrote, 'Lines made entirely of silk, prepared in some patent manner, are now in common use, and seem likely to supersede every other kind'. He praised the ease with which they could be thrown but warned that they should be carefully dried after use, to avoid rot. Cholmondeley-Pennell records the appearance of the new 'cable-laid' or braided silk lines from the Manchester Twine-Spinning Company in the late 1860s, and the unsuccessful attempts to waterproof them. 'The Company, however, informed me that at my suggestion they were about to try experiments with oil dressings, with what result I have not yet [1 January 1870] heard.' There was a field for research here, in which Halford and Marryat were later to involve themselves. It took some time for oil-dressed lines to displace the traditional lines, such was the conservatism of the angling consumer. Perhaps they were taking their cue from Francis, who as late as 1882 was writing: 'I have tried a great variety of lines, and after all, I come back to plaited hair and silk, tapered, of course, but not too long in the taper. . . . Some of my friends prefer the eight-plait silk, rubbed with deer fat.'

Rods were also developing in the middle of the century. Stewart thought that a rod of ten feet, if made stiff enough, would cast further than one of thirteen feet made in the limber, over-supple style so common at the time, but this was a rather radical view and took some years to catch on. It was much more common by the riverside to see ponderous rods of a type not very different from half a century earlier. Sheringham wrote in 1921 that he had once tried casting with one of these ancient weapons, fourteen-and-a-half feet in length and made about a hundred years earlier. He described it as a thing of beautiful workmanship, 'but I should feel very puzzled to catch trout with it today', and recorded 'a feeling of complete helplessness as I held it in my hand'. When Major Carlisle made his debut on the Itchen in 1861 he was armed with a twelve-foot greenheart rod by Farlow. In his recollections fifty years later he admitted that he made a sad fool of himself: 'Those flies on gut, and my floppy rod. Oh! In my frantic attempts to dry the fly, as I saw others do, I whipped them off by the dozen, to say nothing of getting everlastingly hooked up in the grass behind me, owing to the floppy rod.' These earlier rods were often fitted with folding rings, which made packing and unpacking a rod easier, but had no other virtue at all compared to the fixed snake rings which came later. Even though shorter rods were coming in at this time, some anglers retained an almost perverse faith in the tackle of their youth. Francis Francis had learned his trade in an earlier era, as could be seen from his tackle, but his rods, although long were clearly not of the invertebrate kind ('There are not many ordinary trout that can beat my Dickson rod.'). From long practice and natural dexterity he used the long rod to great effect, even for dry-fly fishing. At Houghton in October 1882 R.B. Marston and Alfred Cooper the artist were fishing at Houghton with Francis, and watched his technique with admiration:

> Mr Francis goes in for a long double-handed rod and makes every inch of it do its work too. I shall never forget seeing him fish that stream from the bridge to the fishing house; it was done by inches, every bit of water was searched by his single wee fly, dried between each cast, and so fine was the gut casting line that I could rarely see where it fell on the water.

Major Carlisle was another of the older school who resisted the changes, and as late as 1889 was still using a fifteen-foot rod to command the wider shallows of the lower Test, although he did admit that it tended to pull the fly out of the fish's mouth.

Rods were made of a variety of materials: whole cane, hickory, lancewood, greenheart and other woods. Ogden of Cheltenham assiduously pushed the virtues of his short powerful rods made of Blue Mahoe – a springy wood from a West Indian tree, a member of the hibiscus family and now regarded as the Jamaican national tree. But the new split-cane rods, solidly and heavily built by our standards today, were winning converts all the time, as the need was realized to deliver the heavier lines into the wind without breaking the rods. By the time Halford came to Houghton single-handed rods of ten or eleven feet were available, weighing about the same number of ounces, and of great power in use. They may have been shorter than those of the previous generation but the new dry-fly technique, with its busy routine of false casting, meant that if anything fishing was more exhausting, indeed sometimes painful. There are accounts from this period of anglers having to give up fishing halfway through the day and withdraw to nurse a damaged hand. Marston once recorded that his wrist had become so numb on a chalk-stream expedition that he did not have the strength to strike at a rise, and on a promising mayfly day at Ramsbury in 1894 Halford came upon his guest Thomas Andrews sitting on a stile nursing his right hand and complaining that he could no longer hold the rod. It seems odd that, when the light American rods came in a few years later, there was once again a conservative reluctance on the part of many experienced anglers to adopt them. Several makers as early as the mid-1880s showed that a nine-foot rod weighing as little as six ounces could be made, but such productions were usually described as ladies' rods. The ounce-to-the-foot wrist-breakers were to be seen on British rivers well into the twentieth century.

Halford therefore entered the world of the southern chalk stream at a time of great ferment and fluidity. It is doubtful if his doctrine could have developed and advanced as it did without the new technologies referred to above: in particular, the shorter, more powerful rods, the heavy lines and the eyed hook. And there already existed a number of new ideas, promising experiments and fruitful practices for him to observe and master. Dry-fly fishing was still in an imperfect and somewhat confused state. There were many stray and intriguing references to the new practice in books and journals, but no proper manual for chalk streams. What was needed was a master hand to draw all the strands together, to settle the basic rules of practice, and to codify them in book form for the angling public.

4 Houghton: The Club and the Anglers

Two miles to the south of the handsome old town of Stockbridge in the valley of the river Test, the traveller comes to Houghton and Bossington. The Hampshire lane turns to the east and passes over a series of bridges below which flow channels of sparkling water. The ancient system of watering the meadows has led to a division of the river into a number of channels, and it is a puzzle to know which is the main river. For anglers all over the world this is holy ground, resonant with old associations. The very names are a litany of chalk-stream history: Sheepbridge, Boot Island, Black Lake, North Head, Machine Barn Shallow. The fishing in this choice corner of southern England is controlled by one of the best-known fly-fishing clubs in the world, the Houghton Club, with its headquarters in the Grosvenor Hotel at Stockbridge. The Club began in 1822, and secured the use of a number of river pieces above and below the town. Most of the angling in the earlier days seems to have been done in the spring. As the season advanced weeds would grow apace, trout would become more shy, and the tackle and methods of that era would become ineffective after the first few weeks. Members would come down to Stockbridge and stay for a week in the season of the grannom, go away and return later for the mayfly. After this, the river in summer saw very few anglers.

But by 1877, when Halford came to the Test, the status of the lowest or Houghton reach had entirely changed. For some years it had been held on lease from the lord of the manor, Charles Warner of Winchester, and then from his legatee, Frederick Warner. In 1871 the Club learned that the fishing part of the Houghton manorial rights had been acquired by Dr Charles Thomas Wickham of St Thomas Street, Winchester, remembered in angling history as the inventor of the Wickham's Fancy. The Houghton Club observed the newcomer with some disquiet. An entry for 13 April 1871 in *The Chronicles of the Houghton Club* runs: 'Our new landlord, Mr Wickham, M.D. from Winchester has been here frequently. He avows friendly disposition . . .' There was good reason for this uneasiness, for two years later relations broke down, Wickham took the fishing in hand, and at the end of 1873 the Club lost all its lower water from Machine Barn down to Bossington. Wickham at first pursued the idea of instituting a club with members taking shares, but this project languished, and in 1875 he formed an association of subscribing members called the Houghton Fly Fishing Club. Two years later Halford became a member. It was in fact a proprietary club, better described as a syndicate, for there was no constitution or committee. However Wickham did consult members about policy, even if he did not always take much notice of their views. For a short time John Hammond of Winchester acted as a caretaker secretary, then he handed over to Major Anthony Carlisle. Meanwhile the original Houghton Club, now with much less fishing, changed its name to the Stockbridge Fishing Association.

Francis Francis was well informed about this great change in the Test valley. In fact he had had it under observation before the new club was formed, when Wickham had been still intent on his share scheme. He wrote in June 1874:

> The next day I went over to Stockbridge to see the water of the new club; there was no fly, so we did nothing; but I mean to see it again if possible, and to get out some of those spotted pigs I saw making large waves in the shallows. What a lovely water it is! Simply perfect; the trout fisher's paradise! There are three streams making nine miles. The club is to consist of twenty members; two-thirds of them are already down, and you buy your share out and out, and when tired of it can sell it, the right being vested in trustees.

At Stockbridge there was much bitterness about this loss. The lower water, which had always produced heavy fish, was much prized, and a good deal of hard work had gone into maintaining it.

And the parlour of the Boot Inn at Houghton had been appreciated as an important retreat for the refreshment of tired and baffled fishermen (although one member had complained that the chairs were too hard). The catch record of the Houghton Club showed a sudden decline after the loss of this water, from 135 in 1873 to 70 in 1874 and 62 in 1875. As will be shown, the older club had a long memory, and acted rapidly and aggressively to recover the water when their chance came some years later.

Francis kept an eye on the new club and reported with enthusiasm about the breeding arrangements, which at first were designed by Wickham to maintain as far as possible a natural fishery. In 1876 between 50,000 and 60,000 ova were stripped from some of the best spawners in the river and were kept in sixteen large boxes. When hatched the fish were released quite early on as fry; at this stage there was no attempt to put excessively large, or even just sizeable, fish into the river. The fact that the Houghton Fly Fishing Club was frequently mentioned in *The Field* was useful to Wickham in filling his membership, and in due course Francis was made an honorary member, as he was of several other clubs. He grew to love this part of the Test, particularly the Sheepbridge, where great trout lay out on the shallow ('the wariest brutes in creation', he called them), and the village of Houghton, a subject on which he easily became lyrical. In June 1875 he wrote:

> Houghton is one of the most picturesque little villages I have seen. Every cottage is smothered in honeysuckle and roses. Most of them have capital gardens, and in the bettermost the anglers find lodgings; and here, with home-brewed beer – this being one of the few places I know where everybody, even the public-house keepers, still brew their own beer (and right good stuff it is) – and with home-baked bread, home-cured bacon, fresh eggs, home-made butter and cream *à discretion*, eels from the weir and magnificent trout from the stream, with fresh garden produce, he must be a dainty angler who cannot contrive to exist without other luxuries, though there is of course butcher's meat and poultry whenever you want it. Dr Wickham has worked well to get up a club here, and I think with some success. There are plenty of fish; one member I know has this year killed about seventy or eighty fish that, take one with another, would average 2lb. apiece, so I was told.

At Houghton the fishing conditions did not at first change very much after 1875. Many of the members fished across and down with a sunk fly, sometimes with two flies, as under the former regime. In May, and again in August, minnows could be used in weirs and hatch pools. But the essential difference was that the newly formed club included several thoughtful and expert anglers whose influence was to change the whole face of fly-fishing in the south. Within a decade, Houghton became a forum where discussion accelerated revolutionary ideas, thus challenging Winchester's position as the capital of the chalk-stream world.

It was some time before Halford came to know any of these forward-thinking fishermen. By temperament a shy, cautious man, he was also conscious that he would not at first cut much of a figure on this new and daunting fishery. The Test at Houghton was a fair-sized stream, tenanted by a population of trout and grayling that were large, virtually wild and not easily fooled. With twenty members in the club, the place was well fished; consequently a good deal of patient and informed effort was usually needed to make a bag. By his own account Halford's technique and previous experience were not enough. It was like beginning all over again. It is not surprising, therefore, that for two seasons he worked hard at mastering the fishing and kept out of the way of fellow rods.

At this date a season rod at Houghton cost £20. In 1885 it rose to £25, when the reach at Marsh Court was acquired by Dr Wickham. There is always a difficulty in rendering such money sums into modern terms. Handy figures for multiplying are sometimes suggested, but these quickly become obsolete in our inflationary era. In any case, multiplying is at best a crude method, for Victorian spending patterns were rather different from ours (servants, for example, came fairly cheap). Some of Halford's financial records have survived, from which we can learn his annual expenditure on fishing. In 1882 this included his subscription for Houghton and for a syndicate at High Wycombe (three guineas), the rent for rooms in Houghton (now Bossington) Mill, and expenditure on clothing from Cordings of Piccadilly. The tackle came mainly from Bernard's shop in the West End and from Eaton and Deller in Crooked Lane in the City, a few steps from Halford's office in Cannon Street. The total in that year came to just over £100: a considerable outlay, though well within the means of a man such as Halford, who was prospering in commerce. This figure can be compared with the wages for his coachman in London of twenty-six shillings a week. The drowners, who worked incessantly at the all-important task of floating and maintaining the water meadow system of the Test valley, would have been paid about twelve shillings a week.

Halford's fishing journal did not begin until 1879. His fishing results are more fully examined in the next chapter, but the journal also records, albeit in tantalizingly terse form, his contact with fellow anglers and his reception into the inner circle at the Club. His first meeting with the prince of fly-fishers, George Selwyn Marryat, took place in the spring of that year. Halford had begun his third season in Hampshire on 18 April, and had already fished for eight days at Houghton, before going over to Winchester for a day on John Hammond's ticket fishery on the Old Barge stretch of the Itchen. It was a cold, slow day, and Halford only succeeded in achieving a moderate brace of trout of 1lb on a Blue Quill and 14oz on a Drake's Extractor. He walked back into the town to replenish his stock of flies at Hammond's shop and was there introduced to Marryat.

It was a momentous encounter, and reminiscent of Boswell's meeting with Dr Johnson in Davies' shop in Covent Garden a century earlier. In each case the eager apprentice came into the presence of the master. As we have seen, Halford was by temperament an aloof man who did not get alongside strangers easily, but he must have realized at once that this was no time for a wary approach. He had reached the stage where he knew he wanted to share such knowledge as he had acquired with the right person, to supplement it and to move it forward, and Marryat's reputation as the most skilful fly-fisherman of his generation was already known to him. We do not know how long he stayed in the shop that afternoon. He was only able to tear himself away on learning that Marryat was to fish at Houghton on 1 May, and that Francis Francis would also be there. It was to prove the turning point of Halford's life. He wrote in the *Autobiography*: 'I was most anxious to cultivate the acquaintance of both Francis and Marryat, and it has always been a source of the greatest satisfaction to me that I succeeded in making lifelong friends of both of them.'

The first day of May was windy, with snow and hail. The previous day Halford had secured a good trout of 2lb 12oz on Houghton

Upper Water, but there was no chance of repeating this performance. The party battled with the elements for some time – Halford in fact lost a fish and returned two small ones – and were no doubt glad to fall in with Francis's suggestion of adjourning to the Sheepbridge Hut near the middle of the fishery. Here they were joined by Major Carlisle. The men seem to have spent the rest of the day in fishing talk, no doubt fortified with whisky and tobacco. We cannot help feeling that angling history is the poorer for not having better records of these events: the *causeries* of Sheepbridge have passed into legend, but the detail is lost. Several other ingenious and inventive anglers were, or later became, part of the group: H.S. Hall, schoolmaster, developer of the eyed hook, and co-author of one of the most widely-used algebra books ever to torment school children; William Senior, who succeeded Francis Francis as Angling Editor of *The Field* in 1883, Dr Tom Sanctuary of Salisbury; R.B. Marston, Editor of *The Fishing Gazette*, Major Turle of Newton Stacey, some miles further upstream from Houghton; C.H. Cook ('John Bickerdyke'); Arthur Gilbey; E.J. Power; and W.H. Pope of Dorchester. There were no obvious signs in 1879 that Halford would emerge – or indeed that the other members of this talented coterie would permit him to emerge – as the leader of a new movement. The Sheepbridge Hut on that long-ago May Day arguably contained two people besides Halford who could have placed themselves at its head, and H.S. Hall, had he been there, would have made a third. It is worth looking at some of these individuals in more detail.

By 1879 Major Carlisle had been the popular secretary of the club for several years, presiding over many unofficial gatherings on the banks of the Test, and familiar to a wide public through his articles and reports in *The Field* over the well-known signature of 'South-West'. Much of his earlier life had been spent on military service in the tropics, which meant, in the conditions of that era, that he was lucky still to be alive. Carlisle was of a type now for the most part long-vanished: one of many thousands of servants of empire who endured danger and hard knocks for very little pay or official thanks. He was commissioned in 1853 into a West Indian regiment – not an ideal start to his profession, but no doubt for a man without money or influence there was no alternative. He must have been noticed quite quickly through hard work and merit, for in March 1855 he was able to transfer to the third battalion of the 60th Rifles, a much more desirable post. All his subsequent removes and promotions were without purchase, a sign that his career was being helped along by appreciative seniors. The 60th was a large regiment of several battalions, more nearly resembling a brigade in strength. A few years later it was heavily involved in the suppression of the Indian Mutiny, and Lieutenant Carlisle fought through the operations around Cawnpore until the defeat of the Gwalior mutineers towards the end of 1857, and then through a bewildering list of sieges, battles and pursuits in Rohilkhand and Oudh throughout most of the following year. Much of this was in the burning heat of summer, with savage actions occurring every few days, and a high level of mortality amongst British and native troops through exhaustion, heat stroke and cholera. Carlisle came through these hair-raising experiences without harm, but was later laid low by recurrent fevers. At that date there was little that medical science could do for the European sufferer in the tropics except to evacuate him from the area, and many an officer's record included the words 'Sent to England for the recovery of his health'. It was while he was stationed at the regimental depot in Winchester in the early 1860s that he had his first experience of the trout of the Itchen mentioned in Chapter 2. Carlisle was sent to the East more than once, and subsequently saw service in Burma, but this tall, strong man – he was just under six feet in height – although apparently unscathed in battle, fell victim again and again to microscopic enemies. Of his nineteen years' service half had been spent in convalescence from tropical diseases.

By the early 1870s he was back in England once more, and in 1872 he left the army. In the same year he took a rod on a water downstream from Winchester from Major Turle, a fellow officer from the Rifles (Turle had also been involved in the suppression of the Mutiny, and had been dangerously wounded in the siege of Delhi in 1857). Carlisle never learnt to tie his own flies, and was a little envious of Turle, who was later taught fly-dressing by Marryat. For a year or so he lived on the Thames, a move he afterwards confessed had been a great mistake in his life. Then he was drawn back to Stockbridge by a letter from Turle telling him of Wickham's new club and its need for a permanent secretary. In 1875 Carlisle and his wife quickly installed themselves in a cottage a little way out of Stockbridge on the Winchester road. From here he could reach the fishery that he was to run until 1892 by means of a tricycle – a conveyance much used at that time for those who could not afford to run a pony trap. It was the happiest period of his life, as can be seen from the piece he wrote for inclusion in Halford's *Autobiography*. His reports in *The Field* are in a rather better literary style than Halford was ever to achieve, and two in particular in 1885, entitled 'Spring Flies for Chalk Streams' and 'The Evening Rise', show a deep knowledge of chalk-stream techniques and conditions. But he was not himself an innovator, and his approach was and remained more conservative than that of the new men. He had some ideas for tackle improvement, and at one time Eaton and Deller marketed a fly box of his design, but in the drama of the next decade in Hampshire his part was a cameo one. For the new dry-fly movement he was not leadership material and had no wish to be.

With Francis Francis, the case was different: here perhaps *was* a potential leader. Something of his enormous influence in the Victorian angling world has been discussed in Chapter 2, and he had been thinking about angling problems when Halford had been a schoolboy. In the early 1880s he was beginning to study natural flies and new techniques of making artificials with much greater interest than before. However, his vast knowledge of fishing was too diffused to be brought to bear on the problems of fishing for one, or perhaps two, species of fish in one type of river, as Halford was later to do. From the beginning of his reign as Angling Editor of *The Field* he projected himself as an all-round angler interested in the pursuit of every species of fish – a tradition which was followed by his successors William Senior, C.H. Cook and H.T. Sheringham. Besides, Francis was not going to be active for many more years; in the summer of 1883 he suffered a stroke from which he was only able to make a partial recovery. He was in fact a good deal older than the others, having been born in 1822 in the greatest and last days of the stage-coach. And there is something of the Regency about Francis: his descriptive pieces in *The Field* roar and rattle like a four-in-hand down one of the old white roads of England. Some of these articles are of considerable length, but his cheerful, buttonholing style and his eager pursuit of all sorts of information carry the reader along, and no one could have complained of undue prolixity or wanted a word fewer. He got into a few rows with readers, but one could not quarrel for long with such an engaging character. After his death one correspondent wrote 'Wherever Francis went he carried sunshine with him', and his generosity to others, particularly those in trouble, was proverbial.

Francis may have been accompanied by metaphorical sunshine, but he complained that wherever he went fishing he invariably carried bad weather with him. His reports in *The Field* were full of lamentations about being pursued by rain, sleet, floods, and what he called 'a St Petersburg wind'. This caused a certain apprehension among his friends. C.W. Gedney wrote in May 1886 that the weather was atrocious when he arrived at Winchester; he then discovered that Francis was staying at the Royal, so all was explained. And when Francis arrived at Houghton for three days' grayling fishing in October 1882 Major Carlisle remarked sardonically: 'Oh, you're here. Ah, I wondered the day was so beastly'.

Francis and Marryat were constantly in each other's company. From 1879 until 1882 they fished at Winnal on the Itchen above Winchester. This water – nowadays known as Abbots Barton, and celebrated throughout the angling world by the writings of G.E.M. Skues – was acquired in 1883 by Irwin Cox, one of the proprietors of *The Field* and later President of the Wilton Club. Francis and Marryat continued to fish there after this, also Senior, C.H. Cook, Halford, Skues and indeed most of the chalk-stream big guns of that era.

Of this group Marryat was far and away the master – 'piscatorum facile princeps', as Tom Sanctuary called him – paragon among fly-fishers, all-round sportsman and loyal friend. As a youth he had lived in Dorset at Mapperton House, which his father rented from the Compton family, and had shot snipe over Powerstock Common with Sanctuary, who lived in the next parish. His father Colonel Marryat (brother of the novelist Captain Marryat) was a successful angler in local streams, and is credited with having caught 50½ brace of trout in one day on the Frome at Maiden Newton. Here the young Marryat served his apprenticeship, probably at that date still using the wet fly. After leaving Winchester College he joined the 6th Dragoon Guards (the Carabineers) as a cornet in February 1858. In July 1860 he was able to buy into a lieutenancy in the same regiment (this was in the golden days before the purchase of commissions was abolished). But he seems to have become disenchanted with an army career, and sold out in 1865. Service with a cavalry regiment may have given him one great advantage, however, for learning and constantly practising sabre exercises would naturally tend to strengthen the wrist. His later prowess with the heavy fly rods of the time, and even his ambidextrous casting must have owed something to this earlier conditioning.

Tom Sanctuary records that he lost touch with his friend during this period. Then one March day in 1879, he came upon two anglers by the Old Barge at Winchester. One 'tall, spare, clean shaven . . . with a striking physiognomy', was Marryat; the other, 'short, square, fresh coloured, with moustache and whiskers', was Francis. Characteristically they were deep in argument, into which Sanctuary was immediately drawn, about the extreme range attainable with an eleven-foot rod. In the test that followed Sanctuary managed twenty-five yards, Marryat and Francis twenty-six yards.

Much had happened in Marryat's life since he had last seen Sanctuary. Service in the army had been followed by some wild days of stock riding by the Murrumbidgee River in Australia. On his return he married, and in 1874 moved to Shedfield Grange near Southampton, within easy reach of the premier Hampshire streams. Dry-fly fishing was more widespread than when he had last been in England, and Marryat was carried away by it. He put himself under the tutelage of 'Old John' Hammond of Winchester and imbibed and soon surpassed all the teaching that was offered. He then went to Mrs G.T. Cox of Parchment Street, Winchester. But, again, it was not long before Marryat had absorbed all that she could teach him and become an expert in the field of fly-dressing. By 1878 he was teaching Major Turle how to tie flies, and in 1879 H.S. Hall. A few years later Hall discovered the gifted fly-tier George Holland in Manchester, and in 1886 tempted him to migrate south. It was Marryat however who, with Sanctuary, took the major role in setting Holland up in Salisbury, near to the house in Cathedral Close to which he had recently moved. Hall had already coached Holland in the south-country mode of fly dressing, and with Marryat or Sanctuary frequently calling into his shop with advice or encouragement, Holland and his work force in Crane Street were soon supplying a growing clientele with the latest mark of dry flies. Skues wrote years later that Hammond's flies tied to gut in the 1870s were not built to cock on the surface, had sloping wings and 'would have been equally suitable for wet fly work on the Tweed'. By the mid-1880s Holland's flies on eyed hooks were in most respects the same as the standard chalk stream flies of modern times.

Achieving the highest standards in fly-tying was characteristic of Marryat. He once told Major Turle that when he had taken up a subject he would not rest until he had made something of it. One is tempted to imagine that he would have excelled in almost any field. Gifted with a penetrating intellect, a retentive memory and enormous enthusiasm, he seemed to his friends to possess detailed information on a vast array of subjects: entomology, palaeontology, cell biology, microscopy, photography, horticulture, literature, philosophy and many others. And he was no desk or library dilettante, but a zestful open air athlete, an accurate and very safe man at a shooting drive and, above all, a master-performer with the fly rod. No man, it was said, could do things with a rod that Marryat regularly did. He revelled in the long casts of the sort that some men appear to be able to achieve, although usually at the cost of losing control of the fly. He was also fond of difficult casts into 'impossible' places. George Holland said he had seen Marryat do things with a fly rod that he would have thought 'beyond the power of mortal man'. When Carlisle wished to describe the difficulty of covering a particularly wide shallow on the Kennet it came naturally to him to write that it would need 'the marvellous casting of the renowned M——'. The Rev. Smythe recorded an expedition in a punt on the Avon in June 1885 with Marryat and Tom Sanctuary: 'It was a real treat to see Marryat cast a dry fly and to handle his rod. He can cast 87 feet with it.' Some years later Basil Field recollected

> the clumsy-looking casts purposely and artfully made by the late G.S. Marryat to obviate some apparently insuperable difficulty arising from cross currents, protruding rushes, and submerged boughs, or some such inviting combination. In such straits, after the loss of tackle and temper on my part, I have known him take the rod from my hand, and in two or three seconds it has been restored to my charge bending grandly to the struggles of a well-hooked fish. The trick looks so simple when performed by a master. Luckily we are not all conjurers, or trout-killing would become as easy as the shelling of peas.

Yet, for all his skills and knowledge, Marryat could almost never be brought to publish anything. A letter from him appeared in *The Field* in 1881 about quill bodies for flies, and another in *The Fishing Gazette* about the origin of the dry fly, and as far as is known that was the sum of his publication.* This has created a problem for subsequent researchers. Apart from a natural desire to see deeper into this remarkable man, we wish to know more about areas about which we only have secondary evidence: as for example his work with Deller on refinements of tackle, and with Hawksley, the maker of surgical instruments, in developing a better oil-dressed silk line. This reluctance to publish was perhaps part of a self-effacing habit of behaviour. Although present at one or two of the annual feasts of the Fly-fishers' Club, he preferred to take a back seat, and resisted all attempts to make him hold forth to the company. Major Carlisle wrote that he had seen Marryat the life and soul of the party in great houses, but apparently only when he chose so to be. There seems to have been a certain shyness or sensitivity about him, which turned to resentment when ill-considered attempts were made to bring him forward as a sort of entertainment in a gathering. In 1889 William Senior made a clumsy mistake with Marryat, which he must have regretted afterwards. Thinking to do him honour in the course of a speech from the chair at a Fly Fishers' dinner to which Marryat had been lured as a guest, he launched into heavy-handed praise of him and his prowess:

> You have often read in the angling magazines and newspapers references to a great master in the art of dry-fly fishing, who is always called 'M'. (Hear, hear.) He, I am happy and proud to say, is in our company tonight, and all who know him will agree with what all the keepers in the West of England and all practical men will tell you, that he is the finest dry-fly fisherman in the world. (Applause).

This might have seemed to some men to have been a graceful compliment, but that was not Marryat's way. He never came to another dinner of the Fly Fishers.

The artist Alfred Cooper recorded some reminiscences in 1906 that cast light on the other side of Marryat, and show why anglers valued his friendship. He often did very little fishing in a day on the river, preferring to wander about examining the natural world in general, or watching other fishermen. Francis Francis however was

* The 1881 letter was published by Simon Ward in *Fly Dresser* (Summer 1996). The letter in *The Fishing Gazette* is in Appendix 3.

remembered by Cooper as a persistent 'heart and soul' fisherman who stuck to it for hours. Disagreements between them were amusing – the one noisy and dogmatic, the other agile and witty. He recalled an example of Marryat's droll ways:

> Once at Winchester I had taken a barely sizeable fish, and took it up to where the two were sitting finishing their lunch. Marryat took the fish and looked at it critically, and then carefully arranging it to its best advantage on the seat beside him, and with great solemnity adding some torn grass and leaves to set it off nicely, said, "Now look here Mr C., whenever you get leave to fish on some person's water, and you catch a fish like this, just make much of it, as I have done, and then send it up to the house with your compliments and beg their acceptance of the magnificent fish, and they will think you such an almighty duffer that you will never have any difficulty in getting leave to fish there again.'

Marryat was the ideal man in whom Halford might place reliance as a guide, and in after years he always gave full and generous credit for the help given in the work they did together. In the dedication to Marryat in *Dry-Fly Fishing in Theory and Practice* (1889) he wrote that, if the book had any worth, it was 'due to the innumerable hints which you have been good enough to convey to me'.

Henry Sinclair Hall was not present on that cold May day at Houghton. In some ways he was a more formidable alternative candidate for directing the new movement. In terms of his grasp of the subject and of his practical abilities on the river bank he could not match Marryat – indeed for a time he sat at Marryat's feet and learned all he could. But, like Halford, he was a quick learner, a man of persistent energy and precise mind and, what is more, he was prepared to write down his findings. His work in bringing the eyed hook to perfection has been mentioned in Chapter 3. Having to earn his living, however, restricted his time for fishing and research; for many years he was a schoolmaster at Clifton College, Bristol, where he was Head of the Modern Side. He wrote several books on mathematics, with the idea of supplementing his income (housemasters could make money, but Hall's pay as a teacher would have been unimpressive). This plan succeeded very well. His standard algebra book for schools, which was still in use in the 1950s, made a large amount of money for Macmillan the publisher, and enabled Hall to retire from teaching in 1900.

From August 1879, and perhaps earlier, he and Marryat were conducting joint fly-tying sessions. He had begun to make his own flies from natural models in 1876. In 1882 he wrote: 'I puzzled out fly-making for myself, without any hints from anyone. After making two or three hundred flies, I made the acquaintance of two other amateur fly-dressers, with whom I have compared notes frequently during the past two or three years, and to whom I am indebted for several wrinkles' (see Appendix 4). There is perhaps a trace of vanity here, for Hall had Marryat to thank for more than just 'several wrinkles'. Also, in later years he was to admit that he had in fact used books to guide him in his first fly-dressing. In 1884, as David Beazley has shown, he entered into a shrill and ultimately self-damaging correspondence in *The Fishing Gazette* in an attempt to establish the primacy of his contribution in the development of the eyed hook, and playing down that of George Bankart. But there was no doubting his competence as an angler. His articles in *The Fishing Gazette* in 1883 and 1884 (reprinted in *Fly Dresser* in 1992) were considered by the late Jack Heddon to be 'the first detailed description of dry-fly fishing and the first detailed list of dry-fly dressings'. These articles show a thorough understanding of what the angler needs to do on a chalk stream. But Hall's writings on the subject go back even earlier. He first wrote about the dry fly in *The Field* in 1878. His contribution 'Fly Fishing in Chalk Streams' in *Angler's Note-Book and Naturalist's Record* (28 February 1880), although not so wide-ranging as the later articles, nevertheless contains many of the essential points of the new dry-fly fishing – for example: go slow, be persistent but be content also to wait and observe, search for an individual rising fish and lay siege to him, rather than exploring the water in the manner of the wet-fly fisherman, cast accurately and be independent of the wind, throw short rather than over, and study entomology.

As Skues showed in *Side-lines, Side-lights and Reflections* (1932), Hall learned the best way to make split-winged floating flies from Marryat in November 1882. At first he followed the method used by Mrs Cox, which was to tie in a vertical bunch of wing fibre and use the tying silk to divide it, and he was still advocating this method in *The Field* in August 1882 (see Appendix 4). Marryatt's new method involved removing a double thickness of fibre from the right and left wings of a starling and anchoring the composite strip in the jaws of a long-jawed bulldog forceps, releasing enough when required for each pair of wings. This combined a speedy assembly line with a neat finish. The combination of Hall's new hook and the split wings created the standard shape of dun imitations for the next hundred years.

Hall invented several interesting patterns. His Black Gnat, in which a small piece of pike scale was used to imitate the wing, was first mentioned in an article by him about Hungerford in 1884. It is seldom seen today, but was an ingenious attempt to combine the transparency and iridescence of the wing of the natural fly. He also developed a variation of the Jenny Spinner, and a Detached Olive with an india-rubber body, less long-lasting but more flexible and therefore less likely to result in short rises.

It can be seen therefore that, compared to Halford, Hall was at first ahead in the field. Yet in a few short years Halford was to overhaul him and take up a position of leadership. Hall's earlier contribution seems thereafter to have been forgotten. Skues was aware of this, and tried to put the record straight in an obituary he published in *Journal of the Fly Fishers' Club* when Hall died in 1934. He pointed out that Halford's first book could not have been written if the dry fly had not developed in such a startling way, a development which was itself dependent upon the eyed hook. Also Hall's contribution on chalk-stream fishing in the first edition of Cholmondeley-Pennell's *Fishing: Salmon and Trout* (1885) antedates Halford's first book of 1886. During the 1880s Halford must have been casting anxious looks over his shoulder at Hall, and observing his excellent pieces in *The Field* with as much alarm as interest. Was it possible that this man might publish a major book first? In the event, Halford won through by his dogged energy and persistence. He was able to pursue the crucially-important collaboration with Marryat to a far greater extent, for, although not yet retired from the business world he was much more a master of his own time than Hall could be, and was able to be in Hampshire for a large part of the season. In 1880 he hired rooms at Houghton Mill during the fishing season, and this was a masterstroke in terms of getting accepted into the group. In the absence of a clubhouse, these rooms provided a place of resort at the end of a fishing day, and must also have been important in getting as much of Marryat's time and attention as possible. By contrast, Hall was tied to terms and timetables. In the end he faded from the chalk-stream picture, leaving behind a tantalizing picture of what might have been. He continued to contribute to *The Field*, but in a style more reminiscent than innovative.

However, none of the above is intended to suggest that there was an antagonism between the two men, or that Halford in any way elbowed out a possible competitor. His diary reveals that he fished with Hall for four consecutive days in April 1884 at Houghton and Newton Stacey, and that Hall came back for another four days in September. And Halford was to include three of Hall's patterns in *Floating Flies* in 1886.

That meeting in the Sheepbridge hut on 1 May 1879 was the first of many. They were to continue for many years in various fishing huts, in the evening in the tobacco parliament at Houghton Mill, in London at Halford's house, at the Fly Fishers' Club after 1884, and at Marryat's house and indeed in his greenhouse, where he kept his insect aquaria. In such places ideas would fly about, experiments could be planned and solid advances could be made. These men were in a sense writing their own script from day to day, creating in all its details the dry-fly method that has lasted with surprisingly little modification to the present. Halford and Marryat, and later Dr Sanctuary, with Hall at a little distance, formed the working party. The others, though interested, were less engaged, and at times amused as much as impressed by the solemnity and high seriousness of the process. William Senior later described how he watched the collection and preservation of insects, and the autopsies of fish:

> To stand by while Halford and Marryat with their scissors, forceps, and what not laid out the contents of a trout's stomach, and bent low in separating and identifying the items, putting what were worthy of it under a microscope, and proceeding all the while as if the round world offered no pursuit half as worthy of concentrated attention, was most fascinating. Many a time I was a spectator – I fear sometimes an irreverent one – of this ritual, but always privileged and welcome; always, of course, sympathetic, and always in a way envious of the qualities of mind and extraordinary knowledge which made the whole work a labour of love to them.

But the records of these meetings are sparse. Halford tells us almost nothing. Some scraps of information can be gleaned from the writings of others, from which we get a fleeting impression of the after-dinner sessions at the Mill, with Francis holding forth (as one of them later expressed it) in his 'John Bull hit from the shoulder style', bearing down opposition in a frontal assault, only to find that Marryat had slipped in on the flank with some smart sally destructive of his argument. Both men spoke from a wealth of knowledge and experience, and for a year or two Halford must have sat and listened. As his own experience increased he would have begun after a time to feel justified in making contributions. The conversation did not wholly deal in fishing matters. When tongues were loosened late at night the circle would persuade Carlisle and Turle to speak of the wild times in India, or William Senior to tell of his days as a journalist and parliamentary reporter in Australia. Marryat, who of the group had the best-stocked mind, would sometimes stray into the realms of philosophy, and Halford recalled in after years 'a great night at the dear old mill at Houghton, when we led Marryat on to a series of speeches and contentions upon what he called "the teleology of the infinite" '. But no detailed account seems to have survived of any of these ambrosial nights, nor of the more down-to-earth working sessions so crucial for the development of chalk-stream practice. As lawyers say, the deeds are silent (historians have an even more melancholy phrase: no records, no history). In 1906 Marston approached Halford, suggesting that someone ought to write a biography of Marryat: presumably Halford would have a mass of relevant letters and papers? To his amazement, Halford confessed to having destroyed them all. He said, rather defensively, that he always got rid of non-business correspondence. Marryat seems fated to remain unfathomable, an enigma (even his record of service in the cavalry is missing from the Public Record Office). Perhaps the absence of reportage of the conversations is unsurprising. Many Victorians were careful about what they recorded. Middle-class life was a formal business, and personal feelings were suppressed to a degree unimaginable today. Reticence and privacy were commended, and the phrase 'wearing your heart on your sleeve' was not one of approval. Halford and his friends are difficult to interpret now, but that is how they would wish to be. If Halford left a more personal and revealing account of his day-to-day life and thoughts, it has not survived. If it ever existed it would probably have been destroyed, as have so many other diaries and journals down the ages, by his family after his death in 1914. 'After all,' they would have said, 'that's private', a phrase of considerable weight at that time.

So the historian is driven to inferences and educated guesses. We know that Halford asked Marryat to help him in solving difficulties with fly-dressing in 1879, and that from there they moved on to a much more comprehensive investigation. This does not mean that the collaboration began at once. Halford's angling journal indicates that after that day at Houghton in May 1879 he did not fish again with Marryat until the autumn of 1881 – although it is, of course, not impossible that they could have met away from the river. From then on the mention of 'G.S.M.' occurs frequently. The much bigger puzzle is to decide how much of the material in Halford's first two books is to be ascribed to Marryat. The general feeling has always been that the ideas behind the major part of the content, particularly the more original passages, belonged to him. Halford tells us in the *Autobiography* that Marryat refused to allow his name to appear on the title page of *Floating Flies* but does not really explain why, thus creating a vacuum into which much speculation has flowed. The main suggestions have been either that Marryat, always modest and generous, urged Halford to take the credit since he had done all the note-taking and writing up, or that he had become alarmed at Halford's rigid approach and he wished to distance himself from it. But this is all speculation. The plain fact is that we do not know, and, as with everything else to do with the collaboration, the main actors in the piece had no intention of enlightening us. Halford always acknowledged the help he received from Marryat but leaves us wondering about the detail. Was it *all* Marryat? we wonder: surely Halford must have produced some ideas, at least in the later stages of the collaboration. Was he merely the scribe or chronicler in the matter? To isolate the Marryat factor seems now to be quite impossible, unless a miraculously preserved hoard of crucial correspondence comes to light. The puzzle remains, and Marryat has always seemed an elusive and mysterious figure. Long after his death Skues wrote in the *Journal of the Fly Fishers' Club* that one of the advantages of meeting the great anglers in the next world might be 'to penetrate, perhaps, the secret of G.S. Marryat' – although his choice of words shows that Skues was not confident that the enigma would be solved even then.

One piece of useful evidence is to be found in the obituaries of Marryat in 1896. William Senior went out of his way to emphasize that 'It is not too much, perhaps, to state that Mr Marryat was practically the father of the now fashionable dry-fly school of trout fishermen'. And H.S. Hall added: 'There is, as a matter of fact, very little indeed in the dry-fly fisher's outfit that has not been, directly or indirectly, brought to its present state of efficiency by some clever wrinkle originally due to Marryat.' These are fairly conclusive examples of a determination on the part of friends who knew the facts of the case to ensure that he would receive his proper credit, even though he had never produced a book. But praise of Marryat does not necessarily involve dispraise of Halford. Whatever may be said of the former it was the latter who undertook the considerable labour of writing it all down. If Halford is to be seen as the midwife rather than the parent of the chalk-stream revolution, then it has to be admitted that the accouchement gave him a great deal of trouble. And, on the other hand, Marryat, by his failure to write anything in order to fix and disseminate his knowledge, had lost the chance to take control of that revolution; it was going to be interpreted through Halford, and clearly that interpretation was not going to be the same as it would have been with Marryat as leader. Marryat's disinclination to be his own publicist thus had important results later on. The rigid framework that Halford caused to close around chalk-stream methods would not have been to his taste. In particular he was more open-minded about the place of the sunk fly in the south. Skues once examined a fly book that had belonged to Marryat containing many hundreds of flies, and noted a considerable number designed to be fished under the surface. This evidence is not of itself conclusive (Marryat is known to have fished on the Eden, on the Devonshire Otter, and in many other traditional wet-fly areas), but we know from other sources that he was interested in devising nymphs for chalk streams. George Holland told Skues of some nymph experiments, apparently inconclusive, made by Marryat. The Rev. E.R.J. Nicolls, who knew him well, said years later that he was a keen dry-fly man, but by no means 'an obstinate purist'. There are even signs that in the earlier years Halford shared in this more pragmatic approach, for he included a 'Larva' imitation of the grannom in *Floating Flies* (1886), though without any instructions as to the method of fishing it. It appeared again in *Dry-Fly Entomology* in

1897, by then more properly called the Grannom Pupa. In *Dry-Fly Fishing* (1889) Halford also discusses tactics for fish taking mayfly nymphs, using a pattern devised by Marryat called the Egyptian Goose Hackle. But, as with the Grannom Pupa, Halford seems to have had no real notion of fishing these flies below or even in the surface, in fact he says of the Goose Hackle that 'in any case the fly should be dry'. This fly also reappears in 1897. George Dewar included the 'Marryat nymphae' in his *Book of the Dry Fly* (1897). A comparison of the two coloured plates is instructive. In Halford's book the fly is plentifully hackled for floating: in Dewar's the hackles are much shorter and sparser, and the fly has an altogether more nymph-like appearance. There is unfortunately no way of knowing which version would have been preferred by Marryat.

It is possible that the pragmatic Marryat slipped into quasi-nymph techniques quite easily. Halford recorded an interesting incident in *The Field*, without, one feels, any notion of its real significance. During a mayfly day on Major Turle's fishery at Newton Stacey in 1883 he could only catch one fish, and had failed with a large number; in the *Autobiography* he says he was 'utterly beaten'. He went in search of Marryat, to find that he and another rod fishing together had caught eleven trout weighing 27lb. 'He told me that at the very commencement of the rise he found the only successful plan was to use a very small fly, half dry, so that it commenced sinking just in front of the fishes' noses. . . . He also informed me that both P. and he, fishing in this manner, had done well.' Halford was terribly baffled, and grumbles: 'The reason of this idiosyncrasy neither of us could fathom, as anything more opposed to the action of the fly could not be imagined.' I doubt if Marryat was really puzzled by the behaviour of fish, which must have been taking the hatching nymph.

The above incident, and Halford's imperfect interpretation of it, could stand as a key for understanding the two men. During this heavy mayfly hatch Halford had applied his blueprint: Marryat, on the other hand, had experimented. Halford's approach to angling problems was subjective: once all the parts were researched by long and careful collection and study of the data, they accumulated into an inflexible system, and his mind would shut fast – all the fish had to do was conform. He was a cautious, dogged man, with great powers of concentration and hard work in constructing a system. Much of the time the method worked well enough, but there is no doubt that on occasion it could be rigid and myopic. With Marryat, the approach was more objective and spontaneous, and therefore more capable of varying with the conditions. It began with the fish and its requirements, rather than with the angler and his set ideas. Not for him the persistent application of a technique which, by all the rules, should be working (if only the fish would play their part) - away with it, and try something new! Marryat, although prepared to give endless time to research, was able to store the results in his mind and to deploy them on the river bank in a rapid and flexible way. His studies may have been scientific, but when he picked up a rod he became an intuitive artist. Halford was to remain all his life a scientist and technocrat.

The Halford–Marryat coalition must have been a curious one. But there is sometimes a piquancy in the attraction of opposites, and it can be fruitful in results. One wonders what would have happened if Marryat had stayed in the army, for he had the qualities needful for an inspired cavalry commander. It is revealed in the conduct of his fishing: the preparation, the careful reconnaissance, and the rapid and decisive intervention when natural conditions suddenly come to ripeness. For Halford, a fishing day more resembled a slow siege, with a great deal of pottering, rather than a campaign of manoeuvre. If he had been in the regular army, the proper place for him would have been in the engineers. But the great changes that were already afoot on the chalk streams needed rationalizing and collating. In this process a painstaking and unwearying collector of data, willing to give all his time to the work, might come into his own.

5 The Houghton Years: 1877–1886

Into the pleasant world of the Test valley came Halford at the beginning of the season of 1877, and commenced his campaign with the Hampshire trout. For some years he continued to fish in the streams of the Home Counties – the Wandle, the Colne, the Misbourne and several others – though mainly, it seems, because a quick one-day raid could be made to such places from London, where his business interests still held him. He also made occasional expeditions to streams in the north, and to Scottish salmon rivers. These visits were not very satisfactory. He had some success with salmon fishing, but he indicates in the *Autobiography* that he thought it was a slow business. And his attempts to get on terms with the trout of wet-fly streams, as I shall show elsewhere, were not very fruitful. And so these forays further afield grew fewer and fewer as the fascination with chalk streams grew upon him. Eventually they ceased altogether, and in the last thirteen years of his life he never cast a line outside Hampshire.

For newcomers, the first visit to the Test is often an alarming as much as a delightful experience. The pellucid water with every variety of weed, the plump and disdainful trout clearly in view, the critical eye of keeper or other anglers, the pervasive sense of tradition and of special privilege – all these things put the angler on his mettle at first, determined not to relax until he shall have scored some success. In 1877 the fishing was not easy. Nowadays we associate Test fishing in the nineteenth century with bumper catches and red-letter days. But, as I have shown, except in some closely-preserved fisheries, such events belong more to the records of the early part of the century. At Houghton things were a little different. A population of excellent indigenous fish was only supplemented by turning in stock of fry size – at this date not even yearlings were put in. The techniques of fish-breeding in Britain were already far advanced, but at Houghton the policy of introducing quantities of large stock fish was not admired. Not yet anyway. And these wild or nearly wild fish had seen a good many counterfeit flies. The water was fished by a club that, when at full strength, numbered twenty members. They included some extremely practised performers. And their equipment, as we have seen, was being improved year by year.

It was not surprising therefore that Halford made a slow start. He had imagined after his experience of the Wandle that he knew how to catch fish on a dry fly. The behaviour of the Houghton trout soon put him in a chastened frame of mind. With becoming candour he admits in the *Autobiography* that for him the way forward would only be by 'prolonged study of the river, the fish and their habits, and the insects on which they fed'. The words convey not only the Halford method but also the attitude of mind: for him fishing was to be regarded as a subject of high seriousness, to be approached in an academic and scientific way. Once a rigorous programme of 'prolonged study' had been carried out he (and in due course his followers) would be in possession of a sort of infallible blueprint that would always avail. Halford was to spend the rest of his life pursuing this elusive ideal.

We can know little about his first two seasons at Houghton. He tells us nothing of them in the *Autobiography*, beyond mentioning the vast swarms of grannom which then regularly appeared every spring, the spectacle of which was an encouragement to him to begin dressing his own flies. Major Carlisle recorded that the grannom in 1877 appeared quite suddenly on 20 April. In one thirty-yard stretch at least fifty trout were rising, and 'the river looked as if it were being pelted with big stones, so fast and furious were the rises'. After several accidents Carlisle lost all his grannom patterns. He applied for help to a fellow rod, who gave him some patterns – 'It was not exactly a grannom, but a wonderful killer' – from Holroyd's of Gracechurch Street, a fly with a woodcock wing, ash-coloured dubbing, ginger hackle and a yellow tag. In 1878 the grannom came up again in clouds around 15 April. It was said to be a problem to know which fish to choose to attack, but when the season was over anglers agreed that it had not been so plentiful as in 1877. Halford's journal shows that he never really made much of the grannom. He was frequently in the wrong place, and even when he was present at a great swarming, the tempo of events seems to have been too much for him. Instead of a drawn-out rise, as with olives in spring, it would be a matter of five-minute bursts, and an angler had to act very quickly. After 1886 Halford had no more grannom fishing at all.

In the absence of information about those first two mysterious seasons we are probably safe in assuming that he did little damage to the stock of fish there. No doubt there was a great deal of observation and experiment, as the new man sought to penetrate Hampshire ways and mysteries. The first extant volume of the Halford journal begins in 1879. These volumes were meticulously made up each day from small rough pocket-books (several of which have also survived), that he carried with him while fishing. The system has something of the counting-house ledger about it, as if the catches resembled an amassing of capital (see Appendix 1 for a summary). Its carefully worked-out format leads one to wonder if it was preceded by an earlier record, perhaps suppressed because the tangible results had been so meagre, but at least in 1879 we can know what Halford actually caught. And from then until his last fishing season in 1913 we have a complete unbroken record of every single one of his captures.

Column-headings in the journal for this and several subsequent years remained the same:

Date	*Place*	*Wind*	*Trout*	*lb oz*	*Grayling*	*lb oz*	*Remarks*

The artificial flies used appear in the Remarks column until 1881, when a separate column for flies was added, and years later (when he acquired his own fishery at Mottisfont in 1905), another column was added for fish caught by friends. By that date the multiplication of categories was such that the record ran across two pages.

For the modern researcher, it is a matter for regret that Halford did not follow the excellent method later adopted by J.W. Hills, who wrote an account in the form of a short essay about each day's fishing; some of these are reproduced in *My Sporting Life* (1936). But Halford fished on many more days than ever Hills could have managed – sometimes sixty or seventy days a year, and in three of his seasons over one hundred days – and such a constant literary effort would have been unrealistic. But at least this meticulous and frank record, with the many blank days honestly recorded, enables one to follow Halford closely in his fishing, to observe what he was doing and, to some extent, what influenced his thinking.

The record for 1879 may have been an improvement on the previous two seasons, but it does not show anything very startling in terms of catches. The bare facts are that Halford fished for thirty-seven days and caught fifty trout weighing 41lb 10oz; twenty-eight days were spent at Houghton, producing sixteen trout for a weight of 23lb 15oz. In contrast with his later years, Halford at this date was trying to extend his experience, and still ranged about within and outside the chalk country. Apart from the visit to Winchester mentioned in Chapter 4, he fished twice at McCrae's fishery at Mitcham on the Wandle, and spent a day at Hungerford (a blank), where the future prophet of the dry fly admitted in his journal to using an Alexandra, no doubt in desperation in the last hour of a fruitless day. He also spent a week fishing Yorkshire streams in the summer.

The main effort however was on the Test, where he began on 18 April, fishing almost continuously until the end of the month. The first written record of a Halford fish from the Test appears on 18 April: a trout of 2lb 8oz on a Grannom, in a cold north-east wind. He had another of 2lb 4oz on the 26th and one of 2lb 12oz on the 30th. These were the pick of the April fish; the rest were from 1lb 10oz downwards. The larger fish were probably not in first-class condition. The winter of 1878/79 had been exceptionally severe and the cycle of hard winters continued for several years. Eager as men were to get to the riverside after the winter exile, an opening day of 25 March (changed from 15 March in 1878) was seen to be too early and was changed to 2 April a year or so later. (Major Carlisle would have preferred 15 April, and Marryat was fond of saying that at the beginning of the season the anglers were ready before the fish.) The spawning of the trout that winter had been late and prolonged; Carlisle in one of his reports in *The Field* quoted a keeper who was heard to say 'He never knowed 'em humbugging over it so long before'. The spring that followed was cold and windy, and so wet that the Test was virtually in flood at times.

The first big appearance of grannom in 1879 was on 23 April. Halford returned from a frustrating day on the Upper Water (one trout of 14oz) to learn that Hambrough, one of his fellow rods and deviser of the Hambrough Sedge, had made a great slaughter on the Lower Water. One of those phenomenal appearances of grannom had taken place which are now part of Test history, and Hambrough's fifteen trout weighing 29lb recalled the exploits of a generation earlier; such bags were still possible if the conditions were right. Naturally, Halford was to be found on the Lower Water the next day, artificial Grannom at the ready. Sadly he could only record a blank.

In fact blanks at Houghton were fairly frequent for Halford: only in 1883, 1886 and 1892 did he average more than one trout a day. These figures might seem strange, even astonishing, to modern anglers; we are accustomed to thinking of the men of those days as fishing in a golden age, with opportunities denied to, or unimaginable by us. Several factors may in part explain the puzzle. First, as I have indicated above, Houghton was quite hard-fished, and not heavily stocked with trout from the fish farm. Secondly, rods, though advanced by comparison with those of the 1840s and 1850s, were still cumbersome wrist-damagers by modern standards, and required strength and manual dexterity. Francis Francis, as we have seen, insisted on the merits of a fourteen-foot double-handed rod for dry-fly fishing. Halford did not go so far as that; at first he used an eleven-foot rod by Eaton and Deller, then one of ten feet three inches, weighing 11¼ oz, or over an ounce to the foot. The process of fishing must have been slow, especially as Halford tells us in *Dry-Fly Fishing* that one should false-cast a thoroughly drowned fly at least thirty times in order to dry it. And the rest of his equipment would seem heavy and awkward to present-day anglers. For example, the weight of his fly boxes, which increased in number over the years, varied between a pound and a pound and a half – his Mayfly boxes weighed two pounds. Also in the course of the next decade he was to become fascinated with entomology, and increasingly would spend a large part of an angling day in pursuing insects rather than trout.

Nevertheless, when all allowances are made, it still seems somewhat odd that he caught so little. It is true that Senior wrote that Halford was less concerned than most fishermen to 'make a bag', but this referred to his later years, when he had got his own piece of fishing, was more relaxed about his own achievement, and was helping his guests and friends to catch fish. In his Houghton period he was as anxious to show results as anyone else (the record of visits to private fisheries where the fishing was easier show that he had no objection to the occasional massacre). Even after a number of seasons at Houghton, by which time he was seen as an expert, his results remained much as before: in 1892, his last year at Houghton, with two major books and many articles behind him, he took thirty-four days to catch thirty-nine trout. The most educated guess must be that, apart from the limitations of his equipment, Halford was simply a slow, painstaking performer. His elaborate and carefully-honed method worked well when conditions were right. Given a pleasant day, with a good olive hatch lasting for two or three hours and rising fish to negotiate, or a good mayfly day, that method would pay. But, as discussed in Chapter 3, it was a rigid and rather narrow technique, not adaptable when the trout declined to play the game.

Halford's visits in May, June and July brought even less result. Apart from his blank day at Hungerford he was only able to show one smallish trout for three days at Houghton, and some fish from streams near London. He returned to Houghton for six consecutive days in late July, but this only produced two trout and seven grayling. The evil weather pattern continued throughout the summer: the hay and clover harvests was ruined, and cereal crops turned black and began to sprout in the ear. His last Houghton trout of the 1879 season was caught on a Drake's Extractor on 23 July. In August he made the Yorkshire trip mentioned in Chapter 6, and he did not fish for Test trout again that year.

No proper records were kept by the Club in 1879, or indeed until much later, but it is likely that the other rods did not do very well. Major Carlisle, writing in December, describes the season – one of heavy water in which fish did not move much on the surface – as 'a dismal record' – adding however that his own bag for the season was forty-one trout for 77lb 3oz. The mayfly season was quite good, but Halford had not been able to get to Houghton between 3 May and

21 July. Business interests still claimed much of his time, and he probably missed the cream of the year.

This curious season, which would have discouraged many lesser men, had two interesting pointers for the future. First, one of the July trout was caught on a Silver Sedge. Halford was beginning to appreciate evening fishing, something he was to develop a good deal and which was often to save the second part of the season for him. Later he was to write with enthusiasm in *The Field* about his successes with the Silver Sedge, and with the more sophisticated Dark and Medium versions. Secondly, he came back to Houghton in the autumn and had some success with the grayling. He was on the river for six days in October and three days in November, catching seventeen, the largest being 1lb 14oz (see Appendix 2). This very moderate result was enough to encourage him to persevere in the years that followed, and he soon began to encounter some much heavier grayling.

The next few seasons were no more productive in terms of trout per day. One cannot help admiring Halford's persistence in the face of adversity. Fish on the bank were not the whole story, of course. His grand project was to learn, with Marryat's help, every single thing that it was possible to know about chalk-stream fishing, and this increasingly occupied most of his time. Once he had hired rooms at Houghton Mill he could live on the water for much of the season. There was no doubt that the fascination of the place was very great. Francis Francis wrote in *The Field* in May 1880 that he had never seen a water so improved as Houghton since it had come into Dr Wickham's hands: the banks had been made up, shallows cleared, weed-cutting properly done, and hatching of ova taken in hand. There was a rumour that the rods were to be reduced in number and the subscription raised, 'the object being to have only a snug family of good anglers who may have real good sport, and no muffs to go wandering about all over the water, walloping every shallow and frightening every fish'.

Halford continued to fish the metropolitan streams, and for a time was a member of the High Wycombe Club, which had been set up by James Thurlow. Here he met several anglers who were to become lifelong friends, including Irwin Cox and Sir Maurice Duff-Gordon. The fishing there began to suffer badly some years later from pollution from paper mills, and Halford gave it up in 1884. Fishing these stocked waters was at least a way of catching something. This must have been important in a season such as 1880, when out of forty-four days fishing an astonishing total of twenty-nine were blank. A good deal of slow and careful experimenting was going on as well as fishing, and it is unfair to be too judgemental, but one wonders if Halford was not a little cast down at times. For example, of seven days in June, normally a prosperous month in the chalk country, five were blank apart from some grayling, and the remaining two produced three trout.

He began the season on 7 April 1880, fishing in violent hailstorms, but could only catch four grayling 'with Mrs Brocas' Dark Olive'. During this season and for several more Halford, although developing his fly-tying skills under Marryat's tutoring, was still heavily dependent on commercial patterns. 'Mrs B.'s Silver Sedge' and 'Mrs B.'s Olive Quill Gnat' figure in the Diary, also Drake's Extractor and Deller's Little Wonder. (The more conventional Olives and Blue Quills mentioned in the Journal were probably also bought: a year later, on 29 May 1881, he recorded the killing of a trout at Chilbolton 'with fly dressed by self,' showing that this was a novel event). Later in the season the Black Ant and the Dark Sedge make their appearance. However a noteworthy feature of the 1880 entries in the journal was his interest in natural flies. This showed itself quite suddenly on 29 April: 'Dull cloudy day – very little fly, Iron Blue, Olive and Blue Dun – a few Grannom.' Throughout 1879 there had been numerous entries about flies, but in every case they were artificials. Halford was still at the stage of regarding them primarily as instruments to catch fish. In 1880 we can observe his growing interest in flies as imitations of nature, and the influence of Marryat was no doubt important in this. Entries about fly-life get more complex and interesting as time passes, e.g. on 15 September 1881: 'Olive, Iron Blue, Claret Spinner and a Brown Spinner on water'; and on 28 September 1882 he records: 'Iron Blue, Blue Winged Olive, Green Spinner, Brown Spinner & Willow on water'. We are left wondering what the green spinner might have been, but the reference to the blue-winged olive is interesting, being an early example of a name that had only recently been coined. Francis Francis was on the water that week, and Halford may have picked this up from him. These were the years when the entomology of chalk streams was being worked out, and Halford and Marryat were determined to be at the forefront of that movement.

The fishing in April 1880 continued to be discouraging, although a two-brace day at Clatford on the Anton cheered him. The bad-weather cycle continued, and the spring and summer were generally wet: five million sheep died in Britain as a result, and there was much misery in the countryside. (The Prime Minister, Lord Beaconsfield, considered that the run of bad harvests had cost him the general election of 1880). Apart from a single two-pounder on 16 April Houghton did Halford few favours until the latter end of the season. On 31 July he had a fish of 3lb 7oz (Wickham), on 18 September one of 3lb (Dark Sedge) on a day of gale-force winds, and on 22 September one of 2lb 15oz. His total for the season was thirty-three trout; of these, the twenty-two (weighing 37lb 2oz) that came from Houghton had been forty-four days in the catching.

After the close of the trout season he again turned his attention to the grayling. He had already caught a grayling of 3lb on 20 September. He now fished for another seven days in October and November, raising his grayling score from fifty-three to sixty-two, totalling 91lb. Four of these were over 2lb and two over 3lb, the largest being 3lb 2oz, caught on 26 October. This beautiful grayling took a small Indian Yellow, a fly intended to imitate the blue-winged olive and praised by W.H. Aldam in his curious *Treatise* of 1876. The two largest grayling of 1880 were set up and exhibited for some time in Eaton and Deller's shop in Crooked Lane in the City, a few steps from Halford's office in Cannon Street; the Halford family still possess the bigger of the two.

Halford could not have been accused of lack of keenness. He himself says in the *Autobiography* that, however depressed he was by a blank day, the next morning would find him at the waterside as sanguine about his chances as ever. Although he was now making some of his own flies, he was still relying on Mrs Brocas, to whom he paid £5 12s that spring, and upon Holroyds. He was at Houghton on 6 April 1881, a day of cold north-east wind and no fish. The next five days, however, produced ten trout, including a fish of 3lb 10oz on a Hare's Ear and four two-pounders. Again we may wonder about the condition of these larger fish so early in the season; in his writings Major Carlisle more than once refers to the poor order of the 3lb trout of the Test in April. Halford had another three-pounder on 27 April. By this date *The Field* was able to report the most up-to-date conditions on streams by means of the new electric telegraph: it recorded an immense appearance of grannom on 30 April (almost too much for good fishing, it was said), but Halford had returned to London. Altogether his April fishing had produced thirteen trout with an average weight of just under 2lb, mainly on the Hare's Ear, a favourite with him for many years, and the Medium Olive.

May was less successful; he only fished four days, of which three were blank. June was better, with six trout in five days, including one of 3lb 10oz on a Red Quill on the evening of 7 June. Heavy trout were more in evidence at Houghton this year; Carlisle recorded in *The Field* on 25 June 'an unusual number' of fish over three pounds caught. But for Halford the rest of 1881 saw a good deal of effort for very small return. This was another wet year, and again there was drastic mortality amongst the sheep population in Britain. There were a few small highlights, as on 3 June, when he went over to T.J. Mann's fishery nearby at Horsebridge and secured a pretty trout of 2lb 9oz on a Silver Sedge. The other rods, too, seem to have worked hard to little purpose. Carlisle reported that the summer fishing at Houghton had suddenly become difficult by day, with fish very shy and unapproachable. There would be a small rise around 7 o'clock, then there would be a chance with the Silver Sedge after 8 p.m. At 8.45 thicker gut could be used. And there would be a further opportunity during the last twenty minutes of light with a White Moth or a Coachman.

On 5 September Halford was on the Houghton Lower Water in the morning, catching two small grayling; the journal records 'Only fished until 2 o'clock, then went to meet Mrs F.M.H.' This is one of the very few mentions of his wife, a shadowy figure of whom we can know little. It may fairly be guessed that the wife of such an obsessed angler was not going to see much of her husband, and was left usually to her own devices. This of course was often the lot of the Victorian wife, for whom a large part of her husband's life was a mystery she did not expect to penetrate. Many middle-class couples seem to have conducted their relationships on the 'separate-spheres' basis so much admired by John Ruskin, Coventry Patmore and other moralizing writers of the time. Some wives might have accepted this sort of life without demur, but historians have discovered a good many examples of intelligent women at that time who did not. It seems likely (see Chapter 9) that Florence Halford was in the latter

Trout of 3 lb 2 oz caught by Halford on a Coachman in the Wandle at Carshalton on 20 May 1869. Taxidermy by Cooper

The Boot Inn at Houghton, haven for generations of anglers

Grayling time at Houghton

The Old Barge below Winchester

Horsebridge, where keeper Penton cleared the undergrowth and opened up a fishery for his master T.J. Mann and his guests

Francis Francis.
Watercolour by A.W. Cooper

Marryat playing a fish below the Sheepbridge in the mid-1880s. Watercolour by A.W. Cooper

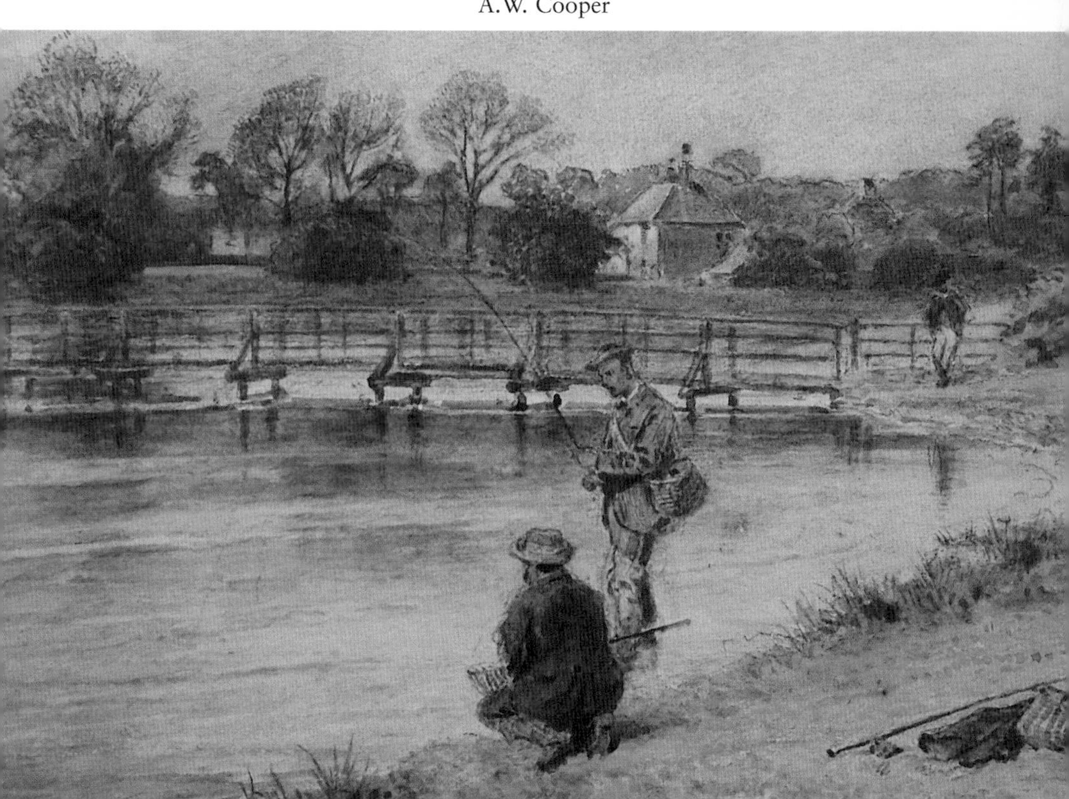

Fly box of Francis Francis (two compartments and two lids), containing Mayflies with gut eyes, probably tied by Mrs Cox of Winchester

Flies to gut, from the fly book of Francis Francis

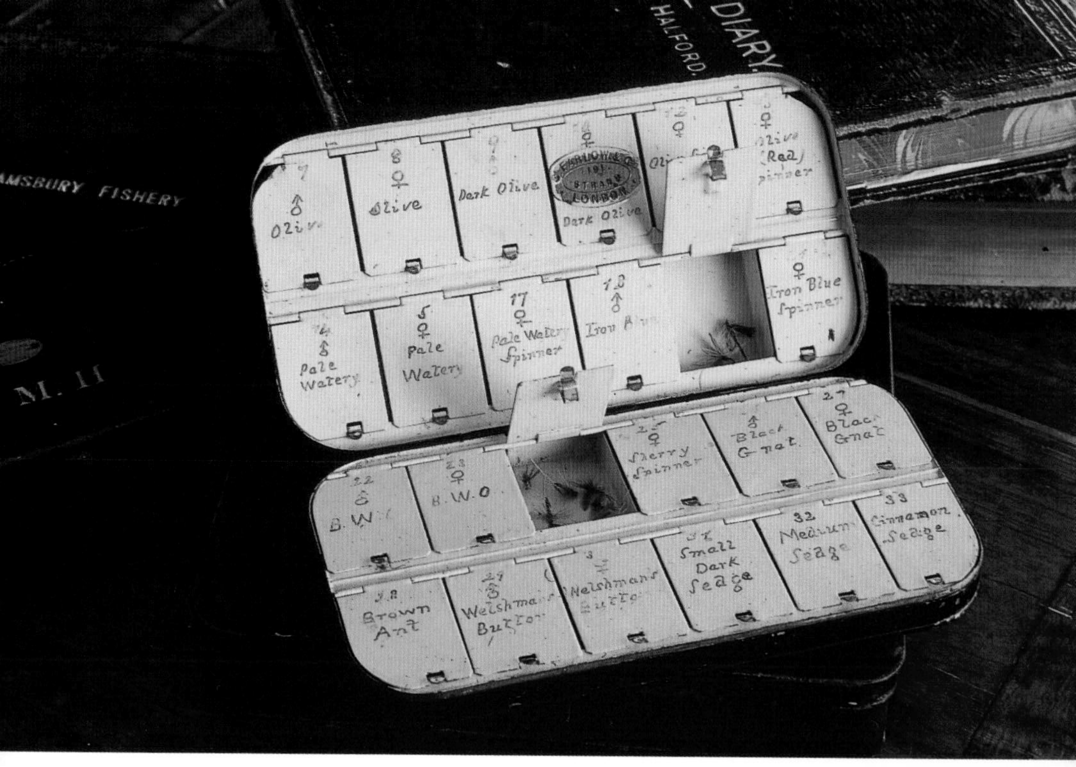

One of Halford's fly boxes, made by Farlows for the New Patterns according to the system described in *Modern Development of the Dry Fly* (1910)

Mayflies: four of the New Patterns, tied by Hardys, from the deluxe edition of *Modern Development*

Houghton Mill, now called Bossington Mill, a little changed in appearance from the nineteenth century but not much

Town Mill at Ramsbury, from across the weir-pool, the fishing box for Halford and his friends from 1893 to 1896

Halford's fishing hut on the Oakley Stream at Mottisfont, built 1911

The leaning oak at Mottisfont, referred to by Halford on page 130 of *Modern Development*

Dr Wallis Jonas and his son by the Oakley Stream in 1912. Colour autochrome photograph taken by Halford

category. (It is fair to add that, as the fishing fell off in late summer, Halford would lay aside his tackle and carry his wife off for a holiday, often abroad. An expedition to Nice in 1882 cost him £167.)

At the end of 1881 forty-seven days at Houghton had produced twenty-four trout weighing 60lb 12oz, a respectable average weight. Throughout these earlier seasons in Hampshire Halford fished almost entirely by himself. He must have arranged it that way: he was still learning how to fish the big chalk stream (and not catching very much) and, as I have suggested, was probably a little sensitive about being observed in action. But from October 1881, when he once again opened his autumn campaign on the grayling, the name of Marryat begins to figure in the journal. Marryat was a kindly and helpful person, who could make even a wary and awkward man like Halford feel at ease. There was a good deal of leg-pulling, but, as Halford later wrote, Marryat's 'chaff' had no sting in it. 'Chaff' in fact was a fairly frequently used word in Halford's later writings in *The Field*, as was 'yarning', which meant walking with a friend who was fishing merely for company and talk (e.g. a typical entry in the journal: 'Didn't fish, yarned with Marryat.') The *Autobiography*, perhaps unconsciously, gives the impression that their friendship developed quite soon after the meeting in April 1879, but the diary appears to show otherwise. Their collaboration may have made a start then, but they were not fishing together, and it was not until the autumn of 1881 that he began to seek out Marryat's society as a fishing partner.

On 21 October 1881 Halford had a baffling day, returning nine small grayling between nine and eleven inches (the size limit had been reduced from thirteen to twelve inches in view of the large numbers of grayling in the water). Marryat had done rather better, and in the evening Halford asked him to add his own contribution into the journal. Marryat wrote, in his customary humorous way: 'Poor duffer G.S.M. had 6 (1¾, 1½, 1¼, 1½, ¾, ¾lbs.) took anything chucked anyhow. – Geo.S.Marryat. P.S. Returned 9 besides.' This small piece of mockery does not seem to have nettled Halford: from then on Marryat is referred to in the journal as 'Poor Duffer' or merely as P.D. The following day the entry runs 'PDGSM had 2 brace' (Halford had caught one grayling), and on 24 October, again in Marryat's hand we find 'PDGSM had 4 brace 1½, 1½, ¾, ¾, ¾, ¾, ¾, ¾ – blue quill & sedge and green woodcock' (again

Halford only caught one fish). For some time this good-natured rivalry continues in the journal. One cannot help joining in the explosion of triumph some time later when Halford was able to record a good bag of fish and add in the margin 'GSM *blank*' (underlined three times for emphasis). By 3 December, his last day, he had increased his grayling score to forty-four for a weight of just over 58lb. Six of these were over 2lb, the largest being 2lb 12oz.

These were the years when many chalk-stream-owners were paying more attention to grayling, encouraging them or even introducing them. However their enormous power of multiplication was being noticed, and some dissentient voices were heard to say that they could become a danger to good trout fishing. Halford clearly valued them highly, writing in 1889 (*Dry-Fly Fishing*, p.202) that 'grayling fishing is quite as good in its way as trout fishing', and it was the subject of one of his early letters to *The Field* in January 1881, long before he had assumed the *nom de plume* of 'Detached Badger'. This early Halford piece deals with the successful flies for the months: July, Silver Sedge, Black Midge, Saltoun; August and September, the same flies, also Black Ant, Yellow Dun, Iron Blue; October and November, Indian Yellow, Blue Quill Gnat, Wickham, Apple Green.

His catches of grayling got better, at least as to numbers. On 20 October 1884 he took fourteen for 14lb 8oz at Houghton; Marryat had nine, and Tom Sanctuary four. He fished far into the autumn, as late as 11 December in 1885 in bitter cold. Two days earlier he fished with Marryat at Britford on the Avon below Salisbury, but records 'Hard frost all day, no fly, no rise'. (The resourceful Marryat laid aside his rod for his shotgun and saved the blank by bagging two plovers, four snipe and two ducks.) Bad days and cold weather did not affect their enthusiasm: a year later, on 3 December 1886, the line constantly froze in the rod rings, in spite of which fish rose well for two hours in the afternoon to a great hatch of olives. Other days were much slower. On 5 November 1887 – a bad day for weather – a party of four (Marryat, Halford, Carlisle and William Senior) could only bag eight small grayling; Halford's one fish weighing 14oz. Truly these men were prepared to work hard!

The largest grayling of Halford's career – apart from a fish of 3lb 9oz in poor condition caught in 1909 (see Chapter 9) – weighed 3lb 5oz, and was caught on 22 June 1884. Its stuffed remains can still be seen at the Fly Fishers' Club. The largest from Houghton at this time, variously recorded as 3lb 9oz or 10oz, was caught by Francis Walbran (see Chapter 6). After 1892 grayling very largely disappear from Halford's angling life, at least until he came to Mottisfont in 1905.

The eyed hook was spreading through the chalk country and elsewhere. London tackle shops were beginning to advise customers that they now supplied flies tied on the new hooks. In early May 1882 Carlisle was invited to Newton Stacey, and noted in *The Field*: 'Our host [Major Turle] was fishing with eyed hooks, and he uses no others – I quite approve of them for dry fly fishing, as it is almost impossible to whip them off.' Later, on 3 June, he wrote: 'These eyed hooks seem to be immensely strong in the bend.'

Fish seem to have been in better order on the Test in 1882, and wild and dangerous when hooked. On another visit to Major Turle's water Carlisle wrote: 'I never met with such powerful fish in my life as these Newton Stacey trout. There is no holding them.' Turle was proud of his fish. A few years earlier his fishery had been well-known in the Test valley for large fish up to 7lb and more, but he had ceased to put in artificial trout of this sort, and by 1882 his fish were much the same size as at Houghton. In fact his earlier experience may have taught him something, for he later wrote disapprovingly of the practice of turning in too many stock fish, as being likely to injure the natural stock. One unusual feature of his fishery were the wooden hides he had placed on some of the wide shallows to provide cover for fish, and so prevent them from bolting too far when startled. These hides were constructed like tables, the legs of which were driven into the stream bed.

Turle was an important member of the unofficial discussion-group referred to in the previous chapter, even though he seems to have invented nothing except for the famous knot associated with his name. In 1892 and 1893 he contributed several articles to *The Fishing Gazette* which cast light on the days before the triumph of the dry fly. His first fishing was at Winchester, with a 'Multum in Parvo' rod built by John Hammond. Like most novices at that date, he began by fishing downstream with a cast of sunk flies. This answered well enough for his first attempt on a day of wind and rain, and he returned to the barracks with a bag of fish to exhibit to his brother officers. Subsequent days were quiet and sunny, and he could catch nothing. Fortunately help was at hand. The proprietor of the local billiard-room, Lloyd Currell, was a professional fisherman and happy to take the young William Turle in hand. First he persuaded him to discard the dropper fly, and to fish upstream. He moved him on to the dry fly in about 1861. But Turle was aware that he still had much to learn, and when he secured his own fishery downstream from Winchester and brought in Anthony Carlisle and several others as fellow rods (see Chapter 4) they invited F.W. Flight, a local expert and inventor of the Flight's Fancy, to make a visit and impart some of his knowledge.

The word 'weeds' occurs with sad regularity in Halford's journal this summer, and 'lost' or 'broke' appear nine times in July, involving the loss of seventeen trout and one grayling. On 10 July he lost five trout in one disastrous evening. Incidents like these enable us to understand why he moved towards ever stronger gut points. The trout of the Itchen were thought to be more shy than Test trout and anglers there felt it was better to use drawn gut, for all its well known unreliability, but on the Test it was considered unsafe.

In 1883 Dr Wickham was able to add the Marsh Court water to the existing fishery. This provided a great deal more left-bank fishing, and therefore better chances of west-facing tactics for evening sessions. Halford was only able to get thirty-nine days fishing this year, probably for reasons connected with his business. Twenty-eight of these were at Houghton. He and Marryat were able to keep up all the arrangements they had made in 1882 to fish at Horsebridge with T.J. Mann, at Newton Stacey with Turle, and at Kimbridge with Mr and Mrs Pincoffs. Generally, results were better on these private fisheries, and for less effort than was necessary at Houghton. They were to fish at Kimbridge for a day or two during the mayfly for a number of years. In 1885 after a difficult day as guests of the Pincoffs they added a new term to their private language: 'Kimbridged'. To be 'Kimbridged' meant to hook and run a fish for a second or so before it came unhooked. It recurs with melancholy frequency in the journal for several seasons in mayfly time, no doubt through a combination of large over-dressed flies and nervy trout.

The grannom came on in the Spring of 1883. Carlisle recorded that on 13 April 'the huge sixty yards wide North Head Shallow was a sight to see – the fish were rising all over it'. Carlisle, Hambrough, Marryat and Francis Francis all had fish. But it was a flash in the pan, and a little later the grannom season was being called a failure. It was in fact the beginning of its decline on the Test. By the middle of May everyone was complaining of floating weed. Halford fished doggedly on, catching a fish here and there. The mayfly came up on 27 May in greater quantity than usual. On 4 June his journal has the alarming entry: 'Griffith May Fly in my cheek and not a knife to cut.' He had some success with Marryat at Newton Stacey, but soon afterwards the sport fell off badly. By mid-June Carlisle reported that day-time fishing on the lower Test had come to a halt, apart from the grayling. He attributed this partly to over-fishing, and advised anglers to slow down: there were not the natural fish stocks of thirty years before, and two brace ought to be enough for anyone on the Test. The Whitchurch Club, he reminded them, allowed each angler no more than three days' fishing a week. This note of anxiety recurs in Carlisle's reports in the next few years, as rod-pressure relentlessly overhauled the regeneration of the river by fry-stocking and by nature.

Francis Francis was again on the river this year. He spent several days at Horsebridge with T.J. Mann, who was concerned to see that his old friend was far from well. Soon after returning to Twickenham, Francis suffered a paralytic stroke which ended his career as a journalist and author. His last contribution to *The Field* appeared on 13 July 1883.

In 1884 Halford continued and intensified his collaboration with Marryat. Other names come into the journal this year, particularly those of H.S. Hall and Dr Tom Sanctuary. Hall was at this date actively propagating the eyed hook to a public that was still strangely wary and sometimes even hostile about it. He had gone to some trouble to explain his ideas in letters to *The Field* and *The Fishing Gazette* in 1882. In March and April 1884 he wrote again, rather irritably reiterating his former arguments:

> As my letter of March 22, about the tying of trout flies on eyed hooks, has induced a large number of anglers to write and ask questions on points which have been constantly referred to me during the last two or three years, it may be worth while to briefly answer, once for all, the different questions which crop up from time to time.

He went patiently over the ground again, as with a class of boys who had not been listening, reciting the obvious advantages of the eyed hook, mentioning again the trusted makers, Hutchinson of Kendal, and describing the knot for fastening it to the cast. Most anglers in the next few years adopted the knot advocated by Major Turle, rather than the Hall knot, which involved passing the gut through the eye twice. It was as a result of the 1882 correspondence, and an intervention by R.B. Marston, that the gifted fly-dresser George Holland, was introduced to a much larger public. Holland had originally set up business in Cook Street, Failsworth (now part of Greater Manchester), as a hat-maker some years earlier, but had found fly tying more profitable. Hall quickly realized that he had found the ideal man to combine the advantages of the eyed hook and the split-winged floater. Holland could already make exquisite flies, but had to be taught the new technique, and about a hundred letters from Hall were necessary before both men were satisfied with the result. Holland then taught his wife and children to tie flies according to the new method. In the spring of 1884 he was marketing the new patterns at two shillings a dozen for hackle flies, and two shillings and sixpence for winged flies. Flies with detached bodies on horse hair bristle or india-rubber – Hall preferred the latter – were five shillings a dozen (this was an unheard-of price at the time, but Holland claimed that they took upwards of half an hour to make). Mrs Cox of Winchester was soon copying the style, but needed help from Hall. He wrote: 'Mrs Cox's people are new to this style; but they will soon pick it up and master it. Henceforth Mr Holland and Mrs Cox will be formidable rivals, but there is room for both, and I wish them both the success they deserve.' Three weeks later Hall was writing of the flood of orders received by Holland, half of them requesting flies by return of post: 'Just at present six pairs of hands could not keep pace with the work.'

Dr Sanctuary was an equally interesting, though quite different, sort of man, and deserves to be examined at some length. His pioneering idea about a floating agent has already been mentioned. His father, Archdeacon Sanctuary, the larger-than-life vicar of Powerstock in West Dorset for forty-one years until his death in 1889, is regarded as the man who brought a somewhat primitive backward village into the modern world. He farmed his own glebe, built and equipped the local school, improved the roads in the area, and did all he could to improve the wretched condition of the local poor. He had been a boxing enthusiast at Oxford and is said to have become involved in bare-knuckle contests with unbelievers and back-sliders in the parish, and also with the navvies building the nearby railway. Young Tom Sanctuary learned to catch trout in the interesting little river Brit at Powerstock and Mangerton in his father's parish, and afterwards on the Itchen when he was sent to Winchester College. He then went to Edinburgh for his medical training. His extraordinary angling journal, which runs from 1875 to 1930, records his early experiences on the Frome near Maiden Newton and Hooke. The upper reaches of this river, with its high degree of spawning success, teemed with trout of the half-pound class in the nineteenth century, and Sanctuary would catch from thirty to sixty trout a day. In April 1877 he fished for eleven days on the Old Barge at Winchester, catching ninety-eight trout up to 2lb 8oz. He returned in March 1879 for a second visit of nine days. It was a time of sleet and bitter north-east wind, and things did not go so well: two days were blank and Sanctuary could only get twenty-one fish in total. However it was during this visit, on 15 March, that the meeting with Marryat took place, as described in Chapter 4: Sanctuary's diary records 'Met G.S.M. & F. Francis – the former I had not seen for 13 years! Fish were taking the curse – & we could not touch 'em.' In fact the trout were probably nymphing – Victorian anglers were too easily inclined to identify trout taking the hatching nymph as taking 'curses' or 'smutting'.

In the following year Sanctuary went to work in Cornwall, but in 1883 he came to Salisbury and for several years practised there as a doctor, with additional responsibilities as medical officer and public vaccinator for the area, and physician to the Alderbury Union (a polite term for the workhouse). The garden of his house, now vanished, in Crane Street was bounded by two arms of the river Avon and is referred to in the diary as 'Crane Loop'. Here he caught many good trout up to 4lb in weight.

Sanctuary's catches of large grayling remain his chief claim to the attention of the angling historian. In 1883, then a newcomer to grayling fishing, he caught 129 grayling, five of which were over 2lb. On 24 October, fishing near Bemerton rectory on the Nadder, he captured a grayling of 4lb 9oz on a Red Quill. He noted: 'My record grayling up to date', as if in a confident expectation of doing better next time. Curiously, he had another enormous grayling a year later, on 14 August 1884. This fish took a Dark Olive and weighed 4lb 8oz. These extraordinary fish are both larger than the currently accepted British record, but there is no way now of authenticating them to the standard required of fish records in modern times. In 1885 he and Marryat caught and returned an even bigger grayling, weighing 4lb 12oz, at Britford on the Avon, but this was while they were netting for coarse fish. Grayling of this calibre are still to be found in northern Scandinavia and Alaska, but are unlikely to be seen again in Britain.

Sanctuary's part in the design of the modern form of the dry fly is less clear. In 1923 Skues wrote a long article in *Journal of the Fly Fishers' Club* about Marryat's enormous fly book, known to his friends as 'the Portmanteau', containing upwards of 1,000 flies. In this article he referred to the importance of Sanctuary's role: 'Marryat, who had been working out the modern floater in concert with Hall and continued his work with Halford, put with Dr Sanctuary's aid the finishing touches on the modern methods which prevail to this day.' But, apart from mentioning that some of the flies in Marryat's *batterie de campagne* were tied by Sanctuary, Skues says nothing to help us on the detail of Sanctuary's contribution.

Marryat brought Sanctuary over to fish at Houghton for four days with Halford on 19 June 1884. On arrival Sanctuary took an early opportunity to ask Halford what he considered to be the best flies for grayling. Questions like this were not generally answered by Halford all at once. The following morning he gave his considered response on paper, and Sanctuary must have been surprised to find that Halford had spent the late evening ruminating and consulting his diary, in order to give a statistical breakdown of the success of every grayling fly he had used since 1879.

The party fished to little effect, although Sanctuary secured a trout of 2lb 8oz on the third day. On the fourth Marryat took him over to Horsebridge. On their return in the evening they discovered that Halford had caught a large grayling of 3lb 5oz. He did not mention this fish in the *Autobiography*, however it was in reasonable shape for a June grayling, as can be seen from its stuffed remains in the Fly Fishers' Club. Neither did he mention his first four-pound trout from the Test, which he caught later the same year. He had been hoping to get one of these prize fish ever since coming to Houghton. Again his silence about this fish, which weighed 4lb 4oz, leads one to suppose that it was one of those crocodilian old trout that are better out of the river, and which give rise to disappointment rather than triumph. During his angling career he had several other fish weighing four pounds and more, but he never caught one of the really large chalk-stream trout of that era. He had some near misses. One of these occurred some days before the Sanctuary visit, on 2 June 1884. Halford was fishing with Carlisle and Turle on a water at Mottisfont leased by Foster Mortimore. He had put up a straw-bodied Champion Mayfly on what he described as 'a stout cast', but it was not sufficient for what followed:

> Almost close to the bank, in the head of a tremendous race, I espied a fish taking down with a gulp every passing Mayfly. Crouching down well below him, and in absolute ignorance of the place, I put the fly over the spot; a quick splashing rise, and with a heavy swirl, the hooked fish ploughed diagonally across the stream; but, before he had travelled ten yards, the point of my rod came back, and I found about three strands left of a 2½ yd. cast. The gut had parted fairly in the middle of a length, and had the appearance of being cut with a knife. Looking down in the water, I noted a primaeval forest of ribbon weed, the edges of which I know to my cost are often as sharp as a razor. I never was so utterly and hopelessly smashed before, especially with gut such as is seldom used on the Test – stout enough to kill a grilse or even a 20lb. salmon at a pinch. Talking the matter over later in the day with the keeper, he said, 'Oh! yes, sir, I knows *he* well – he'd be nigh on 6lb. or 7lb.'; and really I do not think this was an exaggeration.

Halford refers more than once to brief and shattering encounters with big fish, but this may well have been the largest with which he was ever connected. It was incidents such as these that reinforced his determination always to fish heavy rather than light.

Sanctuary continued to fish for several years at Houghton, and became a fairly influential member of the angling community, giving his name to several items of tackle marketed by Bernard's tackle shop in Church Street, Piccadilly. The Sanctuary cast box had two compartments, one for damping and one for drying. It was intended to be an improvement on the Hawksley box, which only moistened the gut. The Sanctuary split-cane rod in three pieces was made in several lengths between nine- and ten-and-a-half feet; it was a fairly solid piece of work of the conventional type, varying in weight from seven to nine ounces. Like many Victorian anglers, Sanctuary could never quite believe in the light rod. There was also a fly for grayling called the Sanctuary, with a hare's ear body ribbed with fine flat gold, and a cochybondhu hackle, included by Halford in *Floating Flies*.

Meanwhile the angling section of *The Field*, deprived of the breezy vigour of Francis Francis, struggled to regain its balance. His successor, William Senior, was a competent journalist but lacked the sparkle and the passion of his predecessor. Others rallied round to help: T.J. Mann submitted several pieces, and J.P. Wheeldon, author of *Freshwater Fish in Great Britain* (1883), tried to make up for the gap in coarse-fishing coverage. In the autumn of 1884 Senior, wishing to enlarge the pool of contributors, began to put pressure upon Halford to do some writing for *The Field*. At first he encountered resistance. For a man who was planning a major book, Halford seems to have been puzzlingly doubtful about his literary abilities. But Senior won him over, and his first full-length piece over the signature 'Detached Badger' appeared in January 1885, on the subject of autumn grayling fishing at Houghton. Once started, Halford became a very prolific journalist. He is known to posterity through his books, but in his own day he was just as familiar to the public through his frequent contributions to *The Field*. By 1912 he had written 219 articles, many of them of considerable length, as well as a number of shorter notices and letters. He also wrote occasionally for *Baily's Magazine of Sports and Pastimes* and for *Country Life*, but not as a rule for *The Fishing Gazette*, except to respond to particular questions from correspondents.

It took nearly a year for Francis to recover sufficiently to fish at all. There was no chance of recovering his place at *The Field*. He found literary work of any sort very difficult, and he only partially recovered his power of speech. Not long afterwards his friends learned the pitiful news that he was suffering from cancer of the tongue. Another two years of suffering lay ahead of Francis before his release in December 1886. He was well enough in May 1885 to get down to his beloved Winchester, piloted by his eldest son, but bad weather kept them indoors for days. At length Senior was able to report (with some relief) that F.F. had secured a brace on the last day of his visit, including a fish of 2lb 8oz. In August he came for a week of grayling fishing at Houghton, and Halford and Marryat were there to give him help and encouragement. Disabled as he was and easily tired, he could still fish to some effect, for he had thirty-one grayling and two trout during the week. Carlisle wrote that Francis had a tough fight with a big grayling: the fish withdrew downstream after the way of grayling and could not be followed, but one helper passed his rod around some railings to a second, who restored it to the angler and the fish was secured. Francis was one of the best-loved members of the angling world, and there was never any difficulty in getting friends to attend him in his sad latter days.

One of his pet projects, which for some years he had been urging on anyone who would listen, was the formation of a fly-fishing club. In March 1882 he had written to Colonel Tickell ('Old Log' of *The Field*): 'I do wish some one would start a club, a real anglers' club, where we simply met, dined and talked &c; but did not vulgarize it with fishing for prizes and all that rot. It would not be difficult. I should back it all I knew.' The Fly Fishers' Club had finally been established on December 1884, largely through the work and persuasion of R.B. Marston, who became its first treasurer. Halford also gave a good deal of help in the early stages, of which he modestly makes no mention in the *Autobiography*, and served for many years as a committee member. A year later the first annual dinner was held in the Venetian salon of the Holborn Restaurant, bringing together what was at that date probably the largest number of fly-fishermen ever to be under one roof. Victorian public dinners were notable for substantial fare and a rather slow tempo. The evening was punctuated by recitations and songs by professionals, and no less than ten speeches. The chairman, Sir Ford North, reported that the membership had already reached 250, and suggested that the club might form a collection of artificial flies, and that some member should write a book to bring Ronalds up to date. The former want was supplied by Halford shortly afterwards, for as soon as *Floating Flies* was published in 1886 he presented the club with a case containing the original patterns used in the preparation of the coloured plates. The latter suggestion was taken up, although not very adequately, by Halford's *Dry-Fly Entomology* in 1897.

In the next few years nearly all the well-known names in the Victorian fly-fishing world were drawn into the club, and discussions, especially on Thursday nights, must have done much to accelerate the process, already begun by books, journals and the increase in railway travel, to bring together and give general currency to all kinds of local and little-known techniques and practices. One notable absentee was Marryat. Marston wrote to him at the outset asking him to join, but Marryat was not to be caught, offering instead, with his usual sly humour, to contribute a big wooden spade as a prize for the man who told the story of the largest fish. Several Americans joined soon after the club was founded: F. Mather, W.C. Harris, editor of *The American Angler*, H.P. Wells, author of *Fly Rods and Fly Tackle* and A.N. Cheney. The success of the club was observed in America with some interest, and two years later *Forest and Stream* was calling for the founding of an anglers' club in New York along similar lines.

There is little to say about Halford's trout season in 1885, except that it was slow to show results. The grayling total of 110, averaging nearly 1lb 8oz, must have been some compensation for the meagre result of twenty-five trout in fifty days of fishing. No doubt the work of the two collaborators was taking up a good deal of fishing time, but the plain fact was that Houghton was getting short of fish, and those that remained were becoming educated hard cases. A certain disquiet was spreading among the members. Major Carlisle, who had some sympathy with them, wrote in July bewailing the fact that with each succeeding season fish were becoming harder to catch. Some writers even suggested that the constant destruction by anglers of surface-feeding fish was breeding a race conditioned to feed on the bottom, a rather odd and Lamarckian notion of the way in which evolution works.

By the early part of 1885 Marryat was living at No. 20 the Close in Salisbury, by the Cathedral and about five minutes' walk from Tom Sanctuary's house, and the two men began once again to fish and shoot together. Sanctuary's journal records their days together on the Frome at Maiden Newton, Bradford Peveril and West Stafford, on the Wylye and the Nadder, and on several parts of the Test. In the same year they took a fishing at Britford on the Avon near Salisbury, to which Halford was several times invited. The three men, and indeed many other chalk-stream anglers, were now enthusiastic patrons of George Holland. Halford had no time to make his own flies, and was happy to order from Holland all his flies for day-to-day use, as well as specimen flies to be used as models for the artists working on the illustrations for his first book, now nearing completion. During 1885 he settled seven bills from Holland totalling £21 11s 8d. In 1886 (not 1885, as Skues stated in *Side-lines, Side-lights and Reflections*), when Hall was able to persuade Holland to move from Failsworth to Salisbury, it was Sanctuary who put up the money to secure him premises in Crane Street, ten yards from the bridge over the Avon. *The Fishing Gazette* announced on 11 September 1886 that the move to Salisbury had at last taken place. Sanctuary also found an assistant for him, Miss Farley, and Holland later took on other women to help. It was now a simple matter for Sanctuary or Marryat to take a short walk down the street for a consultation with Holland about new fly patterns and other dodges. (Holland afterwards admitted that, although Hall had taught him the basic method for the new flies, it was only after further guidance from Marryat that the highest standard was attained.) Halford was also a frequent visitor to Marryat's house in the Cathedral Close. Holland quickly became the leader in the field of chalk-stream fly-tying, and was in an excellent position to dominate the trade. After the publication of Halford's *Floating Flies* in the spring of 1886 he found it necessary for a time to remove his weekly advertisement from *The Fishing Gazette*, because of the tidal wave of orders for flies. After 1886 (and, even more, after 1889, when *Dry-Fly Fishing* was published) anything recommended by Halford or other members of his circle was likely to produce an effect in the market place. Holland once arrived at Newton Stacey for a day's fishing and enquired anxiously if Major Turle had any landrail wings about him (landrail was an important constituent of the Pink Wickham, recommended in *Floating Flies* as good medicine for smutting trout, and Holland had just received an order for twelve dozen from a customer evidently deeply impressed by this). On this occasion Holland was relieved to find that Turle had seven or eight pairs of wings to spare.

He continued to make wet flies to gut as called for by E.M. Tod and the Yorkshire anglers, in fact his business embraced the whole range of fishing tackle. In April 1888 he was able to purchase the tackle business of Gibbons of 10 Bridge Street, a firm established in Salisbury for sixty years. Here he sold fly patterns devised by Hall, Marryat, Halford, Turle and others, along with the Halford double-tapered line, Hawksley and Sanctuary cast boxes, rods by Hardy and many other devices for anglers. Holland, one might suppose, had acquired a constituency and was established for life, but his subsequent career was mysteriously irregular and nomadic (Turle called him 'that famous and erratic fly-tier'), and in the next twenty years he was in business in Liverpool, Winchester, Canterbury, Plymouth, Bristol, and Kingston on Thames. He eventually retired to Wimbledon in 1912.

In April 1886 appeared Halford's first book *Floating Flies and How to Dress Them*. It had been known for some time that the Halford-Marryat project was to result in a book, and R.B. Marston, whose firm Sampson Low were the publishers, arranged for tantalizing advertisements to appear from time to time in *The Fishing Gazette* announcing that publication was imminent, and reminding readers that the firm were also publishers of the most recent work of Cholmondeley-Pennell, Pritt, Edward Hamilton, Cutliffe, Theakston, Greville Fennell and Ogden. The result was that by 17 April the whole of the de luxe edition (100 copies on large paper at thirty shillings) had already been sold out before publication, and also a large part of the standard edition (500 copies at fifteen shillings).

The style of the book was clear and precise, and not as dogmatic as Halford's later works. Perhaps this was because of the influence of Marryat. It may also in part have been a sign of the caution of a first-time author. But, even at this early stage, the lines were already quite hard and fast. Only *floating* flies would do: on chalk streams it was idle to speak of anything else. Colour was all-important, and a colour chart was included in an attempt to avoid any ambiguity. Halford was to remain a colourist all his life, so it is not surprising that he was later to become very rattled by the iconoclastic experiments of Sir Herbert Maxwell (see Chapter 9).

The core of the book was the list of flies with their tying recipes, and the beautiful coloured plates which illustrate them. Halford had originally approached Horace Cox, the publishers of *The Field*, but they had taken fright at the high cost of producing the plates and declined. The patterns were ninety in number, a far cry from the ideas of Stewart and Cholmondeley-Pennell, who believed that a very small number of flies was enough. The point of this colossal list was not to set out to invent new flies – although a number of recently devised ones were included – but rather to identify the main patterns in use on chalk streams and to standardize the mode of making them. The mounting alarm of the unwary beginner coming upon the book might (perhaps) be allayed by Halford's reassurance that 'all the varieties are not absolutely necessary'. Although the list could have been much longer (a number of flies belonging to his earlier days – the Hudson, the Kingdom, the Cocktail, the Peacock Palmer and many others – were rejected), Halford included others that even in 1886 had become rather old-fashioned, and for which twenty years later he would have no use at all. Out of ninety artificials fifty-five are derived from ephemeropteran flies, acknowledging the importance of upwinged flies in Hampshire.

Later writers have dwelt a good deal on the translucency (or, rather, lack of it) in Halford's patterns. He does recommend good-quality hackles, which were increasingly difficult to get at that time: the abolition of cock fighting in 1849 was often blamed. For bodies, though, following Marryat's example, he had a preference for quill, which gives the finished fly a smart and appealing appearance (at least when held in the human hand and looked at from above; held against the light its opacity becomes evident). Twenty-three of the patterns have bodies of peacock or other quill, and a further twenty-four are of silk or crewel (also opaque, and liable to darken when wetted), while the Mayflies all have bodies of rofia grass (raffia). Halford was not unaware of the need for transparency: some of the patterns are of horse hair, which is partially transparent, and others have bodies of dubbing or of herl, which can produce a transparent halo effect, or at least one of broken light. Like all fly-dressers of the period, though, he was hampered by the fact that herl and most forms of dubbing absorb water easily. As C.F. Walker pointed out in *Fly Tying as an Art* (1957), Halford looked forward to the day when a waterproofing agent might be available, and dubbing would supersede quill 'as being so much more transparent and watery in appearance'. It is all the more puzzling, therefore, that by the time he published his next list in 1897, Halford took no advantage of the fact that paraffin had by then come into general use – in fact his use of quill and other opaque materials in this book had actually increased. Again he mentions paraffin, and speculates: 'It is, however, quite possible that in the near future quill, gut, and horsehair for bodies will have been abandoned in favour of dubbing.' However, as I discuss in Chapter 9, he ignored his own advice, and in the list of 1910 dubbing makes no appearance at all. At least in 1886 the form and structure of the typical south-country fly – cocky, split-winged, a little over-dressed, often with two sharp stiff hackles for good floatation – was settled. It had points of resemblance with the rods (and many other artefacts) of the era: very Victorian in its strong solid construction and not liable to wear out easily, and with lightness sacrificed to a solid British reliability. The presentation copy of *Floating Flies* given to George Holland acknowledged 'the patient way in which you have followed me through the various details of fly dressing', and called him the best fly-tier in England.

The response from the public to this impressive book was at first very favourable. Halford's scrapbook contains twenty-seven review notices, in which positive and gratifying adjectives abound: 'Practical, and at the same time delightfully-written', 'Thorough, clear and interesting', 'His almost unequalled experience', 'A real treat to get a book so plain and purposelike, and so beautifully got up in all respects'. *The Field* thought it 'something more than deeply interesting . . . a landmark.' *The Globe* wrote: 'The directions are beautifully clear, and anglers will be specially delighted with the illustrations.' *Punch* awarded its accolade in verse form:

> A capital volume, and no one will doubt it,
> No fisherman now should be ever without it.

In the USA *Forest and Stream* noted the book with some curiosity, remarking

> We do not personally know any angler in America who uses the dry fly, but no doubt many will try it during the coming season. The late Reuben Wood learned something of it from Mr R.B. Marston, editor of the *Fishing Gazette*, while in England a few years ago. The flies used are, as a rule, smaller than those which the majority of Adirondack and Maine anglers prefer, being about the size of those which the educated trout of Caledonia Creek will accept, and they are not allowed to sink in the water. . . . A firm in San Francisco, Kewell Bros., late of London, advertise 'Boyton' floating flies as 'new to the States,' but we do not remember to have seen them mentioned by our Eastern tackle dealers.

But in the midst of this wave of praise a certain note of dissent was present, even in 1886. In after years it was to grow stronger. The notion that Halford's doctrines were accepted without demur in his own day, and that criticism only gained ground after his death through the influence of G.E.M. Skues, is much too simplified. Both Senior and Marston, colleagues and friends of Halford, expressed their reservations in their reviews. Senior, although fascinated by the new dry-fly practice, to which he was a fairly recent convert, warned that it could be overdone:

> Some men make it a hobby, and ride it to death, going so far as to decline to try any other method; nay, even further, for the tendency in some zealots of the school is not to attack any but a rising fish, so that the singular spectacle is sometimes offered of a man with miles of water before him, a clear field and no favour, waiting rod in hand until the rising of a trout invites him to a trial.

Marston's view, following Francis Francis, was that the best plan was to be master of both dry- and wet-fly fishing, and for the rest of his life he stood out against the idea that the dry fly had banished the wet fly from the chalk streams. 'There is no great gulf fixed between the two systems,' he wrote. Towards the end of his review of *Floating Flies* he continued: 'There are days – too many of them – when the fish of a Hampshire stream will not look at a floating winged fly; but change it for a hackle fly, and fish it upstream in the same way, only just under instead of on the surface, and you turn the tables on the fish.' From Halford's own publisher this is fairly direct language. Halford however paid very little attention to these views. Edward Hamilton also assured readers that a sunk Mayfly was much more killing than a dry one. A year later, in the cold spring of 1887, *The Fishing Gazette* wrote that sport in the south was slow, but those who fished sunk fly got some fish, adding with some asperity:

> It is a little the habit of some of the higher lights among dry fly fishermen to look down on those who never cast a fly anywhere but over a rising fish; but it is carrying matters a little too far when they expect an angler who has but a couple of days angling during the season to quietly pace the banks of the river all day without casting his line if no rise is visible.

In a few more years, many anglers with such views began to keep quiet about them, such was the prestige of the new dry fly. It was about this time that several members of the Houghton Fly-Fishing Club, feeling that they were too old to learn new tricks, no longer at ease with the dry-fly men, withdrew from the club. Equally sad was the emergence of a north–south division amongst fly-fishermen, echoes of which are still with us. Halford unwittingly assisted in the process. He was aware that he was emerging as the leader, and felt justified in giving the law to the world of angling. He intended no harm, but he could easily fall into a lecturing style that irritated some of his readers, and anglers in the Midlands and Yorkshire were quick to detect what they considered to be signs of southern pretentiousness. They did not take kindly to being told that their wet-fly methods were of no service whatsoever on a chalk stream. Halford went so far as to inform them that in fact the reverse might very well be the case, and that the dry fly would in some conditions be very effective on their home waters. Dr Sanctuary, writing in *The Fishing Gazette* in September, added for good measure: 'As a rule, the pure and simple North-country fisherman can't touch the Southerner for skill in fly fishing.' In June 1888 a correspondent wrote: 'One hears so much of our scientific southern anglers, with their "half-steeple" casts and "three-quarters undercuts" that we Midland fishermen begin to wonder if we really know how to fish, or whether our southern friends do not put on just a little too much "side".' The leader of the Yorkshire school was T.E. Pritt, a bank manager in Leeds, angling author, and a familiar figure on northern streams. At first he remonstrated mildly in print, pointing out that there were subtle skills involved in the practice of the so-called 'chuck-and-chance-it' wet fly, but the controversy deepened and widened in the next twenty years, bringing in E.M. Tod, Henry Cadman and several other notable men of the north. The one exception was Francis Walbran, who became a life-long friend of Halford; whether his Yorkshire brethren approved of him supping with the enemy we have not been told. Halford's subsequent pronouncements did not help much either, for he repeated his provocative advice to the wet-fly men on a number of occasions. And in January 1889, in an article in *The Field* called 'The Nomenclature of Anglers' Flies' he regretted the practice in the north of England of using local names for flies, mentioning Michael Theakston as the chief culprit. There may have been some justification for criticizing writers who called duns drakes, stoneflies mayflies, and caddis flies duns, but it did give an unfortunate impression that it was in the south that standards and definitions would henceforth be made, to be obediently followed in the north. Halford's determination that the chalk-stream definition of the Welshman's Button should prevail, in spite of what anglers in Wales might say, was another case in point (see Chapter 8). This impression must have been strengthened by the fact that the angling material in *The Field* during this period showed a strong bias towards chalk-stream fishing.

Another and healthier effect of the book was a resurgence of the controversy about the eyed hook. C.W. Gedney, a well-known angler of that time, echoed the feelings of others when he complained of short rises to flies tied on eyed hooks, and complained of their holding powers when a fish was hooked. Marston presided over several weeks of argument in the correspondence columns of *The Fishing Gazette*. Just as he had been a conservative in the matter of the split-cane rod, regarding it as a passing fad, so he was slow to convert to the eyed hook. But in July he reported that Halford had caught a trout of 4lb 9oz at Houghton on a small eyed fly: 'Facta, non verba – eh, Mr Halford? and a very pretty bit of practical testimony to the holding power of the eyed hook it is. Then Mr Hall tells us of scores of trout taken one after another without a miss on the eyed hook. This is the practical testimony we asked for.' Slightly shaken by this and a good deal of other evidence, Marston at least felt justified in urging readers not to give up the new hooks without a fair trial.

The fish mentioned above was in fact Halford's record. He was to catch several more fish in excess of four pounds, a respectable weight for chalk-stream trout in those days. This trout was caught with a Hambrough Sedge on 5 July 1886 at the edge of darkness, and, like his big Wandle fish, was one of those stout parties that weigh considerably more for length than usual. It was for many years in a glass case at the Fly Fishers' Club. From surviving photographs – e.g. Plate 4 in Eric Taverner, *Trout Fishing from All Angles* (1929) – it was clearly a wild fish.

There was no slackening in the intensity of the Halford-Marryat project. The success of the book, and particularly of the final chapter on river tactics (added at Marston's suggestion), encouraged them to proceed with their next project. This was to expand the idea of this chapter into a full-length study of the whole art of fishing chalk streams. Even as *Floating Flies* was being published with acclaim, articles by 'Detached Badger' were appearing in *The Field* on topics which foreshadowed this book-to-be.

In many ways 1886 was a year of triumph for Halford. In July Marston judged the time ripe to publish a full-page biographical piece on Halford in *The Fishing Gazette*, picking out for special mention his talents as a genial host to angling guests at Houghton Mill: 'His one anxiety is to make you comfortable, and the angler who, as Mr Halford's guest, does not find himself comfortable must be indeed a Sybarite.'

The winter of 1886 saw the final act of the tragedy of Francis Francis. Earlier that year it was known that he was beyond any medical help. In May he was well enough to be at the Fly and Bait Casting Tournament, where old friends were still on hand to give him every encouragement. Major Carlisle wrote to him in March: 'Enclosed the usual tickets and hope we shall see you on the Houghton banks this season. We have a very good keeper now,* who is a dead nailer at jack so no doubt the stock of fish will improve.' George Ledger and Dr Ramskill, comrades of the Winchester Mayfly Mess, tried to lure him down to the Itchen, but increasingly he stayed at home, or went over to the Hurlingham Club for an hour or two. He roused himself for a final effort in mid-October and, accompanied by his eldest son and his usual companion the artist A.W. Cooper, he came down to Houghton, where Carlisle and several members were waiting to look after him. To his lasting regret Halford was kept in London and was not able to be there that day. When the party met Francis at the station they thought he looked hardly capable of fishing, but on arrival at the river something of his old vigour returned, and he 'stamped up and down upon the bank in the terribly earnest fashion which many of us had seen to our great amusement'. He then proceeded to catch several grayling, including a two-pounder. But the day had done him up, and he arrived back at Twickenham knowing it had been his last on the river. In the weeks that followed he declined rapidly, and died on Christmas Eve 1886. For the angling world in general much died with him.

* One Morris, successor to William Hall, whose record had been unimpressive.

William Senior quickly organized a committee, of which Marston became secretary and Halford treasurer, to raise funds for a Francis memorial in Winchester Cathedral. His extensive library of angling books, including many scarce and curious items, went under the auctioneer's hammer a few years later. R.B. Marston bought extensively, as did Irwin Cox. The 500 volumes, made up into 311 lots, made £464, and, if this seems a modest sum, it should be seen in proportion to the total of Francis' estate at death of £3,183.

6 Test and Itchen: 1887–1892

Halford was suddenly famous. He acquired a post bag, always a snag lying in wait for people in his position. Readers with problems wrote from all quarters. One wished to know the exact definition of a honey dun hackle. Centre of blue dun, responded Halford gravely, points of golden tint, blue dun being 'a slightly cold blue-grey': the points can be dark, pale or ginger ('Mr Marryat calls the latter sunburnt'). Other questions seemed a little flimsy. Where can I get dioxide of hydrogen? asked another. Try a chemist, said Halford tersely. He was busier than ever now. He had not yet withdrawn from the world of business, and all his spare time was taken up with experiments with Marryat, and with working up the material for his next book. All around him an atmosphere of acceleration and excited tumult was developing on the chalk streams. *Floating Flies* had contributed a good deal to this by demonstrating the enlarged possibilities of interest in the new cult of the dry fly. Recruits to the world of fly-fishing were increasing each year, and on every hand were heard wails of protest at the high cost and diminishing availability of fishing. Messrs Street of Cornhill were instructed to offer two or three rods – all that were left – for a syndicate to fish 'the best part of the Itchen', at the extraordinary price of £50 a year.

The 1887 season began slowly enough, with cutting winds from the East. But May was more prosperous. Halford relied heavily on the Gold Ribbed Hare's Ear, at this date and for years afterwards his premier scoring fly in the Spring. The mayfly was reasonably rewarding, but soon afterwards the fishing collapsed, with low water, bright light and not enough fish to catch. He needed thirty-seven days to catch thirty-four trout (in July he could only catch two in eight days). He left in disgust in early August and did not come back until October for the grayling fishing. He was not the only one in difficulties. The Club's heavy hitters – men such as Hambrough, who in the 1870s had expected an annual bag of between one and two hundredweight – were in much the same case. As Carlisle had predicted, the fishing was becoming more difficult by the year: there were fewer fish to catch, and the extreme caution of the survivors passed belief. The trout of Upper Houghton were less difficult than those of Lower Houghton, he thought, but that was not saying much. As they sat in the Mill on the evening of 11 June, raking over the ashes of a blank and perplexing day, Halford asked Marryat to write something appropriate in the journal. Marryat wrote: 'Finest undrawn gut set every fish down first cast. Cobweb rose every fish once short & set him down except [a] grayling at top of Sheepbridge Shallow who took no notice of gut or fly.' Carlisle wrote in *The Field* in July: 'Quite hopeless to think of fishing. Trout stopped rising, even though one stood four or five yards from the bank with one's shadow behind one.' He was convinced that this extreme shyness was the result of over-fishing, and repeated his plea of the previous year to members to restrict their fishing to three days a week.

Evidently the Test, or at least the lower Test, was reaching the end of its age-long era as a natural fishery. The solution nowadays on a wild trout fishery might be to fish more lightly, to restrict the days of access and the bag limit, to reduce the membership, to create more sanctuary water, and to practise catch-and-release, or at least return females after 1 August. None of these ideas would have been popular in the 1880s: free access and the heavy bag of dead trout was part of the sporting culture of the time. The only other solution – to increase the level of stocking – had been long resisted by Dr Wickham, but he was now beginning tentative steps in that direction. Carlisle's letter to Francis Francis of March 1886, quoted in the previous chapter, continued: 'Wickham has a new scheme for the young fish, and intends keeping them in tubs at the liver until they are big enough to turn out. He breeds yearlings in his greenhouse at Winchester without difficulty.'

For Halford this was too little too late, and he began to tackle Wickham on the subject. Two stubborn adversaries carried on a running argument at intervals for the next two years. Wickham good-humouredly resisted Halford's suggestions, even his offers to cover the cost of a more extensive stocking programme, saying that he was quite satisfied with the river as it was. It was during this period that Halford acquired an obsession about what he came to call 'liberal levels of stocking' from which he never wavered. It should be added that the size and quality of the Houghton fish at this time was excellent – as often happens when stocks decline and there is less competition for territory amongst survivors. In 1887 fifteen of Halford's fish were two-pounders and three were over 3lb. The largest was a beautiful female fish of 4lb 2oz, caught on 1 June on a size 000 Hare's Ear Quill during a hatch of pale watery duns.

A record of a day with Halford and Marryat in 1887 survives from *The Diary of an All-Round Angler* (1956) by the Rev. P.M.Smythe, then aged twenty-seven. I include his account here because first-hand descriptions from this period are all too rare. Smythe had been given a ticket for Houghton for 8 June 1887.

> A friendly water-cress man guided me to the Mill at the bottom of the Houghton water and I put up my rod and nipped into my waders as soon as ever I could. An angler was smoking comfortably on the bridge, with whom I soon foregathered and found him to be no less a person than Mr. Halford himself: and a very good friend I found him. He put me at once on to two trout who were rising at the head of the Mill pond and gave me a fly of his own dressing – (I think it was a Blue Up-right*) – wherewith I rose both fish, but both were only slightly pricked. They seemed about 3lb each. It was not long though before I was consoled, for in a bend just above I got a beautiful grayling of 2lb 10oz., the biggest ever I caught. Above this bend comes the Sheep's Bridge Shallow – *notissima fama* – and above that curves, pools and shallows and a lovely island with a hut on it. So far I penetrated with Mr. Halford in search of Mr. Marryat who had gone upstream and here, not finding him, we lunched. I spent most of the day round the Sheep's Bridge but beyond rising a dace or two and catching one little grayling and once and again getting a meaningless splurge from a trout, I did nothing. Towards evening I foregathered with the Keeper

* It was more likely to have been a Blue Quill. Halford seems not to have had any time for the Blue Upright.

> and we went down to a bit of water called Black Lake. Here were fishing Marryat and Halford, each with a trout of near 3lb. They put me on to a rising fish, but I made two bad casts to begin, one short and one beyond, which caused Marryat to think very small potatoes of me – and to say so! Most kindly they gave me one of their trout to keep my grayling company: and so we parted, they to dinner and the sedge-fly and I to the evening train.

This summer Halford and Marryat were as usual deep in their researches and not always fishing. One of the features of the next book was to be a series of lithographs, derived from photographic plates, of the mechanics of fly casting. Techniques of photography had by this date progressed to the stage where instantaneous images were possible. Halford went to some trouble to get in professional help, and Marryat performed for the camera. (Messrs Elliot & Fry charged £2 8s 6d for the work, which involved a week of photography.) When the book was published in 1889 the public could, in a series of twelve plates, follow all the standard moves of casting as performed by a well-known figure (recognizable even from behind) wearing the familiar Tam o' Shanter.

Such activities were at least more profitable than the fishing. Halford's result for the season of twenty trout in forty-five days seems almost ludicrous, even though there were several three-pounders. Low water could not be pleaded as excuse: 1887 was a wet year, and the planks of the bridge at Boot Island, normally eighteen inches above the surface, were awash. One of Halford's fish that year, a trout of 3lb 1oz, deserves to be mentioned, for it was caught on an Orange Quill. This fly was not mentioned in *Floating Flies* in 1886 and may have been devised by Halford and Marryat soon afterwards as a variation of the Red Quill. The usefulness of the Orange Quill in an evening hatch of blue-winged olive was noticed and publicized by Skues in the 1890s. Skues was proud and rather protective of his discoveries, and prepared a list of them, including the Orange Quill, which he handed to Dr E.A. Barton to be published after his death. Towards the end of his life he was nettled to be reminded (perhaps rather mischievously) by a friend that the Orange Quill had been included by his old adversary in *Dry-Fly Entomology* in 1897. He reacted with some petulance – 'It cannot be the same pattern as mine' – and pointed out that his first use of it was in 1894.

He would have been even more dismayed if he had learned that Halford was using the Orange Quill in 1887.

The disappointing trend continued in 1888. In September Major Carlisle called the season 'one of the worst ever experienced on the Test'. For Halford the quality of the fishing had declined to an unacceptable level. What had been challenging fishing had simply become slow fishing. At the end of 1888 he quit the club, finding that he could make his point with Wickham in no other way, though no overt ill-feeling seems to have been involved. However, in an article in *The Field* on 29 September he could not resist alluding to the shortage of fish at Houghton, adding for good measure the opinion of Thomas Andrews that stocking with fry was quite ineffective. He remained on good terms with 'the amiable proprietor of the fishing' and with 'the capable and indefatigable Secretary', and with a good deal of sadness departed for the Itchen, having acquired a rod on R.A. Carey's fishery above Kingsworthy. This action on the part of such a well-known man as Halford had become may have weighed with Wickham. In 1889 he began work on the construction of a substantial stew pond 180 feet in length. Soon fish of sufficient size to look after themselves were being put into the river at Houghton.

Meanwhile Halford was beginning operations in a new theatre and organizing accommodation for himself and his friends in a cottage at Headbourne Worthy. He tried to keep himself fit in the close season with a tricycle he had bought in 1888 (for £4), which he would ride in the London streets and in the Park. In the spring of 1889 he set about getting to know a new fishery. Fly life was prolific apart from mayfly, which appeared sparsely, and only at the lower end of the reach. He quickly found that there were far more trout to fish for than at Houghton although they were of a smaller average size. On the Test his average catch weighed about 1lb 12oz. Here it was to be about 1lb 4 oz, and the journal begins to record a number of fish of 12oz or 14oz; in the whole season only two of his fish were over 2lb. They were also later to come into condition, but by June were more game on the end of the line than Test trout. There were other interesting differences. They were less shy of man, he thought, possibly because the area was more populated and the banks more frequented, and so the fish were accustomed to seeing people. They were free risers, and came to the fly with less disturbance than Test fish.

During this period the journal records the growing complexity of his fly patterns. His interest in natural insects also increased. As early as 1886 he had begun a close study of the work of professional entomologists such as McLachlan, the Rev. Eaton, and the Swiss naturalist Pictet. He became a Fellow of the Linnaean Society, corresponded with other students of the subject and began conducting delicate experiments, such as dissecting insect eggs under the microscope; his observations were recorded in the pages of a thick, alphabetically arranged notebook. Readers of 'Detached Badger's' column in *The Field* now found themselves confronted with passages of fairly heavy science, sometimes in French. As a result of his reading he began in 1889 to differentiate flies – both natural and artificial – in the diary with the customary scientific symbols for male and female. Ants and Curses in the fly box acquire gender, though it is hard to understand why the Red Quill and the Wickham should do so (it is a relief to find that the Red and Orange Tags have no sex). He was still a pluralist about patterns. His fly boxes at this date must have contained many prototypes and variations, and he used twice as many types in 1889 compared to the previous year.

Halford's views about the relative importance of pattern and presentation changed from time to time. One of his earlier contributions to *The Field*, in July 1885, entitled 'The First Throw over a Rising Fish' begins:

> The majority of anglers are far too prone to consider the particular pattern of fly at fault when they fail to tempt feeding fish, and hence waste the short time during which the rise lasts in continual changes of fly, often changing merely for the sake of changing, and trying imitations of the same insect, only differing minutely in the shade of body, wings or hackle. They forget that the fault is often not in the particular pattern of fly, but in the particular action of the fisherman wielding the rod.

The influence of Marryat can be observed here. The often-quoted tale of the fly and the driver was first mentioned by Francis Francis in 1882 (' "It isn't the fly that is of as much consequence as the driver," once said my old gossip M.') and has come down to us in several different versions. But, although Marryat was a stickler for good presentation, he never seems to have wavered in his belief in a wide range of imitative patterns. By 1889 Halford, although he never relaxed his advice about accurate casting, was fascinated by entomology and the need for precise imitation, and it was the Itchen experience which reinforced this fascination.

Halford paid his first visit to the new fishery, accompanied by Marryat, on 6 April 1889, arriving on a dull morning, with a north-easterly wind and not much happening. Another rod was in possession of the shallow at the bottom of the stretch, standing in the water and patiently waiting for the hatch to develop. The keeper volunteered to show them the fishery, and they spent some time examining Carey's fish house, where 250,000 alevins were being raised. Stocking with fry was the rule, but carried on at a much more lavish rate than at Houghton (they learned that over the previous eight years well over a million fry had been released). A decade earlier this system probably would have worked less well, for the river was then infested with pike. In 1880 Francis Francis had reported that there had been a mass escape of pike into the Itchen from Alresford Pond after some renovation work on the outlet, and he used the pages of *The Field* to declare a holy war against the hordes. It took several years of devoted work by keepers to pull the numbers down again, and by 1889 the environment had become much safer.

Halford and Marryat spent most of the day inspecting the place, and only fished for a short time, catching a fish apiece. Two more days in April produced nine trout for Halford, the succesful flies being the Olive Quill and the Gold Ribbed Hare's Ear. It had been an encouraging start.

Later in the same month Halford's second book, *Dry-Fly Fishing in Theory and Practice*, was published. The intriguing and tantalizingly brief final chapter of the earlier book had now been expanded into a full-length work, whose effects in Britain and the world beyond were to be momentous. The dry fly was an idea whose time had come. The technical advantages of powerful rods, heavy lines and eyed hooks were by now all in place, and techniques of casting, fly-dressing and entomology had all advanced considerably. The time was ripe for something authoritative that would draw them all together and provide a comprehensive practice manual. Many years later Skues was to admit that, apart from its failure to take the sunk fly seriously, Halford's second book remained a complete statement on the chalk-stream art. And even today, with many new inventions and techniques available to us, we are struck by its essential reasonableness. In clear and logical language it set forth the main lines of the subject. Here are to be found, in some cases for the first time, many items of advice which are now standard practices. He insists on the importance of becoming proficient in casting, and to be as far as possible independent of the wind – a rough day may be quite good for sport. Equally it is vital to learn how to circumvent drag: there are five closely-argued pages on drag alone. The importance of entomology is hammered home, also of rivercraft. Go for difficult places that other rods avoid, he urged, and choose the leeward rather than the upwind bank on a day of strong winds. Move slowly and quietly, observe rather than cast until the time is right, and try and work out what the trout is doing, for which the rise-form may help you. When you find a feeding trout, approach with extreme caution, study the fly on the water and note that of several hatching species he may not be taking the majority fly. Observe his feeding pattern, so as to plan the arrival of your fly at the right time; study the set of the current to avoid drag, cast underhand if possible, and if he is a large trout, beware of fine gut. Don't cast too often, and if defeated by his indifference withdraw with the same caution you used when approaching, rather than standing up, scaring the fish and confirming his half-formed suspicions. The fewer over-educated trout in a fishery the better.

Another excellent ingredient was the use of the anecdote to demonstrate a practical example. The idea of stating a principle and then illustrating it with a real episode on the river bank is a standard part of angling books in our time, but it had only been used by a few people before Halford. Ogden had made a good story of defeating three large trout, previously regarded by the local rods as uncatchable, on the Town water at Hungerford, and Francis Francis tells many stories of trout caught and trout lost – though usually to make a good narrative, rather than to point a moral. The device may be said to have come of age with Halford, who had a useful resource in the form of his angling journal, and was later used and extended by Skues (who, it has to be admitted, was a rather better writer than Halford).

There are less sucessful parts of the book, particularly where he enters too much into points of detail – a habit that was to grow on him in his later writings. Readers must have been puzzled, for example, by a long passage about the best way of making a silk line, a process which he had helped to develop with Deller until the latter's death in December 1886, and then with Hawksley. More seriously, we can perceive (with several generations of discussion behind us), the first signs of an attitude to which the term 'purism' has been applied. *Dry-Fly Fishing* was not just a practical guide, it was the manifesto of a movement. Even its assertive title is interesting – he had no intention of using a title such as *Chalk-Stream Fishing in Theory and Practice*. The word 'dry' appears in the titles of three more of his books. He was writing about a revolutionary technique which he confidently expected – indeed intended – would take over on chalk streams and banish older methods that he considered not only less efficient but also inappropriate and even rather a nuisance. It is true that he is careful to make several disclaimers in this and subsequent books, in the form of some tolerant and kindly remarks about wet-fly men, and they have sometimes been quoted as evidence of his open-mindedness. He himself quoted the familiar aphorism of Francis Francis: 'The judicious and perfect application of dry, wet, and mid-water fly-fishing stamps the finished fly-fisher with the hallmark of efficiency.' But a close reading of the chapter 'Floating Flies and Sunk Flies' (and of that section of the *Autobiography* in which he returns to this theme) reveals his meaning. He makes a handsome bow to the wet fly, provided it is practised in the right place. Anglers have to choose whether they wish to practise the dry fly or the wet: if the latter, they had better do it somewhere else, not on a chalk stream. The quotation from Francis is in fact a false example, for what Francis meant was that anglers should be flexible and adopt different styles according to conditions: there should be nothing to stop an angler changing from one to another on the same stream, or even the same day. Year after year on the Test he would fish the dark windy days of early spring with a wet fly, then change to a dry fly as calmer, brighter weather came in; on a wet or windy day he would sometimes change back. That is the real context of the above much-quoted passage.

These disclaimers, of which there are several other examples in Halford's writings, may have been included at Marryat's suggestion.

He never took such a hard line about the wet fly, and Senior and Marston were of his mind in this. It is a tribute to Halford that they remained his friends, and were impressed by his enormous energy and grasp of the subject, even though they recoiled from the purism, and at times allowed themselves a mild guffaw over it.

The puzzle over Halford and the wet fly has never been resolved. Having performed hundreds of autopsies, he and Marryat were fully aware that subaqueous food constituted the major part of the trout's diet, including shrimps, bullheads and crayfish. They had even identified eight different types of freshwater snail in autopsies. And often there were packed masses of nymphs. But his attempts to imitate those nymphs do not appear to have been very successful. In an article in May 1888 he admitted that the sunk fly – perhaps in the form of sparsely dressed patterns as used in the north country – ought therefore to be effective. But he added that, in his experience, such tactics did not appear to work in Hampshire. Even more strangely, Marryat is alleged (at least by Halford) not to have been very successful in this respect, although our knowledge here is very imperfect. Halford did in fact make an imitation of the grannom pupa in 1884, Marryat devised a mayfly nymph (some examples of which he gave to the Rev. E.R.J. Nicholls, who used them successfully for years), and in more modern times there have always been some anglers, such as Oliver Kite, who would not use a Mayfly nymph at all, feeling that it was too deadly to be quite fair. So it is hard to imagine how this pattern could not have been effective in late Victorian times. There was even a shrimp imitation, also designed by Marryat, and possibly a small nymph or nymphs. On a day in October 1883 Halford records in his journal that the grayling were 'shrimping', an early use of a rather modern term. In *Itchen Memories* Skues recalled that George Holland had written to him in 1888, enclosing some of Marryat's experimental patterns, 'They never killed any fish either with larvae or shrimp, which I enclose.' The failure of the shrimp pattern is difficult to understand. In December 1887, in an article called 'Tailing Fish', Halford wrote, 'A really good imitation of the fresh-water shrimp might at times be successful in basketing an odd trout here and there.' This is not something he would have written a decade later.

Halford's experience in this area would seem therefore to have been disheartening. There were days at Houghton when the trout fed on nymphs for hours. On one day in June 1887 he noted, 'Fish on larvae during morning, could do nothing' – one of many such complaints. His usual medicine at such times was the Gold Ribbed Hare's Ear, fished dry. It seems odd that he was content to hammer away for hours at fish that he knew quite well were feeding subaqueously in the hope of a momentary change of mind on the part of the trout. If he tried any wet-fly experiments in this period of his life they have left no trace in the journal, were not perservered with, and produced no result. And yet all through the Halford years other anglers were catching fish on sunk flies. We have observed Francis fishing in this way, and so also did Alfred Jardine, R.B. Marston, Major Carlisle, Lord Granby, Sidney Buxton and Edward Hamilton. In the spring of 1885 William Senior, having observed several trout feeding busily but without breaking the surface on a Houghton shallow wrote: 'Fly-fishing at such times is hopeless, unless you use the imitation nympha, sunk a few inches'. James Thurlow persuaded Farlows to tie and market a fly called the Thurlow specifically for bulging trout. In 1898 George Dewar in *South Country Trout Streams* was stoutly defending the large wet fly fished down stream for tailing trout, and as late as 1907 C.G. Barrington, in *Seventy Years' Fishing*, described taking trout with the sunk fly at Chilland – not an easy water – and pointed out that the famous Panshanger Mayfly was in fact a sunk pattern for the nymph. And yet by 1907 the Halford doctrine, with its well-known disapproval of the wet fly, was familiar to everyone in the chalk country.

So if all these people – and many others – were catching fish on wet flies it is appropriate to wonder if Marryat was doing so, and also why Halford was not. Perhaps the key to much else in his personality is to be found here. His way of working was to conduct extensive experiments until he became convinced that he had discovered a general rule. With Halford such an event was always conclusive, and his mind would shut fast. Skues was to write nearly half a century later: 'Halford was not the man to go back and continually to revise his opinions and to bring them up to date in the light of later experience. Once having established a proposition to his satisfaction it became fact.' There are stray references to – but, tantalizingly, no good descriptions of – verbal confrontations in the Fly Fishers' Club, where he would courteously and firmly state his position and concede nothing. He was careful not to get into conflict outside the club, and almost invariably ignored attacks in the press.

Francis Francis had seen the purist problem coming from a long way off. C.H. Cook ('John Bickerdyke') described an encounter with Francis at Houghton one day towards the end of his life. Several anglers sat in the fishing hut and talked. We do not know exactly what was said, but no doubt much of their conversation was about the new gospel of the dry fly, and F.F. must have sensed an approaching intolerance and tendency towards prescriptiveness, for he broke in suddenly upon the talk to say, 'I wish the dry fly had never been invented!' After which, no doubt, there was a long silence.

It is worth enquiring into Halford's wet-fly experience outside the chalk country. Later writers have assumed that he had no such experience, and that his knowledge of the subject, as set forth in the chapter on wet-fly fishing in the *Autobiography* was second-hand. Colonel Harding wrote in *The Flyfisher and the Trout's Point of View* (1931) that Halford 'knew dry fly-fishing, but he knew no other kind, and that was one of his great weaknesses'. In fact he had visited one or two wet-fly streams, although the results had not been very encouraging. A week in Yorkshire in August 1879 produced his best result: he spent two days on the Helmsley Club water on the Rye, catching sixteen trout weighing 4lb 7oz; on another day on the Ripon Club water on the Laver he caught four trout weighing 1lb 8oz. Two other days on the Wharfe and one on the Nidd were blank. His method was to fish a cast of three flies, but unfortunately the journal is silent as to whether he fished upstream or down. (Halford would of course have given himself a better chance if his wet-fly expedition had been in April rather than August.) In 1883 he fished for very little result in streams around Moffat. His only real success was to catch six trout weighing 2lb 8oz on the river Evan, a tributary of the Annan, but this was as a result of changing to dry fly. In July 1891 he fished the Wharfe near Burnsall on his way to the Driffield Beck, with Walbran as his companion. Francis Walbran, who liked to be called Max by his friends, was a tackle dealer in Leeds, and one of the best-known anglers in the north. He was a prolific writer on angling subjects, and in 1883 he had edited a new edition of Michael Theakston's book *British Angling Flies*. Halford's day on the Wharfe was not very productive, and he could only catch a trout of 9oz and two small grayling on a dry fly. He gave up after a while and spent the rest of the day observing Walbran, who, fishing the upstream worm, ended the day with twenty-seven trout. In an account of this day which Halford wrote for *The Field* it is clear that he admired this subtle technique of northern streams, but that it was not one with which he felt any desire to experiment. He travelled on to the Driffield Beck on the following day. The conditions on this Yorkshire chalk stream were much more familiar to the man from Hampshire, and he began once more to catch fish in some quantity. This expedition, with its interesting contrasts, probably confirmed his own personal inclinations, for he made no further attempts to fish in wet-fly country.

So it looks as if Halford's position about the wet fly in northern and western waters was that it was a skilful art, but not one for him. He simply preferred the dry fly. As for the wet fly on the chalk stream, he honestly thought that its use was not appropriate; the dry fly was not just more enjoyable, it was more effective. The part of *Dry-Fly Fishing* which deals with this topic probably owed much less to Marryat's influence, which had been beneficial in many of the technical and practical matters, and was very much Halford's own idea. Here he was settling the rules of engagement on the chalk stream. He was careful not to deny that fish could be caught in this way in Hampshire, but regarded such captures as flukes, which might occasionally be made on what he called 'happening days' but from which no general rule could be derived. For this reason he was interested in the visit of J.W. Reffitt, who was invited some years later to fish at Newton Stacey to test the efficacy of northern wet-fly skills on the Test. Reffitt was a member of the Kilnsey Angling Club on the Wharfe and was well known in Yorkshire angling circles. The experiment lasted for six days, from 8 to 13 April 1899. The guest from Yorkshire fished upstream with wet flies of the traditional lightly dressed type, trying all likely spots, and in six days caught seven trout weighing 9lb 2oz. Halford was on the water that week, and observed the test of his theory with great interest. One gets the impression that he rather wished the wet-fly man had caught less: 'Candidly, I was somewhat surprised at the result, and have often wondered whether he could repeat the performance.' Skues subjected the episode to a lawyerly analysis, too long to enter into here, in *Nymph Fishing for Chalk Stream Trout*.

In the years that followed Halford's attitude to the sunk fly became more and more complicated and overlaid with detail.

Eventually, what had been a question of inutility became one of ethics. Although, as we have seen, many anglers refused to accept his view, a large number agreed with him, and the rules of many owners and syndicates in the south of England began to include the words 'Dry Fly Only'. The story of how this came about, and to what extent Halford was implicated, is still a matter of some doubt. There is something peculiarly Victorian about it: it could probably not have come about at any other time or place. Halford's view, once it was fully developed, was that the wet fly was not only of no use, it was also bad for the trout and for the fishery, in other words bad for other anglers. It is at this point that the ethical element enters into the matter. An angler who does not consider the feelings and welfare of his fellow rods is likely to become unpopular in any age. In the late Victorian era it was worse: he would not be considered a gentleman.

By 1889 Halford had another and rather startling problem to ponder. The same sort of accusations of scaring fish once levelled against the downstreamers were now being made in the angling press against dry fly-fishing. This was partly due to the increasing numbers of anglers practising the new art. Also a good many of them must have been doing so in a rather clumsy fashion. From all over the chalk country came complaints of fish flogged by floating (and frequently dragging) flies, and of trout made uncatchable. Aware that he himself had done so much to increase the interest in the dry fly and therefore swell the numbers, Halford was shaken by this. The critics seemed to be saying that chalk-stream fishing was getting into a mess, and more than hinting that it was (at least in part) his fault. Much of the later development of the Halford doctrine can be seen as a response to this criticism. His problem closely and curiously resembled that facing Skues in the 1930s. Both men were teaching new techniques that were being criticized, because they opened the door to abuse; both countered by reminding their critics that there would be no problem if these new techniques were properly practised.

Halford's response was to advocate a much more restrained and less intrusive style of fishing. The dry-fly angler following the Halford line would spend a large part of the day wandering quietly and discreetly about, or just sitting on a convenient bench observing and waiting for the right convergence of events to occur in the world of fly and fish. When the olives began to hatch and the fish to rise it became permissible to attack them. In *Dry-Fly Fishing* (p.53) he wrote, 'Some dry-fly-fishermen are such purists that they will not under any circumstances whatever make a single cast except over a rising fish', but added that, although he respected this position, he thought it extreme, and allowed floating a dry fly over likely places as legitimate. But the problem of the tactless and over-active fisherman, which seemed a serious criticism of the dry fly, continued to exercise his mind, and the preparation of a new edition of *Dry-Fly Fishing* in 1899 gave him an opportunity to alter the passage quoted above. Not casting at all until a fish is seen to rise is now no longer called extreme – on p. 63 it is approved of, particularly on club or subscription waters, although if 'an angler on private or exceptionally well stocked water sees a trout or grayling in position for feeding in a likely place, he is perhaps justified in floating a cocked fly over it'. The club water fished by men following this advice would therefore, he hoped, have a population of trout sufficiently wary to present a challenge, but not over-educated and neurotic so as to be impossible to negotiate. In March 1899 he published in *The Field* a piece of special pleading entitled 'The Ethics of the Dry Fly', repeating his advice to wait on events and to refrain from fishing 'on spec.', even if on some days this involved not fishing at all. This was how the members of what he called 'the most advanced school among dry-fly-fishermen' should behave. In 1913, in his last book, he made an emphatic distinction between the purists who will occasionally cast over fish in position but not rising, and the ultra-purists who only attack rising fish. He does not actually say so, but the reader is left with the impression that the ultra-purists get the most approval.

The reception of *Dry-Fly Fishing* in the angling world was one of delight, even of awe. Skues described the effect of the book upon him as 'stunning, hypnotic, submerging'. Hills, looking back to his own formative period in *My Sporting Life* (1936), wrote: 'No fisherman of this age can realise the effect Halford's books had upon our generation. Before they appeared we had heard rumours, but they were vague, indefinite and contradictory. Then suddenly the whole of the new art burst upon us full-grown.' The generation that followed was overshadowed by Halford, and for years authors such as Granby, Dewar, 'John Bickerdyke', Major Fisher and Fred Shaw followed a line of respectful deference to him as the final court of appeal. Lord Grey's book *Fly Fishing* (1899) is another example. Although it is in the main a description and a celebration, rather than a manual, it does contain a chapter of instruction. But it begins apologetically by saying that anglers should read and study *Dry-Fly Fishing*, as he does 'not for a moment pretend to be able to give instruction of value and completeness equal to that contained in Mr Halford's book'. A correspondent wrote to *The Fishing Gazette* in October 1889 asking for advice about standard wet-fly patterns, and was advised that he could not do better than adapt Mr Halford's flies, dressing them after Stewart. The giver of this advice was Skues, writing as 'Val Conson', at a stage when he was completely under the Halford spell. Many years later Colonel Harding, in *The Flyfisher and the Trout's Point of View* (1931), thought that the Halford factor had had an unbalancing effect on fly-fishing by giving undue weight to what was only one branch of the art. He also thought that the books were in fact almost *too* good, in that they brought progress to a halt for some years. But, after this somewhat back-handed compliment, he does concede that no fly-fishermen can afford not to have studied them.

The Field felt precluded from producing the usual sort of critical review of *Dry-Fly Fishing* because Halford was their man, and he had already published some of its material in their columns. But even in a factual notice they managed to indicate to the world that this was a quite exceptional book, with such remarks as 'The brilliant success of the author and his artists has been aptly crowned by the faultless style of the publishing handiwork'. *The Fishing Gazette* could not even get its hands on a copy in the general rush to buy the first edition, and had to wait for a second printing. Its review, rosy but four months late, called it 'the most able and complete monograph on a special branch of the art of angling which has ever been written'. The one quietly-inserted item of criticism in an otherwise unrelieved landscape of praise referred to the dry–wet controversy. However, having raised the question, Marston declined to get involved: he continued to believe that the 'unscientific' angler got as much pleasure as the new experts.

The year 1889 must have been a happy one for Halford. He had been hailed as one of the great angling writers of all time. He was exploring a new and interesting fishing on the Itchen. Also he judged that he had now amassed enough capital to be able to withdraw from the world of commerce altogether and to devote the rest of his time to solving fishing problems.

The fishing at Worthy continued to produce more trout, though smaller, than at Houghton: a two-pounder was a matter of remark. The overall average, as in former years, was improved by some sorties with Marryat to carefully preserved fisheries such as Mottisfont, where he caught a four-pounder. The Pincoffs brought them over to Kimbridge for their customary visit. On the first day Halford could only catch one just sizeable trout, while Marryat had nine weighing 19lb 4oz. On the second day Halford did (and probably felt) better with three trout weighing 6lb 2oz. He may have been fishing even more slowly than usual: the Itchen experience had made him more interested than ever in entomology, and he was now pausing to conduct an autopsy of every single trout caught. (He was inclined to accost other rods on the water with requests to autopsy their fish: it is not known how responsive they were to this.) A few days later he went to Turle's water at Newton Stacey and caught five fish. Marryat appeared in the evening with fourteen from the water at Wherwell Priory. Though usually fairly restrained, Marryat was not averse to filling the bag on occasion.

In August and September Halford spent six days at Abbots Barton, catching twenty trout on that rather difficult fishery. Abbots Barton has been made famous for all time as the birthplace of the nymph methods of G.E.M. Skues. Irwin Cox, the lessee of the water, was one of the proprietors of *The Field*; his cousin James Powell was the senior partner of the firm of solicitors where Skues served his articles, and where he later also became a partner. No doubt this weighed with Cox when he gave Skues standing leave to fish at Abbots Barton. This fishery was impounded by high banks at its lower reach to serve a mill, which in those days was on the edge of the city of Winchester. Further upstream it became more streamy, and there were swiftly flowing carriers in the meadows. The latter were excellent for dry-fly work, but the slower stretches of the main river were ideal for the development of the nymph doctrine. In 1889 this lay in the future, and Halford did not meet Skues until 1891.

Halford left the Worthy fishing a year later, at the end of 1890 season. The tenancy of his cottage at Headbourne Worthy had come to an end, and his search for something suitable near at hand had failed. At first he was at a loss to know what to do for the season of 1891. But by this date Halford was a man with many contacts, and in the event he was able to get fishing in a variety of places: at Abbots Barton, at Clatford on the river Anton, at Munden on the Colne of Middlesex, and at Newton Stacey. In Yorkshire there was the expedition already mentioned with Francis Walbran on the Wharfe and on the Driffield Beck. He wrote in the *Autobiography* that the variety of the fishing made it one of his most enjoyable seasons.

In November 1891 Halford was at Houghton as a guest for several days of grayling fishing, and Walbran was invited to be of the party. Bait fishing was now permitted in the hatch holes in the autumn, and several anglers were on hand to observe the Yorkshire technique on the Test. The results were certainly rather striking. Walbran's account – which with that of Patrick Smythe, is one of the few in any detail we have of this time and place, was, fortunately for posterity, included in his book *Grayling and How to Catch Them* (1895). Senior in *The Field* and Marston in *The Fishing Gazette* also recorded the expedition. From these accounts we learn that Halford met Walbran in London and accompanied him down to Hampshire. William Senior, who was also hoping to come, could not manage to get away from London but insisted on seeing them off at Waterloo. Major Carlisle met the train and took them to their lodgings at the Vine in Stockbridge, 'a real comfortable old-fashioned hostelry'. On the following day they were driven by trap down to Houghton Mill; the river was running high, and the path from the mill upstream to the Sheepbridge was under water. A lad dug some cockspur worms in the mill yard, while the obliging miller shut down most of the current into the pool. Halford looked on while Walbran put his tackle together. 'I should strongly advise you, master, to use something stouter than this,' was his verdict on the gut. However Walbran's worm-trotting soon began to produce grayling of large size. Halford hid the better examples and left out the two smallest fish for Carlisle to admire – only after there had been suitable congratulations were the larger fish revealed. By the time the trap arrived to take them back to Stockbridge, Walbran had caught the most remarkable bag of grayling he had ever seen: twelve fish weighing 22lb 10oz. Halford and Carlisle had made no attempt to fish themselves but had spent their time concentrating on their guest and ensuring that he had a good day. On their return to the Vine they learned from telegrams that Marryat would be with them in the morning, but that Senior was still unable to leave London.

When Marryat arrived next day Halford made him demonstrate some of his casting. The astonished Walbran witnessed the performance of the steeple cast, 'by which he can keep twenty yards of line towering like a corkscrew in the air, and then shoot a midge fly across the stream, when it floats like a thing of life. Then he performed the same feat left handed; then he threw the fly behind his back; and then under his leg, in each case the fly floating perfectly. This was worth going from Yorkshire to Hampshire to see, without anything else.' Sport was quieter on this second day, and in the evening they were joined by Senior, who had at last managed to make his escape from London. On the third and last day of his visit (7 November) Walbran caught a monster grayling in the mill pool. Halford suggested that he give the pool one more try with the worm before coming upstream with the fly rod. At the third swim down Walbran hooked what he knew must be a heavy grayling. Halford, who had glimpsed the fish as it swam down past him, said nonchalantly, 'About 2lb, I think'. Walbran was unable to agree: for some time he felt that he had no control at all over the fish. After it had circled the pool fighting heavily for some time it rolled on the surface, displaying its enormous size. 'No use attempting to deceive you any longer,' said Halford, 'I saw when you hooked him what he was, but did not wish to unnerve you. He is the biggest grayling I have ever seen; now do take care.' Walbran must by now have been regretting using finest drawn gut, as the fish showed no sign of weakening. At one point a swirling mass of weeds fouled the line. The fish was still full of fight when twenty minutes later Halford saw his chance and, lying full length on the wall, managed to scoop it out. A spring balance was produced and the fish appeared to be 3lb 8oz. It was weighed again that evening in London on a more accurate balance by Senior and Hawksley and was found to be slightly over 3lb 9oz. It was 19¼ inches long from the snout to the last scale of the tail, and its girth forward of the dorsal fin was eleven inches. The breadth of the tail was 4½ inches. Several other grayling approaching or just reaching 4lb have been taken on the Test over the years, but this was the largest taken during the tenure of Wickham's club at Houghton.

Well satisfied with this achievement, Walbran laid aside his trotting rod and accompanied the others upstream. A little later he was able to help Halford to land a grayling of 3lb, hooked on a Gold Ribbed Hare's Ear, after a downstream chase over two hedges and a stile.

The big grayling was the crown of Walbran's angling life. It was shortly afterwards set up and made its first public appearance the following February at the Piscatorial Exhibition at the Westminster Aquarium. In the autumn of 1892 Walbran fished again at Houghton with Halford and Marryat, catching grayling up to 3lb, and later recording his experiences in the *Leeds Mercury*. Once again we learn without surprise that his hosts spent more time guiding their guest than fishing themselves.

Walbran remained a friend and disciple of Halford, almost alone among the Yorkshire anglers, and early in 1893 began to market the 'Detached Badger' fly line from his Leeds shop at the price of one guinea. In December 1893 he spent an afternoon with Halford in London. Earlier that year Halford had completed his move to 6 Pembridge Place, Lancaster Gate, a short distance away from his former address in Inverness Terrace. This had given him the opportunity to set up a model angling den. He had already told his readers in *The Field* about this room, 'fitted up in accordance with my own design, providing among other things a convenient working table, fixed in a bow window, facing nearly due west, so that, as far as daylight was concerned, there was practically all that could be desired.' His next care, 'having adopted electric lighting throughout the house', was to provide himself with the best sort of lamp for fly-tying work after dark. Walbran wrote in *The Fishing Gazette* of all these and other wonders: the cabinets, shelves and drawers, the cupboards crammed with rods, reels, nets and lines, the sinks and the table for microscope work. Presiding over all was a picture by A.W. Cooper, with the legend underneath 'The Sheep Bridge, Houghton, on the Test. In Memoriam Oct 16, 1886. Francis Francis' last throw'. Walbran wrote – almost with a sigh, one suspects – 'Never have I seen a more perfect angler's sanctum.'

His invitation to Houghton had given Halford an opportunity of discussing the fishing there with his old friends. In the three years since his withdrawal considerable changes had taken place. Wickham had been won over and had greatly increased the stocking regime to please his rods. Major Carlisle thought that the fishing had improved, recording that thirteen of the trout caught during the mayfly season of 1890 had averaged 3lb 12oz, and the grannom, having almost disappeared, was said to be increasing again. The memories of the good times at Houghton were strong and must have helped Halford to decide to seek re-entry to his old club. At the beginning of the 1892 season he was back on the familiar banks, with his headquarters at the Vine. About the same time 200 fish were turned into the river, some of them 2lb and more. Carlisle wrote on 16 April: 'I can safely say that I have never seen more trout at Houghton at any time.' This part of the Test was moving towards the situation of later years, where the attempt to run a natural fishery would be finally abandoned, and the major part of the fish population in the river provided by artificial means.

The membership had not altered much. During the season he fished a good deal with John Day, William Senior, and two new members, Nathaniel Lloyd and John Leech the lepidopterist. The club also acquired its first (and last) lady member in this year. Halford must have expected to enjoy some years of fishing at a favourite place. Neither he nor any of the members seem to have had any inkling of the disaster being prepared for them.

The fishing in 1892 turned out not to be easy, in spite of the increase in stocking, but this seems to have been mainly due to the weather: the earlier part of the season was spoilt by gales and strong winds. Halford caught thirty-nine trout in thirty-four days, of which nine were over 2lb and three over 3lb. On 6 June he and Marryat went to Mottisfont to fish with the Mortimore brothers. Halford had a prosperous time, catching three fish, one of which weighed 4lb 3oz. But this cheerful day was to be followed by an evening of gloom, for on returning to the Vine for the usual evening colloquy they learned that the Houghton fishing rights had been sold. This alarming news, at first thought to be mere rumour, was confirmed as fact in the next few days. After a long and patient wait the men of Stockbridge had launched a successful cutting-out expedition. Some years earlier under the guidance of banker Martin Ridley Smith they had set up a fighting fund, to which several wealthy members had subscribed. But the transaction still contains some mysterious features. The Houghton men had in fact known that Wickham wished to sell and had expressed an interest in buying him out; they had gone so far as to ask one of their number to act for them. Negotiations flagged when it was discovered what sort of money Wickham had in mind. Then the member who had been asked to negotiate was killed in an accident. Wickham became impatient, the Houghton Fly Fishing Club continued to drag its feet, and the older club stepped in and paid the full price. It probably seemed disproportionately large in 1892, but, with the continuing steep rise in value of good fishing, the transaction must in a very few years have looked like a piece of good business. As Halford said ruefully of the men of Stockbridge in the *Autobiography*, 'They were wise in their generation, and the members of our club were much wanting in foresight.'

And, so after eighteen years, it was to be the end of this interesting club, from which had proceeded so many unusual and advanced ideas. Halford and his colleagues continued to fish through the remainder of their last season with some success but, as he expressed it: 'We had no heart for it. . . . The approaching dissolution seemed to weigh on our minds, and I never remember so dreary an autumn as that of 1892. . . . I really think that when the end came it was in many respects a positive relief to most of us.'

The older club resumed the title of the Houghton Club, and in a somewhat ill-tempered spirit took possession of 'our long-lost water' as if the last eighteen years had been an unnecessary aberration. In particular they complained bitterly about the condition of the banks and the number of pike. The fishery was, they alleged, 'in a shameful state of neglect, and the stock of fish very much smaller than when we gave up possession. All this is being carefully remedied.' The outgoing club insisted that things had been in a much better way under its stewardship than before 1873. At this distance in time it is difficult to judge who might have been right, but from what we can know it seems that the old Houghton Club preferred a much tidier and trouble-free fishery, whereas the Houghton Fly Fishing Club was happy to have something a little wilder. On the other hand, Morris the keeper had undoubtedly let the pike run unchecked. Hills records in *River Keeper* that in 1893 William Lunn and his lieutenants removed between 600 and 700 pike from the newly-recovered water, including fish of 19lb and 27lb.

I have intentionally dwelt at some length on the Houghton experience. This was what made Halford an angler. When he came to the Test in 1877 he was a new boy, and, as we have seen, there were to be some years of swotting before he could feel confident on a chalk stream. By the time of leaving he was an acknowledged authority and law-giver to the fly-fishing world. Houghton had been a hard school – he called it 'no place for bunglers'. But it was worth it. After several years' experience his tested and refined skills were good for export to any other chalk-stream fishery; in fact, on a preserved and lightly fished place, he would have to hold back in order to avoid doing damage to the stock. And the delight of the learning process, and the comradeship and interchange of ideas with some of the foremost angling minds of the age made it memorable for him. It was the *belle epoque* of Halford's angling life. There were to be many other absorbing experiences for him in the future, but somehow things were never to be quite the same again.

On the last day of the year, with icicles on the eel weirs and parts of the river frozen over, Major Carlisle walked by himself over the entire fishery to say a mournful farewell to the much-loved place, and penned his last and saddest of all articles on Houghton for *The Field*. For some hours he wandered about disconsolately, beginning at the Mill, 'where the hospitality of our host was proverbial, and a good deal of the material of the celebrated "Floating Flies" was collected'. Then he went upstream towards the Sheepbridge,

> and then to the hut on the shallows, often the rendezvous of many a joyous gathering of anglers, but now a temple of woe. Gone is the portly notebook of the club, and its bracket; gone is the appliance for making afternoon tea, put there by a benevolent member of the club. Absent also is the ricketty little three-legged table, which one had come to look upon quite as an old friend – a treacherous friend at times, when it stood on one leg and emptied the contents of cup, glass, or ink bottle over one's waders.

He trudged on to North Head and above, where 'I reach Francis' corner, the spot where he lost the big trout out of the crowd during the grannom scramble'. As he crossed the river at Boot Island to make his way home by way of Marsh Court, workmen were in the act of demolishing the western arm of the bridge. It seemed to

Carlisle to be symbolic to reach the other side and to have been cut off from Houghton for ever.

7 Ramsbury: 1893–1896

The collapse of the Houghton Fly Fishing Club had been a bitter blow to Halford. Many of his fellow rods went away in despair and were without fishing for some time. Dr Wickham withdrew to some fishing he had acquired at Chilbolton, some miles upstream. Major Carlisle joined a new club being formed at Leckford, but it was unable to get hold of enough water, and the venture died within a year. Halford had other more ambitious ideas. In the late summer of 1892 he set to work with his usual energy to retrieve his situation. He realized that he would have to work quickly. As Carlisle pointed out in a *Field* article, there were eighteen other fishing-hungry anglers from the dying Club who might also be found in the market place. Characteristically it was Marryat, always well-informed about the availability of waters in the chalk country, who discovered Halford's next fishing opportunity for him. Through Robert Long of Marlborough, a brewer and wine merchant, he was able to open negotiations with Sir Francis Burdett of Ramsbury Manor, who owned a length of about four-and-a-half miles of the upper Kennet. Marryat looked over the water first, and soon afterwards, on 23 September, Halford came down to inspect it, accompanied by a friend from the Fly Fishers' Club, Basil Field. What they saw they liked. Halford asked Field, who was a solicitor, to take over the negotiation, and brought two other partners, also members of the Fly Fishers' Club, into the enterprise.

In an article in *The Field* in the following May Halford described the negotiation as having been 'somewhat protracted', but in the *Autobiography* he seems on reflection to have changed his mind a little, writing, 'For once in a way there was not much delay in arriving at a decision'. In fact it took from September 1892 until the following April to settle what was a fairly complex matter.

Robert Long wrote to Sir Francis Burdett on 14 October explaining how far he had taken matters on his behalf. He quoted Marryat's letter: 'My friend [i.e. Halford] wants some one who is empowered to do so to make him an offer in writing of the fishing at a price, or the fishing and the shooting together.' Long added, 'The man is a very good chap and a first-rate sportsman and I think if you are still disposed to let you will find him ready to take the fishing &c if you will let it for a term of years'. Having brokered things thus far Long handed over to the agent of the estate, E.P. Vaux. Vaux provided Field with a rather curious prospectus, which had evidently been drawn up some time earlier in the expectation that the Ramsbury Estate would run its own syndicate. It was therefore no doubt provided for information and discussion. It proposed letting eight rods at £50 each, with the estate providing the services of its two existing keepers, suggested a season from 1 May to 30 September, a size limit of thirteen inches, artificial fly only and no Alexandras or silver-bodied lures, a limit on guests, and as far as possible no Sunday fishing.

Halford regarded this document as an invitation to treat rather than as a draft contract. He had no desire merely to take a rod on a fishery over which he would have no control. He was teeming with ideas about fishery management and wanted a lease for a reasonable term of years. For this Vaux put on the table a figure of £300 a year, which was substantially less than the estate might have got if they succeeded in finding eight rods of their own, but allowed for the fact that Halford would find his own keepers.

Basil Field's response was a good piece of negotiation. Mr Halford, he wrote in December, was disappointed at the high figure suggested. 'However if you say we must not offer less than £300 we have no right after the open and straightforward way in which all negotiations have been conducted to attempt to induce you to alter your decision on this point.' Having made this concession with much courtesy, he then contrived by way of exchange to get his own way for his client in almost every other particular. The size limit was dropped to a level (ten inches) at which it became irrelevant, and in almost all ways the partnership was left to make its own rules. Upon discovering that Sir Francis Burdett wished to offer fishing to his house guests from time to time, Field not only managed to limit the concession to ten guests a year, but also in return succeeded in persuading the landlord to pay all rates and taxes (otherwise the four members of the partnership might have been liable to jury service). Also, Field pointed out, a local assessment committee, which would not dream of increasing the rateable value against a local landlord, might have no hesitation in so doing if the rates were payable by a stranger. 'As we have met you without further bargaining in respect of the amount of rent, I am sure you will agree to this.' Finally Field was able to get a lease for no less than twenty-one years, terminable at the option of the lessees at the end of seven or fourteen years. Halford had chosen an acute agent to do his work for him. Possession was granted on Lady Day, although the lease was not in fact signed until 10 April.

Marryat appeared from time to time at Ramsbury as a guest, but declined to become one of the partnership, having probably as much fishing elsewhere as he could cope with. In any case, judging from the statement of his effects when he died a few years later, he was far less well-off than Halford and his colleagues.

The fishery had been neglected in recent years, but its potential was considerable, and the quality of the fish was excellent. Dr Hamilton, who knew the water well, wrote that 'The trout of the Kennet are particularly fine, and the nearer you get to the source the brighter are the fish.' They were also prolific. Francis Francis had also known the fishery, and when staying at Hungerford to fish the mayfly had usually made a point of coming up the valley for a day or two on the upper end of the river. In *The Field* of 24 June 1882, he described a day there, fishing the reach at the back of Ramsbury upstream to the Park boundary. By the time the trap came to take him away he had caught forty-one trout between 1lb 4oz and 2lb 4oz, of which he kept thirteen. He learned from the keeper that another rod fishing the previous week had caught 200 fish in six days. (Significantly, even ominously for the prospects of Halford and his partners, Francis had caught nearly all his fish on sunk flies.) The following year, not long before his stroke, Francis had come to Ramsbury again and caught twenty-six fish, of which he kept ten: 'I came on some water which was a good deal rippled by the wind, and here I found the fish take the wetfly better than the dry.'

William Senior was another visitor in earlier days, picking up trout and a *nom de plume* on the same day:

> I have with the wet fly, on days when no floating fly was coming down, caught my two or three brace of trout with some such pattern as Red Spinner, Governor, Alder, or Coachman for the evening; indeed, if I remember correctly, it was on a six-brace day with the 'Red Spinner' on this water that, enamoured of that artificial, I annexed its name for a series of articles contributed in 1874 to the *Gentleman's Magazine*, and have held by it ever since.

The partners in Halford's scheme, Basil Field, William Quiller Orchardson RA, and Nathaniel Lloyd, were from very different backgrounds. Field was a partner in the firm of Field, Roscoe & Co, of 36 Lincoln's Inn Fields. He had first fished with Halford in 1889 at South Stoneham, a salmon and sea trout fishery on the lower Itchen belonging to Halford's relative Samuel Montagu. Field had fished in Norway, and on the Tay, the Usk, and the Test at Romsey, and knew something about salmon. For fishing expeditions he had devised an ingenious coat with pockets, loops and buttons strategically arranged so that the main items of equipment were all immediately to hand. He was still new to the ways of the dry fly, and happy to be tutored by Halford. Contemporary accounts describe him as an urbane and genial man, devoted to his family, at ease with himself and the world, and much sought after for his ability to hold forth with wit and elegance at public functions at the Arts Club and the Fly Fishers' Club. He was also a discerning collector of contemporary paintings, with which he filled his house (called Basildene) in Putney.

It may have been his interest in art that had led to his acquaintance with Orchardson, who at this date was becoming one of the best-known painters of the late Victorian period. In his early sixties, Orchardson was the oldest member of the partnership. Of comparatively humble origin – his father was a tailor in Edinburgh – he had by drive and merit achieved a considerable position in life. Hawley House, his place in the country near Dartford, was within easy reach of the pretty north Kent streams, the Cray and the Darenth. When in London he lived at the impressive address of 13 Portland Place. Apart from the Fly Fishers' he was a member of twenty London clubs. (It was thought quite normal at this date to belong to several clubs – a few years later readers of

Wodehouse would not have been surprised to read that Psmith belonged to six clubs – though twenty might seem a little unusual). Some of his pictures were of historical subjects (*Napoleon on the 'Bellerophon'*, and *The Salon of Madame de Récamier*), others were studies of modern life, often with an element of sadness or discord in loveless marriages (the 'Mariage de Convenance' series, and *The Rift within the Lute*). He was also in some demand as a portraitist, and painted several pictures of members of the royal family. Some years later Basil Field, visiting Orchardson in his studio to view an almost-completed portrait of Edward VII, was amused to observe the arrival of an official from the Palace bearing the royal watch-chain, which was needed to achieve absolute accuracy in the picture.

Orchardson had been introduced to fishing by a fellow Royal Academician, John Pettie, at some date before 1890. He had a fair working knowledge of water flies, but after a brief trial gave up making his own artificials, which he found too trying for the eyes. Apart from his experience on the streams of Kent he had fished a little on the Upper Avon near Amesbury (then a quiet place, before the Army invasion of Salisbury Plain). The Kennet seems to have been entirely new territory for him.

Halford's third partner, Nathaniel Lloyd, was a colour printer with his own works in Blackfriars. He also owned a bleaching business in Manchester. Some years later he turned to architecture, through his association with Lutyens, and lectured and wrote extensively on the subject, becoming one of the leaders in the field. At this date he was comparatively unknown and, at twenty-six, by far the youngest of the group. He had been well coached by Marryat, practised assiduously, and eventually became in Halford's own admiring words 'perhaps the best dry-fly fisherman of the day'. He is still remembered in his family as having been a very thorough man in all that he did. (Skues refers to him as Nat Lloyd, but in fact with family and friends he was always called Tan.)

Clearly there was not going to be much doubt as to who would be the dominant force in this partnership. The successful solicitor and the fashionable artist were self-confessed learners in dry-fly matters: the third member was a young man. For the next four years they were to follow Halford's lead in the running of the fishery, and his theories on river-management were to prevail.

*

One of the advantages of the Ramsbury fishing was that the attractive old Mill House on the lower water was available for the rods, and was large enough to accommodate their families, at least if they did not all come at once. Early in the 1893 season there took place a considerable migration of newcomers from London, which must have caused some curiosity in this quiet village. Family servants were mostly left behind, although the Fields brought Frances, the governess for their two daughters, and Caroline, the lady's maid. They stayed for a time at Park Farm until the Mill House had been refurbished. Later Mrs Field and Mrs Orchardson took over most of the running of the Mill, some local girls were hired for cleaning, and a cook-housekeeper called Mrs Kimber, at £32 a year.

Getting suitable keepers had been a headache. Halford advertised and received a number of replies. Mainly they were from men who knew about salmon, or moorland trout, or barbel, or even just pheasants; one notorious rogue of the chalk country (fortunately already well known to the partners), forged his testimonial. At length they hired two men who honestly admitted that they knew little of chalk streams, but who appeared keen and adaptable.

Something of the relaxed and idyllic element of the Ramsbury experience can be gathered from the charming diary of Basil Field's daughter Daisy, not yet thirteen years old in the summer of 1893. From Halford's somewhat stiff and formal writing in *The Field* and in his books one can get a clear and practical, if somewhat arid, statement about fishing and managing the Kennet, but adding detail about the holiday atmosphere in the Mill House and the village, or the social interaction between partners and visiting friends would not suggest itself to him. Fortunately Daisy has another version to give us. She knew all about the fishing – and no doubt the conversation around her was of little else most of the time – but she was also interested in domestic arrangements, dogs, horses, farm animals and wild life in general. She also involved herself straightaway in the garden arrangements, planting a gooseberry bush on the day of her arrival: some days later she was writing 'I plan a great deal about my lilly of the vally bed'.* Best of all, she was keenly observant of people and their ways. A few more such sharp pairs of eyes in early chalk-stream history would help to fill in many gaps in our knowledge.

* Daisy's spelling has been followed throughout.

Daisy, with her mother and sister Myrtle (aged eleven) did not come down to Ramsbury until 6 May. They spent the evening making themselves at home, installing the dolls' house and the curiosity shop from their nursery in Putney, and unpacking. Daisy wrote: 'We both roll into the middle of the high bed & sleep soundly.' A great deal of work had already been done by this stage. The conversion of bedrooms in the Mill House was still going on (it eventually cost £180); cottages had been made ready for Skelton the keeper and Wilson the under keeper; and an existing stew had been cleaned out and stocked with 2,000 large yearlings from Thomas Andrews' trout farm at Guildford. Half of these were turned into the river on 15 May, with some grayling from Sir William Pearce of Chilton Lodge, a fishery further downstream (Daisy's diary records: 'There is a thunderstorm in the morning & it prevents us from going to see the trout and grayling put into the river'). A further 400 trout were put into the Axford reach some weeks later.

In addition, the pike were persistently harried by every method known at that time. The *Autobiography* does not give the detail of this, but the fishery management journal shows that altogether fifteen men were hired locally to help the keepers. Field could not get away from London for the first netting session, and Halford was ill. Marryat had planned to be there but he also was ill. He wrote encouragingly to Lloyd, who was apprehensive at the idea of supervising without help: 'If I can Ill get down & look after the netting, but at present I am "housed" with a beastly cold, which dont seem to go away. . . . I wonder if Skelton has done much netting, I expect not in water like this, but it is easy enough if he has the hatches & the mill leats so he can let the water off as he wants it.' A few days later, his condition now worse, he wrote to Lloyd: 'We *are* a set of crocks, Im not fit – I believe Ive had a touch of "flue" & had to stop in bed Sunday morning.' Then followed a minute account of how netting ought to be done, and a diagram to make the final drawing-in process clear, with two trammels in place. The head keeper must get in beer for the men, and Lloyd must provide an imperial quart of whiskey, which 'looks thoughtful (for others?) and gives you a good introduction to the country cads!' A few days later Lloyd was no doubt relieved to hear from Marryat 'I am going on all right & I expect I shall be able to go down.' In the event, Marryat, Lloyd and Orchardson were all there, at least in the first few days, until the men got the hang of things. Orchardson wrote to his wife: 'Had a splendid day. Went about all over the upper water with Marryat and the two Lloyds seeing to the netting.' The workmen probably had a less amusing time; for five days in March, twelve days in April and fourteen days in May the exhausting process of hauling heavy nets through cold water went on. At the end of this spring campaign a total of 295 pike had been accounted for. These were distributed among the poorer local families, and the helpers were given a largesse supper, which cost the partners £4 3s 5d.

One of the pike weighed 10lb, and two more were 7lb and 6lb, but the majority were under 4lb, and many in fact were in the 12oz class. Pike of this size are often the most dangerous of all. Halford records finding a small pike in a hatch pool on 18 April. When the keeper had secured it – a fish of only nine inches – they discovered a partially digested trout of four inches protruding from its jaws. Halford wrote: 'The hatch hole contained a large shoal of minnows, of which species the females are at this time of the year heavy with spawn, and hence fall an easy prey to the dash of a small pike, yet this little wretch . . . singled out the active yearling trout nearly half his own length in preference to any one out of the shoal of minnows.'

In fact they had not yet solved the problem: pike were still visibly present, and were wired, trapped, speared and otherwise pursued by the keepers throughout the 1893 season. As soon as it ended Halford urged on another terrific effort of netting, and by the end of the year the total of pike killed by all methods reached 2,087, as well as 1,141 dace.

A great deal of energy also went into introducing more stock, including different strains of trout. Some came from High Wycombe, a short, thick silvery type much admired at that date, and some from Thomas Andrews' hatchery at Guildford. Halford disapproved of the old Kennet type of trout and wished to bring in new blood. (This policy was unlikely to have much effect, though. The Wycombe fish probably adapted to their new environment and lost their distinctive insignia in course of time.) Far more dangerous was the level of stocking, which was too lavish for such a small stream. In our age we know more about the unwisdom of overstocking a fishery that already has a population of native trout and good spawning opportunities – the tragic fate of Plunket Greene's Bourne remains the best-known example. In fact Halford and his colleagues were already well-informed about the spawning at Ramsbury, for they had patrolled the fishery the previous winter and counted a total of 409 redds. But by that date it had become firmly established in Halford's mind that an extensive system of stocking ought to be set up on all chalk streams. It had in fact become an obsession with him, no doubt as a result of his Houghton experience, and readers of *The Field* had got accustomed to trenchant articles by 'Detached Badger' on the subject. The fact that there was a wide difference between the much more confined environment of the upper Kennet and the wide and heavy waters of the lower Test did not weigh with him.

The river at Ramsbury has changed a good deal in the last century. In Halford's day the obnoxious practice of abstracting from the chalk aquifer had not yet begun here (although it was already beginning on the Hertfordshire streams), and there was a more reliable flow of water in the river. Fine trout could be caught for miles above the town of Marlborough. (In more modern times no water flows here at all for much of the year, and only a dry-river bed remains, a sad ghost to remind us of other times.) Springs around the town augment the flow, and just below comes in the mysterious little River Og, which also contained large trout at one time. Consequently the river though still quite small, was now more stable.

The first fishery downstream of Marlborough was Savernake, which, according to Dewar in *The South Country Trout Streams* (1898), was able to maintain a 2lb average without recourse to stocking. Next came the Ramsbury fishery, the top boundary of which was reached at the village of Axford. It fell naturally into three sections, and is so treated in Halford's records, both for fishing and for management. The upper, or Axford, reach contained several long stretches of impounded water above mills and water meadow hatches, so that much of the river was fairly slow-flowing by chalk-stream standards; there were however a number of good shallows. The middle reach included the park of Ramsbury Manor. Here a branch of the river supplied the Broadwater, a landscape feature of the sort popular with the great garden designers of the previous century. This lake, muddy, with almost no flow, and a great retreat for pike, was closed to the partnership, as also was the garden bank of the parallel branch. The further, or southern, bank (known as

Ramsbury Upper), could, however, be fished under the lease. Below the Manor grounds the reunited river passed under a handsome five-arch bridge built in the late eighteenth century, and both banks could now be fished for a further two miles downstream. In the fishery record book this is known as Ramsbury Lower. Here again, quiet, impounded stretches were varied by rippling shallows, where white chalk as well as gravel was exposed. The river was full of food for trout, especially freshwater shrimp.

Ramsbury itself was a large village of great charm. The neighbourhood was unaffected by the London-to-Bath road, which ran a few miles away to the south on the other side of the chalk downs, and even today is notable for its quiet, sequestered atmosphere. In 1893, before the days of motor cars, it was even more so. From many points of view the members of the partnership must have congratulated themselves on their good fortune.

As for the fishing, the 1893 season was, for Halford, friends and guests alike one of astonished delight. It began slowly. The upper Kennet is not an early river, but there was some moderate sport, with hatches of small upwinged flies including, to Halford's surprise, the blue-winged olive – a species which, from Test experience, he would not have expected to see until June. The season was a forward one, and Halford recorded in the first of a series of Kennet articles (*The Field*, 20 May) that the horse chestnuts were in full bloom by the end of April, and speculated about an early appearance of the mayfly. He began to fish on 13 April, and subsequently was on the water on far more days than his colleagues. It is fair to add that he was not always fishing: on many occasions he was occupied with the challenges of river management, at that date a novel thing for him. And, as at Houghton, there was a good deal of observation and collection of insects and data. By the third week in May he had only captured eleven fish weighing 16lb 2oz.

Basil Field made a slow start, which Daisy recorded in her diary with all the candour and natural delicacy of a daughter. 'We go fishing with Papa but catch nothing but huge minnows. He comes home with his tail between his legs.' On 24 May the girls had their first fishing. They had already been given a fly rod with D and M engraved on the butt, although they probably only had a sketchy idea of how to use it. Daisy wrote: 'We go fishing with Mr Halford, but there is no time to fish before lunch so until that time we potter about the mill-house, & Mr Halford gives us illustrated truths on the skill of British workmen.' Halford, at that time still supervising the last stages of the Mill House conversion and hunting for furniture, was living elsewhere in the village; his wife was with him and probably wished to run her own kitchen in accordance with Jewish custom. After lunch Halford collected the girls and took them upstream. Myrtle soon lost interest and rambled off to pick flowers; returning, she became entangled in the back cast ('twice' records the diary, a little sharply). Daisy however was soon caught up in the interest of the game: 'Mr. H: catches a trout & gives the rod quickly to me, so that I may have all the fun, whereupon the fish is promptly lost by me . . . Mr. H. shews us some alder's-eggs & tells me the way to keep them. . . He gets another trout (1lb 9oz) which I land & he says I do it very well.'

This was the first of many expeditions. Halford was fond of young people – it was one of his more endearing traits – and he and Daisy corresponded for years afterwards. On one occasion, when she was about fourteen, she asked him what would happen if she were to marry his son (a leg-pull, for she detested Ernest). He replied, 'My dear, we should all sit around wailing in sackcloth and ashes.' Halford, contrary to the commonly held belief, was not devoid of humour: when gillying for guests and pointing to a particular rising trout he would comment on some less-than-accurate casting by dryly remarking 'There – or thereabouts!'

The long-awaited mayflies began to appear on 22 May – in spite of the weather, the same date as in former years – but for several days the trout paid no heed to them. Halford had worked hard to persuade the others not to rush at the fishing, but to let the fish get well on to the fly; this, he was sure, would avoid shyness and short-rising, and extend the chances of sport into a longer season. He had been preaching this since 1886, and now devoted a large part of his *Field* article of 20 May to this topic. However, with two other partners of the syndicate present, and several friends, it must have been difficult to keep them in leash. He wrote: 'It was not until the 26th that the first loud floop of a trout at a mayfly nymph was heard.' He then persuaded the rods to leave the bottom stretch of Ramsbury Lower completely alone, in order to test his theory – and also for the benefit of Lloyd, who could not get away from London.

Several other short stretches further upstream were treated in the same way. The results appeared to bear out Halford's theory: the parts fished prematurely produced many short rises and similar failures, and fish became wary. Lloyd arrived on 3 June, and, Halford wrote, 'highly appreciated the unselfishness of his brethren, and, to use his own expression, "never found fish so silly" or had such sport as when he waded carefully up this length of the stream during the height of the rise.'

Serious fishing began on 30 May, with a heavy hatch and fish responding well. Halford took his guest Thomas Andrews to Ramsbury Lower. In the space of an hour Halford caught twelve trout weighing over 20lb (it was the sort of day on which the wise angler has to know when to stop); four were over 2lb, the largest 2lb 11oz. Three of them were caught on the Welshman's Button (Halford's favourite alternative fly during mayfly time), seven on the Champion, a pattern devised by John Hammond of Winchester, and one each on the Rouen Drake (three variations of which had appeared in 1886 in *Floating Flies*), and on the Gallina (a fly which Halford had only recently begun to use – it was to appear in 1897 in *Dry-Fly Entomology*). Andrews meanwhile had taken five for 7lb 11oz. The fish were in the highest season, playing in a wild uncontrollable way, and losses had been frequent. Sport at this level continued for some time. The neat columns of the Ramsbury log, faithfully made up by Halford each evening, record a considerable carnage.

All rods were now catching fish almost every day, except for Lloyd, who could only be at Ramsbury at weekends. Daisy records her first unassisted capture, a fish of 1lb 12oz on 1 June and adds: 'Myrtle catches a little one' (in fact, according to Halford's diary, it weighed a pound). Two days later Basil Field again took his daughters on to the river. 'While we are having lunch an old man comes up & tells Father all about the poachers', a tale to which Field no doubt listened with great attention. Arthur Gilbey arrived, as Orchardson's guest, also H.J. Francis and Mr Phelps. The fishing and social tempo increased daily, closely observed by Daisy. She even recorded her own small social mishaps: on 2 June she went out to tea in the village, and returned with a large bunch of flowers in each hand, 'so that when I am introduced to Mr Orchardson and Mr Gilbey I can't shake hands.'

Gilbey, already one of the most expert of the new school of chalk-stream anglers and yet another angler who had been tutored by Marryat, was often at Ramsbury. Soon afterwards E.J. Power, also a well-known performer, came to stay. Both were members of the Houghton Club for many years, and Gilbey was later to become its secretary. Edward Power was an accomplished dresser of flies who, towards the end of his life in 1916, was to pass on his knowledge to William Lunn; his Claret Smut and Spent Olive are both included in *Dry-Fly Entomology*. He was ambidextrous and a long caster, though some thought that he threw too straight a line, creating problems of drag for himself. Horace Hutchinson, in his book *A Fellowship of Anglers* (1925) quoted a remark of one of the Houghton keepers: 'Mr Power's a good fisherman, and Mr Birkbeck's a good fisherman; but Mr Gilbey can catch fish when Mr Power and Mr Birkbeck can't.'

By 3 June the Mayfly fishing on the two lower beats had produced a total of thirty-six fish caught and a number lost in various ways. The survivors were now becoming a little jumpy, and Halford's journal remarks 'Kimbridged 6 times', a sure sign of fish coming short. Most rods discovered that large Mayfly imitations were less successful than quite small patterns on long hook sizes of 2 or 3 (13 or 12 in modern numbers). By 4 June the hatch had progressed up to Axford, and a fresh start could be made on unruffled trout. Another battue day ensued on 5 June, when Halford again caught twelve trout. For day after day the mayfly poured up from the river in numbers that would have astonished an angler who only knew the Test or the Itchen. The hatch generally reached its height between 3 and 6 p.m. Soon afterwards, on many evenings, the temperature fell sharply, almost to freezing point, and late fishing with the Spent Gnat did not answer.

On 8 June Marryat arrived for a three-day visit and immediately began to make himself agreeable to the girls, as Daisy's diary records:

> We go to Mr Halford's to lunch. We meet Mr Marryat. He calls us 'fellows' or 'Johnnies'. He is very funny at dinner. Mr Halford asks me to fill his tobacco pouch for him. When he is out of the room Mr. M. takes the pouch, stufs it with orange peel & one of my gloves. When Mr. H. finds this out he throws the orange peel at Mr. M. who nods his head solemly, so the peel goes over his head. He gives Myrtle and myself two may-flies; so does Mr.H.

Small horseplay incidents of this sort cast a slightly surprising light on Halford – less so perhaps on Marryat, whose love of clowning has passed into history. It was not long before the girls began to call him Aunt Harryat. Soon there were amusing letters, Christmas presents and advice about keeping pets. Daisy talked affectionately of Marryat and Ramsbury half a century later. In his much-loved book *Where the Bright Waters Meet* Harry Plunket Greene describes a similar life at Hurstbourne Priors, a sort of continuous house party, with fishermen, friends, children and animals tumbling down the village street and into each other's houses. For us, on the other side of a gulf of years and two world wars, such scenes have a simple charm and a sad remoteness.

About 10 June the mayfly began to slacken, although they did not disappear for several more days. The rods and their guests had taken 108 trout since 30 May, the largest being 2lb 14oz. A further eight trout were caught between 10 and 14 June, at which point Halford made the authoritative entry in the fishery log 'End of Mayfly'. Inevitably there was the usual summer anticlimax, but fish continued to be caught throughout the rest of the season. Daisy and Myrtle were taken back to Putney for several weeks. They returned on 16 August, and once more threw themselves zestfully into Ramsbury life, riding, fishing, blackberrying, building a den of branches, and romping in the lanes with the dogs. August 24 was a busy day. Basil Field and Nathaniel Lloyd went off shooting, leaving T.B. Vernon and the Rev. G.E. Mackie to fish. The three dogs were restrained with difficulty from joining in the shooting expedition, and one of them lost his collar (a hint in the diary made it Myrtle's fault). After lunch Field took the girls to the local saddler, Mr Wren, to get a new collar. Daisy writes: 'A poor, old, red-eyed man serves us. He asks F. if he is "one of the fishing gents" & says that he has been very poorley & wants to know whether F. can give him a fish. He says he would'nt mind even if it were a pike.' Happily her diary the next day records the capture of a trout of 1lb 6oz, 'which Caroline takes to the poor old red-eyed man'.

This trout had been caught by Myrtle, and the log shows that pike tackle had been used. A certain latitude crept in from time to time. Several fish were caught with minnows in this and succeeding seasons, though usually by young people and beginners who needed the encouragement of a fish on the bank. Other trout fell ignobly by accident to the keepers' trimmers. But the most startling breach of chalk-stream decorum at Ramsbury also came to be the most publicized, for a jocular account of it was included by Basil Field in his speech at the annual dinner of the Fly Fishers' Club in 1897. He described to his audience how he once arrived unexpectedly at the Mill House, penetrated through to the kitchen looking for signs of life, and found all quiet 'save the rhythmic snoring of the housekeeper'. He pressed onwards towards the back garden.

> All was still. Unlikely as it seemed, I began almost to fear that my friends had been struck religious and gone to afternoon service, when a wild shout of triumph, followed by a loud chorus of excited voices, told me that those I sought were at the Bathing Pool behind the Mill! The Bathing Pool! What could they be doing in that sacred spot, taboo to us by general consent and reserved for visitors only arriving by the evening train, too late to don brogue and wader, and wander further afield? . . . I will tell you in confidence what I saw at that pool. I saw "South-West" of the *Field* newspaper, float fishing for trout with a live minnow for his bait. He was, at the moment of my arrival, attempting – unsuccessfully, I am glad to say – to land a lightly hooked and apparently undersized fish.

Field's mock-horror account of this distressing scene makes it clear that no less than four members of the committee of the Fly Fishers' Club were present, aiding and abetting, including Halford and William Senior. Even in 1897 purism did not always reign! All those implicated in the crime were present at the dinner and may have joined in the merriment, if somewhat hollowly.

By contrast, Daisy was determined to master the art of the dry fly, and during the summer of 1893 she began to make flies. Halford probably watched over these early attempts. In August he records that Field caught two fish 'on a fly dressed by Daisy'.

The weather became very hot, and a serious drought developed in southern England. In some places in northern Europe excellent white wines were made in areas normally regarded as marginal, an indication of an exceptional summer. The Kennet held up reasonably well, though it became very low after the end of the season before the winter breaking of the springs.

Halford was the highest scorer for 1893, with 115 trout for 173lb, eighteen of which were two-pounders. (He was of course more often at Ramsbury, being the only member of the quartet who did not have a working life.) Lloyd caught thirty-one trout, of which seven were two-pounders. Both Field and Orchardson filled in the fishery log in a careless manner, giving totals aggregated with those of their guests (which must have greatly irked the meticulous soul of Halford), and it is not easy to know in detail what they caught. Orchardson made the least use of the fishing and was only at Ramsbury for a few days. The grand total for the year was 343 trout weighing 561 lb. Fifty-four weighed over 2lb (though there were no three-pounders). A great many of these were caught by the numerous guests, including many well-known anglers of the day: H.S. Hall, Captain J.J. Dunne ('Hi-Regan'), James Rolt, the copyright barrister and friend of Skues, and the Rev. G.E. Mackie.

That first season of 1893 was the bright morning of the Ramsbury experience. Although more fish were caught in 1894 something began to go wrong. Partly this was due to the fading of something that had been a novelty, but other reasons for disenchantment began to show themselves later. The mayfly was never again to appear in such numbers during Halford's tenancy. And the disinclination of the trout to rise to small flies once the mayfly was over was noticed by all the rods. Other and more serious problems emerged because of the policy of over-generous stocking.

Halford was for the time being contented enough. Apart from his time and money, he had invested a good deal of himself in this project. Here at last was a chance to get to work on a stretch of his own – for his partners left him very much to himself in forming policy. It was characteristic of Halford to throw himself with tremendous drive and numbing enthusiasm into a work of this sort, and also to begin writing about it at once, as if making a report upon it to himself as well as to the world. His book on river-management *Making a Fishery* was not in fact published until 1895, but much of the material had already appeared in *The Field*. The first of these articles had been published on 23 May 1893, a date which, with fishing only just starting, might be thought rather premature.

The 1894 season produced a bigger total bag than 1893, but this was partly the result of many more rod-days: 415 trout were caught weighing 612lb, an average of about 1lb 8 oz. Of these Halford secured sixty-one for 95lb, fishing on forty days or part-days. As before, he was a generous-minded host, giving up time to ensure that friends got fish. Also a good deal of his time was spent in looking after some detail of river-management, or merely in studying aquatic life, and indulging his passion for autopsy. On 6 April Mrs Field wrote to the girls, who were at their lessons in Putney, 'Mr Francis caught a pike this morning, which Mr Halford has just opened & found a stickleback & a bullhead inside it'. He devoted a large part of one mayfly day to observing the egg-laying flies, and recorded that one female imago dipped to the water fifty-seven times before she had shed her quota of 6,500 eggs.

Once again the guest list reads like a roll of honour, with many leading names of the world of fly-fishing at that time: J.J. Bolding, R.E. Booker, W.F. Brougham, T.P. Hawksley, W. Pingo Horton, C.A. Payton ('Sarcelle' in *The Field*) and T.B. Vernon, as well as many of the 1893 guests noted above. The mayfly was regarded as a failure. Nevertheless many more large fish were caught this season, forty five being over 2lb, and eight over 3lb. Halford secured one of 3lb 6oz (*Autobiography*, p.207). The two largest of the season and indeed of the entire tenancy were fish of 4lb 1oz, caught by Field on June 10, and 4lb 6oz by Booker on 16 June.

Halford's Mayfly patterns do not seem to have changed during his four years at Ramsbury. The main types, as noted in his journal, were the Egypt (by which was meant the undyed Egyptian Goose Hackle, a soft floppy fly he found useful when the trout were bulging); the Green Egypt, with wings dyed according to one of Marryat's recipes; the Rouen, a pattern devised by George Holland; the Green and Brown Champions; and the Gallina, first used by Halford at Kimbridge in June 1890. This last had a limited usefulness: it looked well for a few casts and then took up too much water. All these patterns can be found in *Dry-Fly Entomology* (1897). Spent Gnats are not differentiated in his journal, so must have been of Marryat's pattern with the grizzled blue dun hackle points, variations of which are still made today.

May and early June produced the main fishing effort and the great bags. The partners and their friends then began to leave, and by the third week in June the Mill House was empty. Apart from Basil Field who made a brief visit from London in July, and Robert Long of Marlborough, no one fished until August. Halford did not return until September, to find the fishing much more testing: it took him six days to catch seven fish. Already the pattern had become established of abandoning the more stubborn summer fishing, when substantial hatches of small fly were ignored by the fish. The Field family came back in August, and so did Orchardson, who stayed for several days, catching twenty-nine trout for 43lb.

Marryat came over from Salisbury in late August and amused Daisy and a small friend by catching a frog, landing the fly on the unlucky creature at a range of fifteen yards. It was characteristic of Marryat the humourist to record this feat, for the further entertainment of the girls, in a mock official document, which read:

> KNOW all men by these presents that I, G.S. Marryat of the Close Salisbury did lawfully take and catch with the fly known as the Mayfly in the water known as Moon's Mill pound in the river Kennet, in the parish of Ramsbury one reptile to wit a FROG in the presence of the undersigned this 20th day of August 1894.
> *Signed*: Geo S Marryat
> *Witnesses*: Flora Kelson X her mark
> Daisy Field

The fly that caught the frog is hooked into the paper, and more than a century later provides for us an interesting example of the small, discreet patterns Marryat and Halford had come to prefer by the 1890s. The vast Mayflies of the previous decade, with wings of solid feather a full inch in length, look decorative in the beautiful plates of *Floating Flies*, but they were poor tools for hooking fish and evil to cast. This small, neat fly is a wingless version of the Brown Champion, with a golden pheasant hackle wound in front of a ginger cock hackle, and a body of raffia grass ribbed with scarlet thread and gold wire. It was a variation of one of Marryat's recent designs exhibited by Holland at the Fisheries Exhibition in April 1891.

The stocking continued apace in 1894. Thomas Andrews provided 250 of his largest yearlings, which were released on 11 April. Another batch came as a gift, as Halford explains in *Making a Fishery*:

> A friend fishing the water, as the guest of one of the lessees, expressed a desire to present 1000 yearlings to the fishery. He explained that a

> relative had erected and fitted up a small hatchery, taking the ova from a strain of large trout, and had arranged a series of small carriers in which some good yearlings were reared. This kind offer was accepted, and on the 27th of February 1894, they were conveyed to the water.

The friend was Arthur Gilbey, and the fish had been bred at Denham by his cousin W. Crosbie-Gilbey, who some years later raised the salmon parr for the Thames salmon experiment of 1901; Thomas Andrews arranged the carriage. The fact that five were found dead on arrival probably raised no eyebrows, but ten more died the next day, and Skelton reported that 'they did not feed well' and some were marked with fungus. A stronger flow of water was directed through the stew, but this had no effect. Halford and the keepers tried immersing the fish for five minutes in a strong solution of brine, but the mortality continued for some weeks before dying away. The remainder eventually prospered. They were fed bullocks' liver and lights, at first at the rate of 15lb a week, then 30lb a week in June, and finally in September 60lb a week, which was the most that could be provided by the local butcher. When counted just before Christmas 1894 the numbers were found to have fallen to 745. One half of these had grown to eight ounces or more – some reached 1lb 2oz – and were released into the river; the remainder were held back in the stew for another month's feeding. Apart from disease in the stew the ill effects of over-stocking began to show themselves in some parts of the river, and during pike-netting operations in October some black or otherwise sickly trout were caught. Others were wired or otherwise secured from carriers and ditches. Altogether 108 diseased trout were removed during 1894.

Running costs rose during this second season. Halford had fixed on a sum of £600 a year to cover all expenditure, and this was fairly closely kept to in 1893. In 1894 expenditure was £696, and Halford as manager had the embarrassing task of calling for an extra £25 each from his colleagues. The running of the Mill House and garden had cost £41 in excess of estimate, and the immense programme of netting had added an extra £31. It is pleasant to be able to record that the wages of the under-keeper had been raised, but this didn't strain the budget greatly: seventeen shillings a week in 1893 now became eighteen shillings.

The autumn of 1894 was one of prolonged bad weather. At first the aquifer soaked up the water, but in November, after four weeks of almost continuous rainfall, the river rose alarmingly, and the Kennet valley was inundated with widespread floods. Halford and the partners feared for their fish, imagining that they would have been whirled downstream or lost over the meadows. When the water subsided, however, there seemed to have been no great loss of stock, and alarmist prophecies of heaps of fish-corpses on the land proved unfounded – one dead trout and one dead pike was all the result.

In 1895 Halford did not get to Ramsbury until 8 May. He had been persuaded by John Day and John Leech to travel to Germany to try the fishing on the River Ilm at Weimar, and so in April he departed on the only fishing expedition of his life outside the British Isles. This fishery, rented by Leech and Day with two German partners, produced an astonishing weight of trout, and they must have held out tempting prospects of its possibilities. They were both keen on big catches, 20lb in a day or more. Leech, in an article about the Ilm in the *Badminton Magazine* in 1898, wrote a little disparagingly of the lack of fish in the Test in 1892:

> On joining the Houghton Club, during the last year of its existence, I first became aware of the state of perfection to which fly fishing can be brought, and the extreme shyness of which trout are capable. It took me some time to realise that on the Test, the most celebrated of English trout rivers, anything like a big bag was an exceedingly rare occurence, and that one ought to be satisfied with a brace of 1½lb trout. Although the charm of Test fishing is supposed to lie in the skill required to get the better of such highly educated fish, I have never come across the man who did not look forward to the times of the grannom and the May fly, when the trout are supposed to be less wary.

And he refers, in terms that must have struck a chord with Halford, to the style of the typical Houghton day, composed of 'loafing, yarning, an excessive contemplation of nature, [and] endless waiting for a rise of fly that wouldn't come'. In Germany, Halford was assured, they did things differently; blank days would not happen, and it was all due to management and stocking.

No doubt fired up by the tales he had heard, he joined the party at Weimar on 17 April. He began his campaign the following morning and fished hard for seven days. Perhaps the anticlimax that followed was inevitable. He was only able to catch thirteen fish up to 1lb 15oz; Day and Leech had thirty between them in the same period. In the *Autobiography* Halford describes this result, when compared to the usual pattern at Weimar, as 'contemptible'. But the weather had been poor, the water somewhat coloured from melting snow, and such fish as he did find were undiscriminating, taking large flies, wet or dry, and sometimes trailed downstream. Leech and Day kept the water for several more years, on occasion obtaining some striking results (in August 1896 Leech caught ninety-eight trout up to 5lb in three days) – Halford had not been there at the right time. He went away to prepare for his Ramsbury season, and planned no more German trips.

It may be that Halford's enthusiasm for his Wiltshire fishery waned a little in this third season. He began once more to accept invitations to other places, and during 1895 he fished at Munden on the Middlesex Colne with the Hon A. Holland-Hibbert, at Clatford on the Anton, and on the Wylye with the Wilton Club. He only fished for seventeen days at Ramsbury, a strong contrast with 1894 (thirty-three days), and 1893 (fifty-two days).

Orchardson came on 1 May and stayed for most of the month. He at least was as keen as ever. For much of the time his sons Quentin, Ian, and Gordon were with him. He wrote to his wife, 'The boys are looking quite rustic . . . They are all over the place, but we come into every meal and go to bed every night,' and, later, 'This afternoon I was out with the boys and got a brace before lunch, besides losing three others, one of which Quentin muffed with the net, poor chap – he took his misfortune very quietly and landed the next one well.' On 23 May he wrote: 'Went out after tea, had good sport, got 2, one a very big one which I returned as not in condition. The other a game fish – I saw him under the opposite bank and had him first chuck.' He came back in July and had more fish, but he seems, as in other seasons, to have caught much less than the other partners. This did not dampen his enthusiasm, or his pleasure in the success of others. On 2 July he wrote: 'Gilbey got a very nice fish, nearly 2 pounds, after I left, and Halford got two'.

The Fields stayed much less at Ramsbury this year. Basil Field made a number of short visits when he could get away from his office. His best day was on June 13, when he had five fish, the three largest being 3lb 1oz, 2lb 9oz and 2lb. The girls spent most of their time in Putney, and their absence was felt. Halford wrote to Daisy:

> All your pals here are pining for the society of Daisy and Myrtle. When can we expect them? Your pet trout are getting tame again. [These were the fish in the mill pool, accustomed to being fed by Mrs Field.] A little bird told me that the Orchardson boys made them shy trying to delude them with a hook in the bread – however we are all glad to hear that they failed ignominiously.

Marryat was only able to come once in 1895, on 14 June. Later he wrote mournfully to Lloyd:

> It is awfully good of you chaps to ask me so often over to Ramsbury, & I'll come when I can but I am afraid it wont be till some time in Augst. as we have a run of silly visitors just now – theres one coming to stay and I dont know yet how long she'll stay – and after the 20th we have two lots one my S American brother & his wife.

And after some advice about dealing with the summer weed cut he returns wistfully to the same subject: 'Im just thinking that if this woman doesnt stop for more than a day or two I might come on Wednesday & back here on Thursday just to have a "glance round" the new palace of Fish [i.e. the extended stewponds] – Ill wire as soon as I can find out.' In the event he was not able to get away, and never fished at Ramsbury again.

Lloyd and E.J. Power fished together for a fortnight in the first half of June, taking fifty fish between them, but once again the falling off in the fishing after the mayfly was noted. Such hatches of small fly as occurred were generally ignored by the fish. Halford and Marryat had observed in previous years that a trout lying out in position in the summer, even though not rising, could often be brought up to an artificial. It did not seem to matter unduly what the pattern was. This behaviour they considered to be markedly different from trout of Test or Itchen, and it was again observable in 1895. This would probably not strike a modern angler as a particularly unusual thing, but Halford was mystified by it, writing in the *Autobiography*, 'To Marryat, as well as to myself, this peculiarity of the trout was, and still is, quite unaccountable.' Worse still, it was not how he wished the trout to conduct themselves. He had by this date settled in his mind how chalk-stream trout behaved, and how anglers should respond. Trout that rose (that is, if they rose at all) in a casual way at any sort of general pattern held little interest for him, either at Ramsbury or Weimar, or anywhere else.

The final total for the 1895 season was 310 fish for 439lb. 20 were 2lb and more, and three were over 3lb, the largest being 3lb 6oz. One was caught by Basil Field, as mentioned above. The other two were taken by David Wilson, the secretary of the Fly Fishers' Club.

Halford's third book, *Making a Fishery* was published in September 1895 by Horace Cox. The ordinary edition was priced at seven shillings and sixpence; customers wanting the edition de luxe in morocco had to pay twenty-five shillings. Although a good solid discussion of what was then regarded as best practice on south-country streams and mainly derived from his Ramsbury experience, it is perhaps his least lively work. It had been two years in the writing. The first article entitled 'Making a Fishery' in *The Field*, in May 1893, had been followed by a number of others, and the whole had been widely redrafted in book form.

It began with safe and unexceptionable advice for the would-be tenant about selecting a suitable water and gauging its value. He added: 'If he prefers the company of his wife and children when away from home' (and, pretty clearly, Halford did not), 'he had better inquire into alternative sources of entertainment for them, such as walks and drives, and whether the condition of the villages nearby is healthy.' This last was not a thing that could be relied upon: some villages were much more dangerous than others. He continued: 'If his better half has no love for comparative solitude, he must discover something about the social status of the neighbours, and of their disposition towards newcomers.' Most of his middle-class contemporaries would have nodded approvingly at such sentiments – unwise contact with 'socially impossible' people was to be avoided – although the Field family seemed to have mixed cheerfully with everyone in Ramsbury. He would also have carried his late-Victorian readers with him in his strictures on the poacher ('idle, loafing vagabonds', etc). Attempts to reform or help him by offering him casual work, he insisted, did not answer: he would refuse such offers, or scamp the work, after which 'it is safe to predict that he will be found at the village pothouse on Saturday night, more or less intoxicated.'

The chapters on stocking and on the management of the stew are interesting, for here we come close to the reasons for the eventual failure of the Ramsbury experiment. Halford's obsession with this subject has already been referred to, and it was one upon which his mind had locked shut. Here he began, in his best lecturing style, to harangue his reader: 'There are possibly a few owners of water who still cling to the exploded theory that the natural reproduction alone in a river is sufficient to keep up the stock.' More than a century later we can see that there is some truth in Halford's view, at least on the big waters of the lower Test. There will always be in such places a reduced chance of successful spawning, and a greater activity of predators, including Man. But it is not a safe principle to apply everywhere, particularly in a more restricted environment such as the Upper Kennet. Some modern experiments have shown that wild trout fisheries are sustainable in southern England, but usually in smaller waters, and then only if they are lightly fished and the majority of the trout are returned to the water. Few anglers in the 1890s would have been willing to carry on their fishing in such a way; the majority of them resembled Day and Leech and would have wished to leave the water with a satisfactory weight of fish. There is a close analogy here with the shooting world. Many an old browned photograph has survived from the nineteenth century of sporting parties at the end of a hard day on mountain or moor posing with an immense heap of dead mammals or birds. Seeing these pictures nowadays makes us feel a little queasy. Victorian culture explains much of this: it was an age of imperialism, and men regarded the natural world as something to be exploited and colonised in much the same way as the world beyond Europe. If fisheries were not producing the heavy bags of earlier times then they must simply be made to do so. A management plan with ample stocking would restore the situation. Terms such as 'going with nature', 'ecological balance', 'biomass', and 'carrying capacity' were not in vogue at this date.

He continues:

> It is said that this stocking, or, as some say, overstocking, with tame fish is producing an artificial state of things, but it is too late to advance this

> argument. The necessity for such stocking is brought about by an even more artificial state of things – viz., that of having thousands of anglers frequenting waters that are not fairly capable of accommodating a tithe of their number, and still further aggravated by the spread of the dry fly, by which every rising fish on every day in the season is more or less educated by the sight of artificial flies floating over him.

As we have seen, he came to Ramsbury with his ideas on stocking firmly thought out. As early as March 1891 he had published an article on stocking in which he indignantly rejected the misgivings of critics:

> A small minority honestly believe that putting artificially bred fish into a river has some dreadful and unexplained effect on the old inhabitants of the stream – in fact, some go so far as to say that, if not the chief, this is one of the chief causes of the serious and progressive decline in sport during the last few years.

In *Making a Fishery* he quoted, as an example of a success story, the case of the old Hungerford Club, which on migrating to a new fishery on the Wylye in 1891 commenced a heroic campaign of netting and stocking. In the first four years the new club, now called the Wilton Club, had slain 3,619 pike and 13,056 other coarse fish, and had stocked ('on a most liberal scale'), putting in 4,000 two year olds, 16,000 yearlings, 45,000 fry and 24,000 ova. Thus a stream formerly in a neglected and derelict condition had been brought up to scratch, a club with a long waiting list was now flourishing, a substantial rent was being paid to an owner who before got nothing, and money from outside was being spent by visitors in the local area.

Before we judge Halford too severely we should remind ourselves that, if some of his policies sound unsubtle, working against rather than with the natural order, we are hindsighted and more experienced. The practices and the failures of the Halford era provide lessons from which we now can profit. At least he was not guilty of putting in the oversized monsters nowadays found in some chalkstream fisheries. Halford's preferred fish for release into the stream were big enough to look after themselves but usually at or just under the size limit. And he was insistent that a good sportsman should always release fish if they were only doubtfully sizeable.

The deterioration at Ramsbury was not on the same scale as that of Plunket Greene's Bourne, which was a much smaller stream with a more fragile natural balance. But it remains an object lesson in angling history. Both cases were discussed by Jack Hills in the second (enlarged) edition of *A Summer on the Test* in 1930. Hills was well acquainted with this part of the Kennet. He rented Ramsbury Lower in 1902, and between 1899 and 1922 he was able to fish all three reaches as a guest. He was critical of Halford and his friends and their attempts to develop the water on 'scientific lines': 'Coarse fish were killed: yearlings and two-year-olds, chiefly barbarians from High Wycombe, were poured in by the bucketful: everything was done to improve the river: and yet the fishing, which had been so good before restocking in 1893, had got so bad by 1896 that the tenants threw it up in disgust.' During the twenty-three years that Hills knew it, no trout at all were put in, and the river soon achieved a natural balance and was full of good healthy fish.

Many years later history curiously repeated itself, for in 1969 the Piscatorial Society took a lease on the Axford reach. They took over a water seriously overcrowded with fish, many of them small and not a few black, which latter they removed. They made no attempt to stock, and in the years that followed the quality of the trout improved enormously. In 1973 one of the members had by August caught sixty wild brown trout weighing 100lb, including fish of 4lb and 3lb 4oz. Once again the fishery had been saved by a policy of deliberate inactivity.

In February 1896 the angling world reeled from the shock of the untimely death of George Selwyn Marryat, pattern of fly fishers for all time. For many it was unbelievable that this apparently indestructible man could die from a common illness. At the age of fifty-six he still had the vigour of a young man, seemed impervious to fatigue, and was fond of spending long hours in winter weather pursuing snipe over frozen marsh and moorland. But a dangerous strain of influenza began to show itself in Britain in the New Year of 1896, and in the latter part of January it struck at Marryat. He seems at first to have made light of it, dosing himself with lozenges and staying indoors. He had in fact been ill in February 1893, and again in February 1895, with persistent cough and influenza, but probably of a milder strain. This was different, and after some days he took to his bed. He wrote to Daisy Field, apparently puzzled at his own condition: 'It feels so queer being ill – I havent spent a day in bed since I can't remember.' But his letter is full of the usual Marryat drollery, describing the antics of a kitten rescued by his daughter Dolly from a tree in the garden, and relishing the recollection of a recent triumph at billiards over Daisy's mother. He adds: 'I hope you are getting on all right with the bicycle and not falling about at every corner like the philosophers after the FFC do [i.e. the annual dinner of the Fly Fishers' Club] coming home'. It was the last letter signed 'Aunt Harryat' that Daisy was ever to receive. His state worsened, though with occasional remissions, which gave hope to his alarmed family. Then a serious stroke left him paralysed and unconscious. Basil Field reported the seriousness of his condition to members of the Fly Fishers' Club on the evening of Thursday 13 February, and as William Senior recorded, 'The news had the effect of placing the club-room in a sympathetic atmosphere of silence.' After some moments, however, the members chose to take the optimistic view. A strong, hard man like Marryat could surely not be in imminent danger. Sadly they were wrong: Marryat was in a coma, and died the next day, Valentine's Day 1896.

A badly-shaken William Senior wrote in *The Field*: 'To say that the news of his death will create consternation and sorrow amongst anglers in the South of England will not at all convey the feelings which follow the sad event.' Other well-known anglers joined in to add their contributions – Major Turle, H.S. Hall, R.B. Marston, Major Carlisle and Dr Tom Sanctuary. The obituaries in *The Fishing Gazette* on 29 February run to more than three pages. Throughout there runs a sense of disbelief as well as a terrible sadness: how could a man who, above all others, seemed destined for a long life be taken away with such appalling abruptness? Halford alone did not join in these sorrowful tributes. He seems to have been struck dumb by the tragedy, and in any case was not a man much skilled in handling his emotions. His silence need not be construed as lack of feeling: he made ample amends in the preface to the 1899 revised edition of *Dry-Fly Fishing in Theory and Practice*, where he wrote that Marryat's death 'was as severe a shock as if I had lost one of my dearest and nearest relations'. And in 1903 he wrote in the *Autobiography*, 'Even now I cannot write about this sad event'. The Fields, who loved him, were grief-stricken. Daisy remembered

Marryat all her life – the kindness, the amusing letters and the presents at Christmas. Marryat's daughter Maggie wrote to Daisy and Myrtle: 'I must write, dears, just to tell you that I know no one will feel it more than you two & yr people will . . . You know it was *much* better as it is – no pain & no consciousness, only the painfulness for us'.

After February 1896 Halford and his friends always referred to him as 'poor Marryat'.

This tragedy seems to have cast a gloom on the Ramsbury partnership. Young Nathaniel Lloyd, who owed so much to Marryat's teaching, seems to have been more affected than most: he did not appear at Ramsbury at all in 1896. Halford had been ill himself, and needed a long convalescence at the seaside. He came to Ramsbury on 21 May, fished for two days, then for a further ten days during the mayfly. But it was a poor hatch, and the weather was unkind, with days of glittering light, blustering winds and low water. Some of the fish caught were soft or black. Halford thought it was a sign of backwardness in the insect world, but it is more likely to have been a result of the overcrowding discussed above. He took forty-four trout weighing 61lb 12oz. A good many of these were caught on Sedges and the Welshman's Button, and nothing resembling the great mayfly hatch of 1893 was seen. He wrote in the *Autobiography*, 'I did not fish hard that year, as my health was not very good, and the remembrance of poor Marryat was ever before me'. The sense of depression attaching to the fishing this year even shows itself in Halford's records: normally meticulously kept; the Ramsbury log and even his own personal journal become careless and tail off with no attempt to do the usual totalling up of numbers and weights. He left on 16 June, and, apart from a single day in August, seems to have given up at Ramsbury.

The Fields came down in May, determined to try and make the best of things. Orchardson appeared for a few days in July, having installed his family in holiday quarters in Felixstowe. But he was restless and missed his wife. He wrote: 'Don't be surprised should I turn up on Sunday evening. Sport is not good and *you* are not here', and the next day: 'I hope you are having a good time – we are not! No sport though company in plenty. The Fields, the Lloyds and others all fishing or duck shooting.' Soon afterwards the family descended on him, having been driven out of Felixstowe by mosquitoes. The Mill was full, and they went up the valley to stay at Axford Farm. The fishing continued to be slow, with fish feeding well below the surface throughout the long summer days, and Orchardson could only catch nine trout in five days.

In the autumn of 1896 Halford wrote three articles in *The Field* entitled 'Free Rising and Sulky Rivers'. He covered the characteristics of the Test, Anton, Wylye and Driffield Beck, all of which he considered free-rising, the Itchen less so, and finally the Kennet, which – unsurprisingly after four post-mayfly summers – he placed firmly in the sulky category. He must have recalled with some bitterness the original prospectus supplied by the agent in 1892, with its attractive description of the Upper Kennet as 'eminently a dry fly river' with the innocent addition 'though the wet fly is also very successful'. As the season limped to its close he became aware of an undercurrent of discontent among his partners. Boldly he called them together, and after some discussion they agreed to end the tenancy if they could (it still had three years to run to the first date of option). The lessor raised no objection, and the lease was duly determined. The end of the season melted away in heavy rain and south-westerly gales. The season's total was only 202 fish. There were no three-pounders, and only nine two-pound fish, the largest being 2lb 10oz. Halford had only been able to catch one of them.

And so, on this rather sad and minor note, the Ramsbury experiment came to an end. Writing of it years later Skues wrote of 'the foredoomed attempt to convert what is essentially a wet-fly water, though not of the rough stream type, into a water of the type of the Test or Itchen'. No doubt with hindsight it was easy to see that the stocking level was ill-advised, and that a more flexible angling style could have yielded sport in the summer months. Modern fishery owners are more careful (though not perhaps always) in estimating a river's capacity when stocking. And the present-day angler on such a fishery would attack rising fish with a dry fly, or, if they were feeding beneath the surface, with various nymph strategies. This Halford and his friends were not prepared to do. It is true that the twentieth-century doctrine of the nymph had not yet arrived, but, as we have seen, there were anglers in the 1890s who were no stranger to the use of small wet flies discreetly used. William Senior, an open-minded man interested in all styles of angling, records an instructive incident:

> One evening we met at Ramsbury, after an afternoon without sign of fly or rising trout. Halford and Basil Field were there, and we stood and bewailed the absence of duns and lack of sport. We loitered with our rods spiked, and smoked sadly. I then, and not for the first time, repeated the tale of my former experiences, and at last begged Halford not to be shocked, not to think me an unforgivable brute, but would he give me free permission to try the wet fly in the old way, and without prejudice.

After some good-natured wrangling, Senior was allowed to do his worst, mounted a small Red Spinner, fished it wet and down, and in a short time caught the only brace of fish taken that day.

Halford, the prime mover in the project, was left with a sense of frustration. At least, he felt, the water was in a better state than in 1892, after the introduction of 5,500 stock trout. It was not likely that he was going to admit that his carefully-planned practices had had a bad effect on the place. The official reason for quitting Ramsbury, as stated in the *Autobiography*, was the disinclination of the fish to take surface fly in the summer. For the other partners, however, the passage of time operated to erase much of the sense of failure. Perhaps they had in a sense benefited more than he had. Orchardson, though not often there, had enjoyed himself enormously (his daughter devoted a considerable section of her biography of him to the good times at Ramsbury). Both Basil Field, who always generously acknowledged Halford's role in tutoring him, and Lloyd had improved greatly in their style and effectiveness as anglers by 1896. Field in fact on several occasions contrived to get himself invited back to his old haunts by the next tenant, one Atkin Fraser. And Mrs Field had loved the place, the walks in the Wiltshire lanes and the Mill House garden to which she had devoted so much time. Years later, in a letter to Daisy, she remembered the flowers, in particular the sweet peas, and wished the whole family back in Ramsbury.

8 Towards Exact Imitation: 1897–1904

By the mid-1890s the chalk-stream world had undergone a radical change. The revolution was in being, with Halford's own stamp recognizably upon it, and his notion that the dry fly rendered alternative techniques on the chalk stream ineffective and inappropriate was becoming widely accepted. He had by now a considerable following, many of them personal friends such as Dr Cheadle, W.H. Pope ('one of the best of modern dry-fly men'), Nathaniel Lloyd, Dr Wiblin and B.W. Smurthwaite, an ardent enthusiast for exact colour in fly patterns. Like many revolutionaries, they had by now been carried away by the pure creed and would admit of no exceptions. Perhaps they thought that their revolution was an accomplished fact, but, as we have seen, there remained a number of malcontents and wet-fly rebels in the outside world who refused to surrender entirely to it. Marston's views have already been mentioned. The books by G.A.B. Dewar and Lord Granby, with their descriptions of fishing large wet flies downstream, were the subject of urbane reviews in *The Field* which were in no way critical of these practices, though it should be added that these reviews were not written by Halford.

But even here change is observable. Dewar and Granby may not have been cowed by the purists, but they made it clear that they regarded the wet fly as a makeshift tactic on chalk streams and not 'the real thing', and they acknowledged that the dry fly was more interesting and more exciting. As time passed, those who preferred a more liberal approach, such as Senior and Marston, were finding themselves increasingly marginalized, and became reticent about their opinions and somewhat furtive in their practices. By 1900 on most parts of the larger chalk streams – with the exception of the Houghton Club, which held aloof from trends – the wet fly had largely disappeared, whether there were rules banning it or not. Hills, writing many years later in wry amusement at the absurdities of another age, confessed to the use of improper methods in the Halford age, as if it was a sort of prank when Authority was looking the other way:

> In 1902 [the purist] reigned a despot: nothing was admitted but the dry fly. At least openly, for we did get fish, though rarely big ones, on a sunk alder or march brown or hare's ear in stiller waters when ruffled by wind, and an occasional heavy one in mayfly time on a sunk hackle; but we did not talk about it, and always left off when there was a chance with the floater.

All the same, the battle was never over, and the enemy, even though they appeared to have lost the main battle, continued to carry on a sort of guerilla warfare for years. It would be a mistake to imagine that Halford and his followers carried the day during his lifetime and for some time after his death, until the Skues doctrine began to take effect. The true picture has a much more ragged and untidy look about it.

When the revised edition of *Dry-Fly Fishing* came out in 1899 the reviews, as usual with Halford's books, ranged from the respectful to the enthusiastic, but some contained a note of criticism of his intolerance towards the wet fly. Alfred Jardine wrote that he had read the book with pleasure, but warned against the extremism of the dry-fly anglers 'who fret their theories to pieces'. He insisted that the sunk fly was just as useful, depending on weather and conditions, and referred to some of his own staggering bags of fish caught by wet-fly methods on the Colne and the Windrush. Marston attempted to introduce a lighter note by comparing the fly-fishing world to the Anglican Church, in which there were High-dry-fly men, Broad-dry-fly-men and Low-dry-fly men, that is to say, Halfordians, opportunists and Alexandra-users, and suggesting that they are 'all jolly good fellows'. The harshest review in 1899 came from E.M. Tod, the spokesman for the Yorkshire school since the death of Pritt in 1895. He straight away identified Halford's tactic of disarming criticism by saying that he has nothing against the wet-fly man, and then proceeding to imply in an oblique way not only that he has no place on chalk streams, but also that he is practising a lower form of fishing. Tod's review was written in the strongest language yet used in any review of a Halford book: 'I cannot refrain from commenting upon the self-satisfied complacency with which the experts of the "dry" fly view us of the "wet" fly; while entering a disclaimer, Mr Halford is not quite free from this almost patronizing tone, especially if one reads between the lines here and there.' He rejected the idea that the experienced wet-fly man merely fished the water: 'the knowledge and skill and intuitive perception displayed by a really skilful wet-fly fisherman when fishing a river where no sign of a rise is visible is a sealed book to those of the dry-fly school.' And he reserved his greatest scorn for the idea that it is not quite correct behaviour to cast over a fish in position but not actually rising ('How funny and ceremonious. . . . Really, I think this is going too far'). And he finishes rather witheringly: 'I am inclined to feel that there is a good deal that is rather artificial in the dry-fly business, with all its punctilio.' Halford pasted this long review of five-and-a-half columns into his book of press cuttings, along with over twenty others, and, as usual with him, made no attempt to respond. But in fact Tod had marked out the main lines of a battle that was to go on for decades. It was the first real sign that the hypnotic state of 1889 had worn off a little, and that some anglers were not just defensive, they were prepared to fight back.

Some members of the Houghton Club – such as Arthur Gilbey, who joined in 1896 – soon became past masters at the dry fly, but the evidence is that the club as a whole retained a relaxed and broad-minded approach. In *A Fellowship of Anglers* (1925) Horace Hutchinson mentioned a trout of 6lb 8oz caught by Robert Newman, Deputy Governor of the Bank of England, on a large hackle Mayfly fished downstream in a gale of wind and rain. This happened in 1916, by which time dry-fly orthodoxy might be supposed to have established itself everywhere in the south of England. Hutchinson remarks, not without a trace of irony:

> Mr Newman made confession that he had, that day, been fishing wet-fly, down-stream. It was an awful, a most daring confession, to make in such a company, all reputed purists of the pure. But its effect was

> singular. Several, quite unsuspected persons, dared to confess, the lead being given, that they too, in such circumstances of weather were not above the use of the wet-fly and the 'chuck and chance it'.

The *Chronicles of the Houghton Club* mention a number of other lapses, even more startling: the eleven-pounder caught by Herbert Norman in 1898 on a piece of meat, the seven-pounder caught by General Wigram on a slice of bread, and several other such crimes (but, be it said, these were all large fish not so likely to feed on flies).

Halford would have regarded such misdemeanours with amusement. They had no real bearing on his teaching, which was still spreading and conquering. He continued and redoubled his journalism in *The Field*, while avoiding getting into conflict in the correspondence columns. At times he seemed to go out of his way to avoid arguments. In 1898 he reviewed C.E. Walker's book *Old Flies in New Dresses*. Walker had some advanced views about the use of patterns to imitate shrimps and corixae, for which he had already been criticized in the angling press, and in his book he called for a clear definition of what a legitimate trout fly really was. But Halford's review entirely ignored this coat-trailing and the fact that much of Walker's ideas struck at the root of his doctrine. Instead he confined himself to a minute examination of the entomology in the book. His own copy of this interesting work, which has points of resemblance with the writings of Cecil Mottram, is inscribed 'To F.M. Halford, whose criticisms on my little book have been most kindly and impartial, in spite of the fact that I have gone for him badly in it'. Three months later, though, in March 1899, Halford appears to have had second thoughts, for he condemned Walker's shrimp pattern: 'The more accurately it represents Gammarus pulex the more certainly should it be prohibited on a fishery where floating fly only is used.'

The revolution was not confined to chalk streams, or even to England. (In 1887 Marston reported, not without some astonishment, that the dry fly had made its appearance in New Zealand, and in 1888 a writer to *The Field* described his success with floating flies in Norway. In time it was to spread all around the world, and each area would engraft its own particular characteristics upon it. In France, Petit's book *La Truite de Rivière* leant heavily on Halford's first two books for much of its material. In America, fly-fishing had been established for years, and a movement in the direction of the floating fly can be traced back at least to the days of Thaddeus Norris in Sullivan County, when false casting was sometimes practised. As Paul Schullery has pointed out, it is not quite true to say that the dry fly was introduced in America by Theodore Gordon (in 1885 J. Harrington Keene of Greenwich NY and several other writers mention it), but, as in Britain in the middle of the nineteenth century, it was not a shared and widely used method. Rather it was a case of inventive but isolated individuals coming upon a practice which had not yet come into general use. So when books of coherent doctrine from Britain began to appear in America they caused considerable interest, and more American fly-dressers began to tie flies designed to float. The well-known exchange of letters between Theodore Gordon and Halford took place in 1890. Halford's response to Gordon was friendly and helpful but cautious; he was well aware that he knew little of the fly life of American streams. He sent a set of his own patterns, but his letter showed that he realized that they might not be relevant, and he suggested that Gordon send some local natural flies preserved in spirit to George Holland in Salisbury to get the right imitations made. But Gordon was less interested in the question of precise imitation. It was the build of the Halford fly with its superior floating qualities that seems to have impressed him.

In 1894 A.N. Cheney reviewed the Halford influence in *Forest and Stream* and called for more entomology in American fly-fishing. Halford had written to Cheney after observing a newspaper item about the success of a Vermont angler who had been a recent convert to the dry fly. Halford wrote:

> It is certainly a source of gratification to find one's little efforts appreciated by anglers in the United States, the more so as my work was more specially devised for the use of our chalk stream fishermen here. However it goes to prove that the habits of our *Salmonidae* do not differ greatly in different climates, and that the popularizing of the sport is tending to work the same improvement in the education of your trout as it has already here.

In the next two decades Americans absorbed the idea of the dry fly, and their ingenuity and open-mindedness soon began to transform it for transatlantic use. They had already moved ahead of Britain in rod-building, and were not likely to accept Hampshire teaching in its pure form. There are some placid streams, such as those of central Pennsylvania, which have a resemblance to waters in southern England, but much American water is rough and turbulent, requiring a different design of fly. Nor were American anglers much impressed with the English habit of hanging around and waiting for the rise. Gordon, although fascinated by the new art, shows in his writings that he regarded dry and wet techniques as being of equal status. In spite of this he and other anglers retained an admiration and an affection for the English fly-fishing school, and appreciated the research and hard work of the theory and the delicacy of the practice. Unfortunately, although Gordon wrote a good deal, including a number of articles for the *Fishing Gazette*, he did not produce a book. It was left to Emlyn R. Gill in 1912 to produce the first full-length book to treat of the dry fly in America.

Halford's doctrine changed in a major way in the period 1897–1905. At the beginning of this period his published work was in line with his previous thinking. There is nothing surprising about his *Dry-Fly Entomology*. He had been promising the world for some time that he would close the last important gap in his theoretical edifice and tell the angler all he needed to know about natural flies. One may admire the hard work of assembling and reducing to a system in one place a number of scattered facts, but the material in the book is derivative rather than original or dynamic. By 1905 Halford had adopted the much more unusual and radical plan of equipping the chalk-stream fisherman with a reliable outfit composed of a set of essential flies of his own design. The experiments on the Itchen and his relationship with Edgar Williamson had by then produced the final statement of doctrine in its most pure form.

Dry-Fly Entomology (1897) was a curious book. In the first place, it was divided into three sections, only the first of which was on entomology. The second section was a list of fly patterns – all, of course, floaters. This was partly based on the list of ninety flies of 1886, with a number of patterns removed and others added, so that the total was now one hundred. The third section was on fly-dressing.

The entomology was based on Halford's studies over a number of years. He was well aware that there had been numerous calls for a good authoritative book on river flies. At frequent intervals there would be letters in the angling press from men despairing of distinguishing between the various olives. At the first annual dinner of the Fly Fishers' Club in December 1885 the chairman, Sir Ford North, had suggested that it was time a work appeared to bring Ronalds up to date. And in 1892 'Pelagius' (a *nom de plume* adopted by the Rev. M.G. Watkins) complained in *The Field* about 'the utterly unscientific state of anglers' entomology'. By the middle of the 1890s Halford considered himself to be in a good position to fill this gap. He was now well-versed in the techniques of microscopy for his own research, and had consulted the monographs and lists of McLachlan, Pictet, Eaton, Westwood, Verrall, Kirby and others, all of which were the best of their kind at the time. He had also approached the Rev. A.E. Eaton directly and received help from him. He now proposed to boil down some of the material from these heavy works, which no fisherman would normally read (even assuming they were aware of their existence), and present them to the angling world.

The standard edition was a good-looking book, although the colouring of the plates is less fine than those in *Floating Flies*. It had been hoped to market it at a guinea, but Vinton and Co, the publisher, found that the cost of production made this impossible, and it appeared in the shops in the summer costing twenty-five shillings. There was however a magnificent two-volume special edition costing five guineas, the second volume being entirely filled with actual specimens of the 'Hundred Best Patterns', all tied by George Holland and his team. Skues records that these flies were tied on particular hooks of a blued, rather than bronzed, finish that were not very suitable for practical fishing because they were too fragile. (As the de luxe edition was of one hundred copies, it enabled Holland to rid himself of no less than 10,000 otherwise unwanted hooks in this unusual way.) This edition was fully subscribed before publication, and so vanished immediately. The list of the subscribers included many of the grandees of the chalk-stream world: R.B. Marston, the Rev. G.E. Mackie, Nathaniel Lloyd, J.J. Bolding, Dr J. Wiblin, Sir Samuel Montagu, Albert Petit, Sir William Pearce, Hedley Norris, and four members of the Gilbey family.

For all that the book looks impressive, however, the first part of

Dry-Fly Entomology does not quite work. What was wanted was a practical guide that would enable anglers to make quick identifications. Once again there were no representations of naturals and artificials side by side – which had been the great strength of Ronalds' book. Only artificial flies were reproduced in colour; natural insects were depicted in a series of black-and-white line drawings, in some cases very large and with much detail, as if under a low-power microscope.

Five olive duns are identified (*Baetis vernus*, *B. tenax* and *B. buceratus* – all three nowadays called the medium olive – *B. rhodani* and *B. atrebatinus* – now large dark olive and dark olive respectively); four pale watery duns (*B. binoculatus* – later *bioculatus* and now *fuscatus* – *B. scambus* – which is odd, in view of its colouring; we would now call it the small dark olive – *Centroptilum* (now *Pseudocentroptilum*) *pennulatum* and *C. luteolum* – now called the large and small spurwings). Two iron blues, *B. pumilus* (now *muticus*) and *B. niger* are mentioned, as was the blue-winged olive, *Ephemerella ignita*, and the three mayflies, *Ephemera danica*, *E. vulgata* and *E. lineata*. He also describes the turkey brown, *Leptophlebia* (now *Paraleptophlebia*) *submarginata* which figures little on chalk streams, the march brown, *Ecdyurus* (now *Ecdyonurus*) *venosus*, now called the late or false march brown – he did not seem to have been aware of *Rhithrogena haarupi* (now *germanica*) – and the yellow may dun, *Heptagenia sulphurea*, common in the south of England but not often taken by trout. What we now call the broadwings (a term which covers several species of *Caenis*, receive a mention, but, having never found an example in an autopsy, Halford had become convinced that they had no significance for the angler. (Major Carlisle wrote of a mysterious evening rise on the Marsh Court reach in the summer of 1892: 'I think "Detached Badger" pronounced it to be cenis or coenis – something.' Halford replied in *The Field* a fortnight later that the white curse was *Caenis rivulorum*, but he doubted if fish ever ate it, in spite of the evidence of the evening rise.) Other flies which can become important at certain times or in certain local areas, such as the yellow evening dun and the pale evening dun, were not mentioned – nor, of course, were a number of other ephemeropteran flies found in more acid waters, and therefore in his view not likely to be of interest to the fisher of the dry fly.

The other orders were dealt with more selectively. Six of the more frequently-seen caddis flies were singled out for special mention, and other common representatives of the stone flies and the two-winged flies.

The ideal person for the heavy programme of reading that this book involved would have been someone who could spend a great deal of time on the river and whose hobby was insects as much as fishing. This description fitted Halford, who by this date was saturated with the love of water entomology, but it is doubtful if many of his readers had the same level of enthusiasm (although as anglers they were probably not averse to learning a little natural science). For Halford entomology had achieved equal status with fishing in his mind, and he was prepared to follow it just as far. It would have avoided much later misunderstanding with his public – as well as being a considerable relief – if he had explained that, although he personally found entomology immensely absorbing, he was quite aware that only a small part of it was relevant to the ordinary angler and his needs. True, he did not actually *insist* that the chalk-stream angler should master all the detail, but somehow the book implied it, and this helped to add to the impression that fishing the dry fly involved mastering a subject that was both laborious and daunting.

The 'Hundred Best Patterns', making up the second part of the book, gives an interesting indication of the direction of Halford's thought on the subject since 1886. In the introduction to the section he defended himself from the charge of recommending anglers to carry *all* the patterns: it was intended simply to be a full-length list of the well-known flies available. Also, aware that the 1886 list had been criticized for its haphazard arrangement, he now divided the flies into natural-fly categories, e.g. Olive Duns, Pale Watery Duns, etc.

Duns and Spinners were the staple of these artificials: thirty-four were duns, twelve were spinners, nine were Mayfly duns and one was a Mayfly spinner. So more than half were of ephemeropteran types. There were ten sedge flies, five two-winged flies and a small number of miscellaneous flies, including Ants, the Alder, the Willow Fly and the Cow Dung. There were also twenty fancy flies, amongst which one is puzzled to find the Golden Dun, the Apple Green, the Badger Quill, the Greenwell and the No.1 Whitchurch, all of them fairly specific and sober imitations of up-winged flies.

The list showed Halford's growing enthusiasm for hackle pattern – which, in the case of Sedges, was intended to make the fly lighter and so allow it to fall on the water with less disturbance (there had been no hackle Sedges in the 1886 list). Many of the other patterns carry a soft hen hackle at the shoulder to impersonate wings. The Red Quill, described by Halford in 1886 as 'one of the sheet anchors of a dry-fly fisherman on a strange river, when in doubt', now appeared with a medium blue dun hen hackle in front of the usual red gamecock hackle. There is also a move towards better patterns of spinners with the inclusion of E.J. Power's Spent Olive with its hackle point wings tied flat (Power, one of the most admired fly-dressers of the Fly Fishers' Club, used to make a variation of this fly using tiny shavings of whalebone for wings).

The question of body material is also intriguing. Very little concession was made to the principle of translucency. Bodies were for the most part made of opaque materials such as silk, crewel, flat gold, raffia (for Mayflies), and, in particular, of quill. Only eight were made of fur or other dubbing, materials which had presented problems of floatation a few years earlier. As paraffin was widely used by 1897, it is a puzzle to know why Halford did not move away from quill in the direction of dubbing. He was not as unaware of the value of transparency as his critics have imagined, but apart from the use of horse hair in the bodies of a small number of flies there is not much sign of it here.

This interesting list had already been published rather inconveniently in three different numbers of *Baily's Magazine* in the summer of 1896. G.E.M. Skues, who was by now becoming better known through his journalism, published a review in the *Fishing Gazette* minutely analysing the value of this classification. He acknowledged Halford's 'characteristic thoroughness', then proceeded to pick a number of holes. He disliked the use of gallina for whisks as being unnaturally thick, and treble-cipher hooks were, he thought, too small for flies carrying three hackles. Soft shoulder hackles were not new – they went back to Hammond's time. 'If they are a success,' he added, tongue in cheek, 'it is safe to say that they strike a bad blow at the "precise imitation theory".' He finished by doubting the wisdom of the widespread use of quill, and believed that 'the time is not far off when we shall get back to dubbing and floss for dry flies'.

This review, which Halford probably thought was not as respectful as it might be, nevertheless made him think. He was aware that Skues was the rising star of the fly-dressers at the Club, and he had included in his list one of Skues' own patterns, a Red Spinner with a gut body. The year before the publication of *Dry-Fly Entomology* the two men had shared two pages on fly-dressing in *The Field*, Halford covering floating flies and Skues wet flies, with Skues' part running to 5,000 words (nineteenth-century *Field* readers were accustomed to long informative articles and almost nothing in the way of pictures). Halford was sufficiently impressed with Skues to ask him to contribute a section on fly-dressing in the third part of *Dry-Fly Entomology* – he also made a similar request to W.F. Brougham. Skues' method was to use the fly vice, whereas Brougham was 'a strong and consistent member of the school who condemn the use of the vice and work with their fingers only'. Skues had therefore been in the odd position of reviewing a book in two different sections of which his own work figured.

Altogether eighteen reviews survive today in Halford's news cutting album. In general critics were impressed by the industry behind the book, but there were one or two rebukes. *The Daily Chronicle* thought that 'his work, as an effort of literature, is deplorable'. *Land and Water* allowed that duns and spinners were well covered, Sedge flies less so, but why was the Alder not valued more? And why were its wings upright like a butterfly? 'Their evolution [i.e. the artificial patterns] seems to have stopped short, as they are practically those which have been handed down for the last fifty years without being altered in any important point.' (The convention at this date was for the anonymous review, but it is likely that this was written by Charles E. Walker, whose book, already referred to, came out a year later.) Whether or not Halford was influenced by remarks of this sort, it is certain that he wrote no more about current flies then in use. When he next discussed fly patterns they were to be something new and of his own invention. Other critics were a little bewildered by the entomology section, as if wondering what all the detail was for. Years later, in *A History of Fly Fishing for Trout* (1921), Hills indicated that he had little time for the book, and thought Halford far too inclined to get over-involved in matters of detail. Reading it now, after the lapse of over a century, one is impressed by Halford's mastery of a good deal of recondite information, but the entomology part savours more of the study and the microscope than the riverbank.

For five years after quitting Ramsbury Halford fished mainly on the upper Test. Major Turle gave him a rod on his water at Newton Stacey for thirty guineas a season, and from time to time he contributed sums up to £25 towards restocking, which was carried out from E.V. Corrie's fish farm at Chilland on the Itchen. There were five other paying rods, including Nathaniel Lloyd, and Turle kept some days for himself and friends. Halford was able to vary this fishing with invitations to Wherwell, Testcombe and Leckford, with the occasional visit to big-fish places such as Kimbridge. In 1898 he fished for six days on the Frome of Dorset under the guidance of Walter Pope, who knew the river well. The waters above the county town of Dorchester he found well stocked with plenty of pretty trout, mostly under the pound mark. Below Dorchester, due to the pollution from the town (see Chapter 2), large fish were to be seen. He witnessed the capture of a trout of 4lb 3oz by a local angler but decided that he did not care to fish in the place himself. He recorded an interesting day, with fish averaging 1lb 8oz, on George Floyer's fishery at West Stafford, which was far enough downstream for the worst effects of the Dorchester effluent to have died away. Patrick Smythe described the lower Frome at this date as being 'chock-full of trout', which is not the case today.

This period was something of a lull in Halford's life, and a sense of sameness appeared to descend on his fishing. Each season began with a similar pattern: the Gold Ribbed Hare's Ear scored above all other flies, the Red Quill succeeded it, the Iron Blue got its chance on the right day, the mayfly would continue to decline and the Welshman's Button would be the effective fly instead in late May. He devoted much of his time to insect-collecting, and fished rather less than in former years, as if his enthusiasm was declining. The marginal comments in the journal become more and more brief, disappearing altogether in places. The *Autobiography* passes fairly rapidly over this period, as if he found it difficult to present any facts of interest to the reader; the chapter closes with a reprinting of an article he had written in *The Field* in 1899 called 'The Decadence of the Test', a jaded production, as of a man now getting on in years and feeling that the best was now past. Moreover, his health had begun to suffer, and he found the upper Test fishing, widely dispersed in several channels over a large area and not accessible by pony trap, increasingly burdensome. He records that after a long day's fishing he would return to his inn at Wherwell in a state of near-collapse.

In the late autumn of 1898 he had an operation and a month in bed, followed by a convalescence at Margate. He then set about the task of getting up his strength for the next season by riding his tricycle around London. He wrote to Daisy Field in January, hoping that by Easter he would be fit enough to 'propel that old tricycle to Basildene'. He was cheered at becoming a grandfather, Ernest having married Constance (née Manville, and known in the family as Connie). Halford's letter continued:

> I suppose you heard that Connie has a son. She is awfully proud of him & thinks of course of nothing else. He is called 'Cecil Frederic' & Ernest adds 'mind – Frederic without a K'. They are at Hastings for a few weeks. Mrs Halford is quite sad at not being able to see him about twice a week & seriously suggested a day trip there & back for the purpose. Just like a grandmama, eh!

He ends by complaining that he has to work five hours a day on the revised edition of *Dry-Fly Fishing*, adding archly: 'which for a lazy man like myself is a horrid nuisance.'

He was strong enough later that year to go on one of his occasional salmon-fishing trips. Edward Power had rented a reach of the Spean, and Halford joined him at the end of September. He was always a little ambivalent about salmon fishing. While admitting to the thrill of playing a large fish in a wild river, the fatigue of working down a pool and the absence of the sort of interest he prized in fly imitation and all the attendant minutiae of the chalk stream took away much of the pleasure. In fourteen days he caught four fish weighing 35lb together, and Power, an accomplished salmon angler, had sixteen. Halford found it sufficiently amusing to decide on another visit in October 1900. Conditions were much less favourable this time, and Halford and William Senior fished for many days with no success at all. On the last day of their trip Senior had two fish of 11lb and 14½lb, and Halford, after a hard struggle hauled in a salmon of 34lb. It had been in the river some time, a coppery male with a huge kype. In spite of this success the main impression left with Halford was of the slowness of salmon fishing. He wrote in the

Autobiography, 'Whether, however, a journey of 1,000 miles and seven consecutive blank days are compensated by the capture of a 34lb. salmon is a question to be answered by each individual according to his own ideas.' After 1900 he did no more salmon fishing.

He was back in London in November in time to see Ernest and Connie, who had been on a leisurely cruise around the world. Ernest recorded in his diary that they were 'received with much joy at Pembridge Place' on the evening of their return, and that after supper 'I played a game of picquet with the guv'nor'. Father and son spent the next day companionably together, strolling in the Park, taking a Turkish bath in Jermyn Street, and then going on to inspect 'the pretty new premises of the Fly Fishers' Club over "Epitaux" in the Haymarket'.

In 1899 Halford published another article in *Baily's Magazine*, this time on his catch results over the previous twenty years. The idea may have occurred to him as a result of reading several similar articles in *The Field* written about this time by James Englefield ('Red Quill'), a somewhat wooden and pedantic author with a bent for statistics. Halford's journal had been kept with minute exactness since 1879, and he was therefore able to reveal that he had caught 1,151 trout weighing 1,746lb 13oz, an average of about 1lb 8oz, and 598 grayling weighing 821lb, an average of nearly 1lb 6oz. Having released these statistics Halford became slightly apologetic in the accompanying text; perhaps he felt that the public might expect that a man who had tendered so much authoritative advice over the years should have a better result to show. A notice of this article in *The Field* by Senior indicated mild surprise, pointing out that the total came out at something like 83 trout and grayling a year, which 'does not strike one as being great for so noted a fly fisher'. As I have shown before, Halford was never as effective a performer as some experts of the time – at least by the crude yardstick of fish on the bank – and there were several scorers of considerable prowess, such as Turle and T.J. Mann, who had their own well-stocked fisheries, and Arthur Gilbey, who was fast becoming the most successful angler of the Houghton Club. (In 1888 T.J. Mann caught a hundredweight and a half of trout up to 4lb 8oz in ten days in the mayfly season, but with small flies, the mayfly having been a failure. On another occasion his keeper Penton landed four trout weighing 16lb for him in one fishing session.) Significantly Halford's trout-count had risen a good deal when he secured his own close preserve at Ramsbury, and 1893 was up to that time his record year, but he never achieved the results of some of his contemporaries.

Senior, in *The Field*, put a generous construction on these figures: 'Mr Halford, like his friend Mr Marryat, was never eager to catch fish for the mere sake of making a bag. We have on many occasions known both these gentlemen, having a brace and a half of trout in their baskets, roam the meadows thereafter, content with what they had.' In the *Baily's* article Halford explained, a little defensively, that much of his time by the riverside was spent in pursuing insects rather than fish, and that for the first decade until his retirement he could only spare occasional days for fishing. Unfortunately this is not quite borne out by the hard facts of the journal, which shows that in the first decade he averaged sixty days a year on the river, whereas in the next eleven years the average was thirty-eight.

Although his fishing activity declined between 1897 and 1902 Halford worked hard in other ways, particularly for the Fly Fishers' Club, as a member of the committee from its beginning, and as President in 1903. With Skues and Dr Wiblin he helped collect materials for the members' fly-tying bench. (Wiblin was a leading amateur in the field. In 1888 Marston visited him at his home near Southampton, and had been astonished at his collection of feathers for salmon flies from rare birds from every part of the world: 'I am sure that Major Traherne and Mr Kelson would go into raptures over them'. Wiblin also kept a collection of honey dun chicks at a nearby farm, some of them the progeny of eggs he had obtained from Mrs Aldam.) In 1901 Halford presented his natural fly collection of 324 examples preserved in formalin to the club, where it still remains. It was an obvious next step for Halford in 1902 to accept the chairmanship of the Natural Fly Committee, of which C.E. Walker was also a member. Halford raised no objection to this, although he disliked Walker's pragmatism about sunk flies, for he was a fair-minded man: in 1898 he had advised 'all my readers' to get hold of a copy of Walker's book, which he considered interesting although subversive of his own doctrine. His own theoretical thought did not advance much during this period, but his journalism in *The Field* and in *Baily's Magazine* continued unabated, usually in the form of factual reminiscence of recent experience with useful hints. Readers were given a variety of instruction, from the use of the field glass to identify the genera and even the species of flies at a range of thirty yards, to the best method of hand-lining a trout out of weeds ('Take the line between the left thumb and forefinger and apply a gentle strain, accompanied by a backward and forward or swaying motion'). And there was another wave of articles on river management, derived from the Ramsbury experiment, which were put into practice when he acquired his own fishery at Mottisfont.

Halford's two last seasons on the upper Test in 1900 and 1901 had convinced him that the nature and layout of the fishing there was too tiring for him to manage any more. In both years he ended his season in June, and in 1901 he only caught fourteen trout in twenty-three days. He searched for something more congenial and put out the word amongst his acquaintance that he was in want of fishing for 1902. Eventually Edgar Williamson offered him a rod on the St Cross water on the Itchen below Winchester for £100 a season. This was a much more convenient situation for Halford, and there was ideal access to most parts of the fishery by pony cart.

Williamson is a retiring and enigmatic figure in chalk-stream history. His distant and solemn countenance stares out at us from the frontispiece of *Modern Development of the Dry Fly* (1910), giving little clue of the man. He was the founder of the firm of Williamson and Murray, with brewery and other interests, and chairman or director of several other companies. Most of what we know of him comes from Halford, who was an uncritical admirer. His lease of the fishery was about to end in September 1902, and so towards the end of Halford's first season there Williamson was beginning active negotiations for a new agreement with the head landlord, the Hospital of St Cross.

The massive and imposing pile of the church of St Cross is one of the sights of Winchester. Founded in the twelfth century, it dominates the meadows to the south of that ancient city like a second cathedral. Adjacent to it are the buildings of the hospital, where the pensioners, called the brethren, have their lodgings and keep. The trustees of the hospital had the freehold of the adjacent fishing on the river. Mindful of the growth in the value of good trout fishing and of their duty as trustees to the finances of the hospital, they proposed to increase the rent from £235 a year to £285. They may have been surprised that Williamson raised no objection and even proposed to spend not less than £2,000 at the start of the new tenancy. This sum would mainly be spent on practically rebuilding the Mill, which was in a poor state, and in constructing hatcheries. The hospital's solicitor advised the trustees to agree to this, as the outlay would materially increase the freehold value of both mill and fishing, so that on the determination of Williamson's tenancy it would be worth at least £100 a year more than before. The trustees however were accustomed to doing things rather slowly, and they had no objection to Williamson holding over after 29 September 1902, but he refused to expend any money until he had secured his new lease. They discovered that he had further ideas in mind. He insisted that fourteen years was not enough – he wanted twenty-one – and refused to take a repairing lease, saying that his word and his own plans should be sufficient. He further said that he had no intention of defraying the charges of the trustees' solicitor, and produced his own draft deed for discussion. If he did not have sufficient assurances by 10 December, he threatened, he would withdraw altogether, because he would lose the fish-breeding season. By now the trustees must have decided that they did not much like Mr Williamson, and thought him no gentleman, but the solicitor, seriously alarmed, advised them to agree at once. Williamson's offer had been unique in his experience, and if he withdrew they would lose their best candidate and would also have to repair the mill themselves. The trustees grumbled, and the solicitor admitted that Williamson's behaviour had been rather irregular, but they caved in and he got his way on the basis of his own draft document. Our knowledge of him may be defective, but we can see that he was a tough man at the bargaining table. If he had lived to see it, his hard-won tenancy would have lasted until 1923. As it was, he was only to enjoy it for another two years.

Halford was not directly involved in this, although he must have known all about it, and the hard line taken by his patron probably increased his regard for him. The preamble to *Modern Development of the Dry Fly* (1910) not only pays Williamson a handsome tribute, it indicates that Halford's work for that book was strongly influenced by him (for a man with such a powerful intellect Halford could be surprisingly suggestible). He had found in Williamson a convinced disciple who had not only absorbed all Halford's teaching but had taken an even more extreme line on it – who was, in short, *plus royaliste que le roi*. In 1910 Halford wrote: 'He had for many years been a firm believer in the paramount importance of reproducing in each part of the artificial fly the precise shade of colour of the same part of the natural insect, and at the same time dressing a fly as nearly as possible of the exact size and shape of the living subimago or imago.' It certainly looks as if Halford's final progress (or descent) into super-purism was encouraged by Williamson. His attitude towards the relationship between natural and artificial flies was hardening, and he was about to embark upon another creative programme which, however misconceived it has since been judged to be, was at least original. This was to produce an entirely new and final series of flies for the chalk stream. They have been long superseded, and the verdict of posterity is that, although ingenious, they are based on a doubtful principle. The programme nonetheless casts an interesting light on the direction of Halford's thinking in the last dozen years of his life. The influence of Marryat in the early years had been almost wholly beneficial: it is doubtful if we can say the same about Williamson.

The New Patterns, as Halford liked to call them, are known to us now from the pages of *Modern Development*, but readers of *The Field* had been aware of them for some years before 1910, and their origin goes back to 1902. He began the season by using his usual patterns, and it was not until 22 April that a fly called New Olive ♂ made its appearance, attached to a trout of 1lb 13oz. Thereafter the journal records New Olive Spinner ♂, New Iron Blue ♂, and New Pale Watery Spinner ♀. In late July there was also a Williamson Red Spinner, a fly with blue dun hackle points tied spent. Williamson may have got the idea from B.W. Smurthwaite, who had pointed out in an article in *The Field* that trout sipping something very small at the surface were not always smutting, as had been thought, but might be taking spent fly. It took a long time for good patterns of the spent spinners to become available, although several designers, such as E.J. Power and L.J. Graham-Clarke ('Glanrhos' of *The Field*), had made attempts. Gilbey's Extractor, a fly that once had a considerable vogue, was a flat-winged spinner with a red body. Hackle points had also been used by Marryat for his Spent Gnat, and had been suggested for flies in general by Francis Francis as long ago as 1867, though not, of course, tied spent. The real failure of the earlier fly-dressers, as Hills later complained, was their inability to reproduce the splendid body colours of the female spinners.

Halford considered these patterns to have been successful enough for him to decide to use them in 1903 to the exclusion of all others, and he spent the winter devising more of them. Eventually all the main types of chalk-stream flies (with a few odd exceptions) were covered, and he seems to have used nothing but this new series for the rest of his life.

He spent time during 1903 working on a contribution to *Fishing*, a comprehensive multi-author work in two volumes edited by Horace Hutchinson and published by *Country Life* in 1904. The New Patterns were not included – no doubt because Halford, with his customary caution, felt that they had not yet been sufficiently field-tested. Instead he fell back on the Hundred Best Patterns of 1897, extracting thirty-six flies and including coloured lithographs of them (if *Fishing* had been produced two or three years later there would have been no sign of any representatives of the 1897 series). The book also included a number of photographs of Halford fishing with E. Valentine Corrie and his brother W.M. Corrie, taken on 14 and 15 September 1903.

Halford had two happy years in 1902 and 1903 at Itchen Valley, as Williamson called his fishery. The contrast with 1901 is striking. The new fishery invigorated him, and he threw off his jaded mood (he even joined the Winchester Golf Club). His contributions in *The Field* became more lively again, with a long-running series called 'The Log of a Dry-Fly Man'. In 1901 his usually frequent appearances in print had fallen to one: in 1902 he published thirteen articles. By 1903 his journal had become more minutely analytical than it had ever been. Every trout caught was identified by pattern-type, pattern-sex and hook size, in order to achieve the most accurate record of the New Patterns. The Gold Ribbed Hare's Ear, successful in the spring of so many seasons, was last used on 2 June 1902 – when it was responsible for the demise of a trout of 1lb 6oz at Itchen Valley – and was never again attached to Halford's cast. Several writers have since stated that he discarded it because he did not know what it represented. This is only a half truth. He had on more than one occasion suggested that it looked like a hatching nymph, because of the resemblance of the fur to the abdominal appendages of the natural (which perhaps means that Halford was more modern and knowing than some have allowed), but that is not the main point. It has not been sufficiently noticed that Halford gave up *all* formerly-designed flies at this date, not just the Hare's Ear. The season of 1903 saw a radical break with the past, and he now wanted as much precision as he could get. Mere impressionist flies were for opportunists: the ultra-purist henceforth would only fish with pre-Raphaelite exact copies. Therefore literally dozens of flies that he had been using since the 1870s were rejected. Fancy flies were proscribed; so, too, were more sober flies with fancy names whose lack of descriptive precision he now disliked, such as Drake's Extractor, Hammond's Adopted, Flight's Fancy and the Harlequin. His new system of nomenclature had an austere clarity about it: every artificial simply had the same name as the natural it represented. Indeed so hard had he laboured for accuracy in the New Patterns that for him natural and artificial had blended and become almost the same thing. The two worlds thus came together – it was to be the triumph of Art over Life. An angler finding a male olive dun on the water would now attach to his cast a Male Olive Dun – or, as Halford liked to express it in his journal, Olive Dun ♂. However illusory the attempt may have been, at least Halford was beginning with nature before going to the fly-tying bench. The Halford fly box, soon being marketed by the trade, was designed to accommodate this system: japanned black outside and ivory white inside, each compartment had a metal spring-loaded lid with the name of the fly in indelible black on it.

By March 1903 the New Patterns were twenty-four in number, all of ephemeropteran flies. Sedges, gnats and ants followed. Fishing at Itchen Valley that year was a serious business, as the two men continued the work of the previous season of collecting insects and matching colour, shape and size at the fly-tying table. Some prototypes were rejected at an early stage. Although he was convinced that he was close to arriving at the perfect solution of the fly problem, Halford was careful not to be too dogmatic: 'I must caution the reader that, like most enthusiasts with the fly rod, I am prone to develop preference for individual patterns, and one of the most important factors determining the success of a fly is the degree to which the angler pins his faith on its superiority.' At the close of the season of 1903, after many conferences, Halford and Williamson considered that enough work had been done on both entomology and fly-tying to be able to say that the New Patterns were settled, although they were not to appear in book form for some years. Westley Richards was quick to copy the patterns from the recipes given by Halford in *The Field* in October 1904, and began to market them at three shillings a dozen (three-and-six for those requiring horsehair eyes) and five shillings for Mayflies. Hardy and Farlow soon followed. In March 1905 *The Field* praised Farlow's tying: 'We believe that Messrs Farlow have taken the greatest pains to follow Mr Halford's instructions with regard to the exact shades and colours, and that the ultimate result has been approved by him.' By the time *Modern Development* was given to the world in 1910 the entire list of thirty-three flies had been worked out and tested by some years of fishing, so that Halford was able to give anecdotal evidence of their success on the river (see Chapter 9).

Williamson was determined that St Cross would be a well-stocked fishery, in fact he boasted to Halford that he was resolved to see if it was possible to overstock a stream containing natural food in such quantity. On 28 March 1903 his men took delivery of 1,000 fish of ten to twelve inches from the fish farm at Chilland belonging to E.V. Corrie, and carried out the weary work of dropping them at the rate of twenty trout in each can all the way down the fishery. Williamson, meanwhile, was pressing on with his own stocking plant. He had sought the advice of Corrie, who had designed a plan for his rearing ponds; the hatching house had not been completed because of the delay in dealing with the hospital trustees, but Williamson had managed to hatch 60,000 ova in an outhouse by St Cross Mill. Needless to say he insisted on having progeny of the Wycombe strain. Halford's views on stocking accorded with those of Williamson. He may have been a strong advocate for a liberal stocking policy but (as at Ramsbury) he preferred the idea of putting in fish below the size limit to grow on: a policy he was to carry out later at Mottisfont.

In the same year the controversy over 'light rods' came to the boil. Fly rods in Britain had been steadily shortening over the previous twenty years. Some old die-hards remained faithful to the longer rod,

The Mayfly Mess at the Royal Hotel, Winchester, *c.* 1880. *From left, back row:* Watts, Saunders, T.M. Doddington, Francis Francis, S. Lloyd Stacey. *Front row:* R.C. Bushell, George Ledger, W.M. Corrie

Season ticket for the college fishery on the Itchen, issued by John Hammond in 1870 to Tom Sanctuary, then aged 18

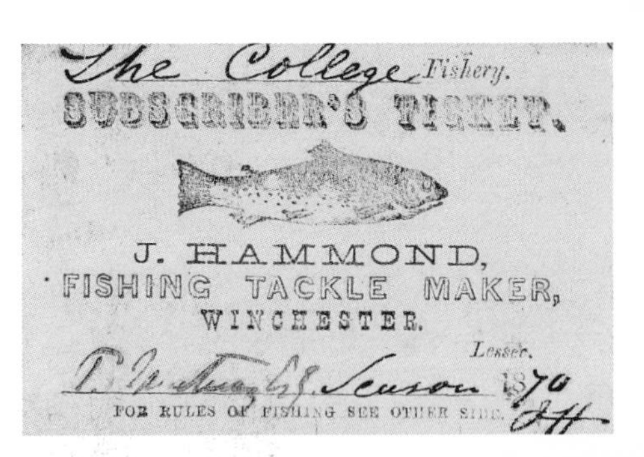

The College Fishery.
SUBSCRIBER'S TICKET.

J. HAMMOND,
FISHING TACKLE MAKER,
WINCHESTER.

Lesser.
Season 1870
FOR RULES OF FISHING SEE OTHER SIDE.

Winchester College boys fishing in 1889. College buildings in background. Etching by F.P. Barraud

Houghton Mill in the late nineteenth century. The side door led to Halford's accommodation, where he lodged during the season from 1880 to 1888

The Sheepbridge at Houghton a century ago

R.B. Marston, editor of *The Fishing Gazette* from 1878 to 1927, and his father Edward Marston ('Amateur Angler')

George Selwyn Marryat in 1895

Major Anthony Carlisle ('South-West'), date unknown

Henry Sinclair Hall in 1913

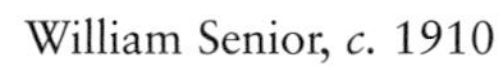

William Senior, *c.* 1910

Page from Halford's fishing journal – Autumn 1881. Two of the entries in the remarks column are in Marryat's hand

Dr Tom Sanctuary (sitting on ledge with landing net), *c.* 1885. His house is out of sight on the other bank. Crane Bridge (Salisbury) is upstream

A thirsty day at Ramsbury: G.S. Marryat and maid

Drawing of Marryat by Basil Field, 1893

Daisy Field fishing in a hatch pool on a carrier at Ramsbury in 1893, with Amy and Basil Field. In the background Myrtle with (probably) Frances the governess

Marryat advises Nathaniel Lloyd about netting the Ramsbury fishery in a letter, January 1893

Saturday

THE CLOSE,
SALISBU

Dear Lloyd
If I can I'll get down & lo
after the netting, but at pres
I am "housed" with a beastly
which don't seem to go aw
let me know nearer the ti
& I'll see how I am – I mu
be here any way for the 12th
15th April – you'll find the
Otter pit fisher, a lot, tho
the Ramsbury ones – we saw
a fair lot of fish when
been down there from 1 to 2

Know all men by these presents
that I G. S. Marryat of the Close
Salisbury did lawfully take
and catch with the fly known
as the Mayfly in the water known
as Moons Mill pound in the
River Kennet, in the parish of
Ramsbury one reptile to wit
a FROG in the presence of
the undersigned this 28th day of
August 1894.
Signed { Geo S. Marryat
Witness { Flora Rebson – X her mark
Daisy Field

Marryat's mock-legal record of catching a frog at Ramsbury in 1894

Halford and Senior on the Itchen below St Cross in 1903

Halford and his keeper Dick Coxon, at the fishing hut on Oakley Stream, Mottisfont, *c.* 1909. Halford wears mourning band after his wife's death

Halford at work in his fishing den at Dunbridge, near Mottisfont, 5 May 1912

Halford at his winter retreat in Tunis, 22 February 1913. The last photograph taken of him. He left for home on 28 February and died on shipboard on 5 March

such as the Rev. Veitch (known as the 'Honorary Chaplain' of *The Fishing Gazette*, who in 1888 used a rod of eleven feet but liked to go back to a sixteen-footer in mayfly time if long casting was called for, and Major Carlisle, who as late as 1900 felt he needed a double-handed rod to reach across a wide shallow of the lower Test. And there remained an irrational but strongly held view that a big rod was required to kill an obstinate fish: an idea that can be found as late as 1929 in F.D. Barker's book *An Angler's Paradise*, which is about lake fishing in County Clare. But many of the new generation appreciated the shorter rod, and by 1895 rods of ten feet were common, although they still had plenty of cane in them. Halford was one of those who persisted for years in the belief that a light rod, however pleasant to use, would not be adequate in mayfly time, but, after a mayfly day in 1902 when he defeated two good trout in a gale of wind, he wrote: 'It has certainly resulted in my determining never again to burden myself with a longer and heavier rod than the one used when fishing Mayfly on a Hampshire chalkstream of only moderate width.'

However the term 'light rod' is a relative one. Some anglers in America were using rods which were much lighter than anything normally seen in Britain. British tackle-makers were well aware of this, but believed that such rods must be unreliable in use. They were also inclined to belittle American claims to have been first in the field with the split-cane rod. In *The Fishing Gazette* in 1888 Thomas Aldred insisted that he had been making split-cane rods for forty years, and had been awarded medals for them at the Great Exhibition of 1851 and at other exhibitions on the Continent. C. Irwin, one of Aldred's craftsmen, remembered making them in 1848 and mentioned repairing a split-cane rod belonging to the Earl of Craven in 1851 which was then twenty years old. (No doubt these early examples were of the four-section variety.) Marston intervened in the correspondence to remark that he believed that the Americans were the first to ensure that the rods were built with the hard enamel of the cane outside. But whenever the subject came up there was a general and patriotic agreement that the American rods were not adequate – the products of Leonard, Conroy & Basset and Shipley looked well enough but in practice, apart from bass rods, 'we can well hold our own against these far-famed American tacklers'.

G.E.M. Skues, having permanently damaged his wrists in a boyhood accident, was more inclined to regard casting a fly as something easy and comfortable, rather than strenuous and athletic. It was natural that he would emerge as the champion of the light rod, and he sallied into print to compel the tackle trade to match the American achievements – the story is well set out in Donald Overfield's book *G.E.M. Skues: The Way of a Man With a Trout* (1977). Halford entered the argument in 1905 in an article rather provocatively entitled 'The Light Rod Craze', describing a comparison he had made by fishing alternate days with one of the heavier Leonards of nine feet nine inches weighing eight-and-a-half ounces (with spear attachment), and with his favourite Eaton and Deller, now cut down to nine foot six inches and weighing twelve-and-a-half ounces. The test convinced him that he preferred the British rod: he thought that the Leonard required far more exertion in casting into or across the wind.

British firms continued to insist that the advantage of weight lay in the light fittings and handles of American rods. Nonetheless, their work was influenced by the advocacy of Skues and others, and by a number of tests and tournaments at the time. By the eve of the Great War, therefore, it was possible to buy good British rods varying from nine to ten feet in length and weighing from five to six ounces. Halford seems never to have found such light rods credible, but in the last years of his life he was influenced to some extent by the new ideas. J.J. Hardy worked closely with him to produce an ideal weapon. This resulted in the three-piece Halford Dry Fly Rod in 1905, nine feet six inches in length. It was modified in several particulars in 1912, so that it weighed less – eight ounces, fourteen drams – and had a better balance, agate rings and an improved reel fitting. Hardy met Halford by the riverside on 17 May 1912, and between them they caught eight fish. Halford's journal recorded: 'It might have been an ideal day, but we were testing rods, reels, lines, and other paraphernalia & did not fish heavy. All over by 2.30. Hardy's new rod (given to me) the very best I ever handled.' This rod remained in the Hardy catalogue until 1948. The inexpensive Halford Knockabout, intended as a second rod to leave in the hut in case of breakages, was the same length but lighter in weight (six-and-three-quarter ounces) and was marketed at half the price. Halford caught fish with it up to 3lb 14oz, and probably liked it as much as the expensive rod. It continued in the Hardy catalogue until 1971.

It was also in 1903 that Halford published *An Angler's Autobiography*. By this date his previous works had been reissued, in a project called 'The Halford Dry-Fly Series' by Vinton & Co, who had been compelled to buy the copyrights of his first two books in order to publish the complete series. The material of *Floating Flies* was absorbed into a revised form of *Dry-Fly Entomology*, and his other two books were reissued in separate volumes. The *Autobiography* was therefore the fourth in the series. His admirers and followers took up the book with interest and perhaps some relief – no doubt this well-informed but somewhat remote authority figure was going to unbend a little. William Senior had been leaning on Halford for some time to write this book, and it is revealing to learn that Halford at first resisted the pressure. This was not just the show of modesty that was customary at that time: he clearly looked upon the task as something novel and alarming. As we have seen, he was good at writing the didactic manual, but the style of his writing is a reminder to us of his training in life – he was a man of commerce, and his books in many ways resemble the business letter: clear, unambiguous and to the point. Anything else he would have regarded as embroidery. Matter, not manner was his strong point. George Dewar praised his 'love of plain, unvarnished truth'. His approach to angling had always been scientific, and the appeal for him was that of a complex subject containing an immense number of puzzles and problems – of tactics, fly-dressing, entomology, tackle-improvement, trout breeding and river management – which, by patient and dogged application, one might solve (he wrote that his fear was that his life might not be long enough for the solution of all these matters). Now he was being asked to do something that would place him in a false position. There is no doubting his enthusiasm and deep love for fishing and the places where fishing happens. As he himself tells us, he was from boyhood regarded by his family as fishing mad. But he must have known that fine writing, like that of Richard Jefferies or W.H. Hudson, was not possible for him. He would not be able to describe the intense and palpable atmosphere of the chalk-stream valley, the misty morning, the dreamy noontide, and the evening rise under a luminous sky. We need not imagine that he was impervious to these beauties, but he had no language for them. His dismay was evident even in the apologetic introduction to the *Autobiography*: 'I am but too conscious that my powers of descriptive writing are but limited and my appreciation of witty and pithy anecdotes far below the average.' The result is that the reader would never guess that Halford had fished in some of the most beautiful places in the south of England. Reviewing the book, Marston regretted that he had not 'let himself go' a little more.

Another problem with autobiographies is that the reader expects a certain amount of self-revelation. This did not suit a very reticent and self-protective man such as Halford. The *Autobiography* tries to give an honest picture of the development of an angler, but it is wary on the personal side, and those who expected Halford to demystify himself were disappointed. Family life and the world of work are only referred to very briefly, and many of the individuals are not named at all, or in some cases are given an initial. The book was the subject of a number of reviews, which generally extended a welcome to it, but in the event it did not sell well. It remains however an invaluable source book for the period, and its fine series of photographs are an excellent record of places, most of which have changed for ever.

The new season was marred for Halford by the death of Edgar Williamson on 21 March 1904. His death was not entirely unexpected. Recent events in his business life had caused him a good deal of stress, and heart disease had announced itself the previous December. On 26 March Halford chaired the annual general meeting of the Fly Fishers' Club as retiring President, and made his preparations for his season at St Cross. On 1 April his journal records: 'My first day's fishing since the death of poor E W.' Later he wrote that the day was 'one of sadness and gloom' as he observed the improvements made everywhere by Williamson's ample injection of capital.

The season of 1904 in fact produced Halford's largest annual bag: 180 trout weighing over 221lb. For the sake of testing the new patterns he also recorded the nearly sizeable trout returned, of which this newly stocked fishery had plenty. Of the total of 306 trout retained or returned 148 had been caught with duns (including

Mayflies) and 111 with spinners; the rest with sedges, gnats and others. It was his last season at St Cross. With the demise of his patron he was once again in the wilderness.

9 Mottisfont: 1905–1913

In the early years of the twentieth century Halford was at the height of his fame and influence, and his books, at least for his disciples, were the sacred texts of the new cult. Some experts might quarrel with his more extreme views but the majority of anglers were glad to listen and accept. His maxims had passed into the realm of accepted and permanent fact – an evening mist puts the fish down, bulging fish are best left alone, smutting fish should be attacked with a Pink Wickham, a fish which runs under a bridge generally stays there, a north wind is best for bringing on a hatch on the Test, and many others. So ingrained did they become in the collective angling mind that even original-minded men like Skues accepted them as unassailable truths for years before allowing themselves to have doubts. His name was constantly before the angling public: tackle shops marketed Halford rods, Halford lines, Halford reels, Halford fly boxes and other items of equipment. A man of his prestige and numerous contacts in the chalk country was not likely to be without fishing for long, and he was soon able to establish himself at Mottisfont on the Lower Test. It was here that he was to spend the last part of his angling life.

This fishery had at first been leased by his friend E. Valentine Corrie of Chilland. In 1905 he began to share it with Halford, but at the end of that year he withdrew, leaving Halford in sole control of it. It was the second great chance of his life to carry out his own ideas on river management. The fishery was small and compact, but under his care it improved and developed so that every part of it became productive. It consisted of a stretch of the right, or western bank, of the main river Test, and a by-stream, smaller but still substantial, called the Oakley Stream. (The land belonged to the Russells, a branch of the family of the Duke of Bedford, and the Oakley Stream was named after a part of the family estate at Woburn.) There was also an adjacent series of ponds called the Peat Pits, made by the extraction of peat years before, where a population of rudd flourished, also some pike transferred from the river during netting operations.

Halford soon established himself in the new district, securing rooms near the railway halt at nearby Dunbridge. From there it was only a short ride by pony trap, driven by Mr Moore from the village, to the bridge over the Oakley Stream, followed by a stroll up to the fishing hut. Mr Moore would return with the trap, and Mrs Miller, his housekeeper, would send him back in the late afternoon with food so that Halford and his friends could dine in the hut. The pony was released to graze in the meadow, and was harnessed up to bring the party back after the evening rise was over, sometimes after ten o'clock. To the many guests who enjoyed his hospitality over the next few years the place seemed a paradise. A pattern was soon established in Halford's life which was to endure for the next decade. He would take up his quarters in Dunbridge in April and remain in Hampshire for weeks into the season, spending much of the time in conference with his keeper Dick Coxon, and in concerning himself with the fine detail of the fish stews, the river or the bank work, or in gillying for his friends. Being constantly on the water he was able to take his own fishing in a very leisurely way. He also spent time creating a small colourful garden next to the fishing hut, full of summer flowers, and dominated by arches over which grew that quintessential rambler rose of the Edwardian garden, the Dorothy Perkins.

Before he came to the Test, Dick Coxon had been employed at the Sowley Fishery near Lymington; from there Corrie had brought him to Mottisfont in September 1903. Halford soon discovered that he was the ideal type of keeper, and kept him on after Corrie's withdrawal. Always generous-minded with employees, he went out of his way to encourage Coxon and to praise him to his friends and even in print. In 1910 he wrote: 'I have been fortunate in finding a keeper who, to my mind, is a pattern of what such a man should be, and I mention this here because I should like to place on record my full appreciation of the success which has rewarded his unremitting exertions in carrying out his and my own ideas for improving the sport of the fishery.' In the next few years he presented signed copies of his books to Coxon, who by 1914 had a full set. Halford seems to have sympathised with keepers in general and their life of relentless toil round the year. Weed-cutting, he knew, was an exhausting task, and yet in a well-kept fishery it was vital. He would urge Coxon and his usual part-time helper Eli Pragnell to spread the load – 'Do a little each day,' he would suggest. Visitors remarked on the artistry of the weed-cutting, saying that the place resembled a garden. And Halford seems to have been aware, to a greater extent than many in his position, that the close season can be a lonely and demoralising time for a keeper, and would make a point of coming down to Hampshire at intervals in the winter to help with some of the tasks and to provide companionship.

Coxon moved into a cottage in Back Lane and settled his family into Mottisfont society, putting his sons Bobby, William and Charles into the local school. Here they learned their letters and survived the usual regular epidemics of mumps, scarlet fever and diptheria. There was a strong tendency for children in this as in other rural schools to vanish in droves at the time of harvest or hay-making, or when there was a big shooting party, and the headmaster was often at his wits' end over poor attendance – Mr Balfour's Education Act was clearly battling with ancient village custom. Entries in the school log such as: 'many children absent because of shooting parties' are common. As the son of a keeper Bobby might have been more exposed to such temptations than some of his friends, but in fact towards the end of his school career the record shows that he was presented with a medal 'for regular attendance' by Mrs Barker-Mill, the local lady of the manor.

The fishery at Mottisfont, like Horsebridge in the early 1880s, had been suffering from neglect when Corrie took it on in 1903. The work of rehabilitation ran on for several years. By the end of 1905 Coxon and his helpers had cleared excess vegetation and killed around 800 pike (the tally of pike killed diminished year by year, until by the end of Halford's tenure only about fifty a year were being taken). William Senior watched the netting of the Oakley Stream in October 1910. Several keepers from nearby properties were helping, including Hoskins from Arthur Humbert's fishery, with several volunteers from the village and the keepers' boys –

whose task it was to tend the pails of live trout being transferred – but eight tiring hauls of the net only produced seventeen pike, one roach and three dace. By 1910 the predator problem was well under control. By contrast, in 1905 the trout were few in number and large in size, because of the pike infestation. During that season a limit was imposed of 1lb 8oz for male trout and 2lb for females: fifty-two trout were caught, averaging over 2lb, and thirteen grayling averaging 1lb 11oz. At St Cross, finding that Williamson fished on Sundays, Halford had done the same, but he was careful to avoid this at Mottisfont.

The Halford family soon became well known in Mottisfont. Ernest was an occasional visitor, but he had never really become a committed fisherman (he is said to have given up fairly quickly if things were not going well, and to have retired to the hut to read the paper or to look over his investments), but with Ernest's son Cecil it was different. A strong bond of affection grew up between Halford and his grandson, and in after life Cecil cherished his memories of early exploits at Mottisfont. His fishing began in 1907. Knowing how important it would be for the boy to achieve some early results, Halford did not attempt to launch him into the mysteries of the dry fly on his first day, but took him over the meadow to the Peat Pit. Here all went well and Cecil bagged fourteen rudd on float tackle.

Within a year Halford had instituted the pleasant custom of an annual dinner in the village shortly after the autumn netting. As the number of helpers grew the event expanded to include the nearest keepers and other neighbours such as Arthur Humbert and the vicar of Mottisfont, and ultimately the village hall was needed. Employing casual labour to help Dick Coxon, and holding a banquet every year made Halford a sort of alternative squire in the district. It was through Coxon that he got to know of cases of hardship with some of the poorer families in the village, where he was able to give help. There was nothing patronizing or showy about these acts of charity – in fact they were so carefully and discreetly managed that knowledge of them only emerged after his death.

This period was the afternoon of Halford's middle age. His life had achieved an agreeable equilibrium, and the routine was fixed and predictable. He would fish until late summer, then go on holiday to the Italian lakes or Switzerland or to the Austrian Tyrol. He would return in the autumn for the grayling fishing, although he was less inclined to fish into the colder weather than in the Houghton times. As he got older he took up the winter holiday habit, slipping away from England after Christmas to spend the worst months of the year in warmer places abroad.

His personal habits were simple. Like R.B. Marston he was an addict of the cold bath. In an age when members of the more fortunate part of society were obsessed with food he seems to have been fairly moderate, content with ordinary rations while on campaign in Hampshire, and only going to some trouble when entertaining guests. He would bring a flask of coffee (cold and without milk or sugar) with him to the river in the morning. There is a tradition in the family that he was fond of whisky, a crate of which was kept in the hut, but this may date from a period of depression after the death of his wife. He was certainly a heavy smoker, and the figures for his yearly expenditure on cigars were striking.

As to his character, there were during and after his lifetime numerous testimonies to his kindness, courtesy, love of fair play and sportsmanship, as well as to the fondness for children to which I have already referred. In familiar company he could be relaxed and join in what he called 'chaff' and larks in general. But these amiable characteristics were noticed by people who were close friends, and the rest of the world was aware only of a polite but remote manner. There were in fact two very distinct sides to Halford, and many people were never able to penetrate past the first to be able to perceive the second. As William Senior revealingly said of him, 'He took some knowing.' The angling world, which saw his public face and was aware of his achievement and of the weight of his research and public work, was in awe of him, but does not seem to have liked him very much. As with many authority figures who appear aloof, Halford was in fact a shy man, and having become the head of a movement was bound to create problems for him at times. An example of this had occurred some years earlier, at the 1892 annual dinner of the Fly Fishers' Club. As a leading light, it was natural for him to be called upon to take the chair, but by his own admission this weighed heavily on him, and he did not enjoy the evening very much. He confessed to his audience that he was overwhelmed by the responsibility, apologized for his lack of oratory and wit, and spent an unnecessarily long time comparing himself unfavourably with previous chairmen. He then struggled through a speech – amongst other things defending purism – that was evidently read from a script. It was significant that Basil Field, a much more accomplished after-dinner speaker, rising to propose Halford's health as chairman, referred not only to 'the fame of a man whose works are read and prized in every quarter of the wide, wide world, wherever the English-speaking angler casts his fly', but also to 'the pride we all take in him, the love we all bear to him'. This sentiment was loudly applauded and showed that a somewhat awkward platform technique was no bar to the warmth of the regard of his fellow members. During a similar speech-marathon at the next annual dinner, when Halford performed the rather easier task of proposing a toast from the floor, he admitted that the year before he had been suffering from 'a somewhat severe attack of what, in my schoolboy days, we called "funk", engendered, no doubt, by the anxiety inseparable from the position I was occupying'.

We have scant record of how he conducted himself in verbal controversy, but the impression we receive is of someone very difficult to convince or beat down, and perhaps a little annoying in his quiet, good-humoured inflexibility; he had done so much investigation into fly-fishing problems that he honestly believed that he had arrived at the right conclusions. A discussion with a fellow member of the Fly Fishers' Club was less likely to have been an equal exchange of views than the issue of a bulletin to be accepted. If, as Anthony Quintin has suggested, the distinction between a philosopher and a sage is that the former welcomes dialogue and discussion, whereas the latter imparts his wisdom and expects people to listen, then there is little doubt which category Halford belonged to, and this was particularly so in his latter years. As for attacks in print, as we have seen he ignored them all. His method was to lay down the canonical law and leave it at that.

But some at least found him prepared to give ground. R.B. Marston wrote that 'we had one or two fairly big rows in the course of our thirty years friendship, but very soon made them up, for although he was hasty and dogmatic, he was good-tempered and reasonable, and if he saw he was wrong he made no bones about admitting it'. It would be fair to say, however, that those who could persuade Halford that he had been wrong were few in number. He also fell out with T.J. Mann, probably after giving him unsolicited advice about how to run his fishery at Horsebridge, but Marston got them both to have lunch with him and to make it up. Old friends knew that allowances had to be made for tactless behaviour on occasion. For example, however well-intentioned, he was a difficult host on the river: too ready with advice to a guest who wished himself alone with his mistakes. Senior described one of his early visits to Houghton in 1885, when he had not really mastered the dry-fly technique:

> The backward cast caught buttercups and daisies, the forward throw fouled the sedges, the underhand cut landed line and cast in a heap on the water, the fish was put down, the whole shallow scared. Halford stood behind amiably commenting upon the bungling operations, and then I uprose from a painful knee and delivered myself of remarks. Well; yes, I let myself go, and let *him* 'have it.' The amazement of Halford; his contrition; the colour that spread across his countenance . . . these sufficiently told me that he had not the ghost of an idea of the perturbation that had been seething in me.

Senior immediately regretted his hastiness. He probably regretted it even more when Halford continued to apologize profusely for several days.

The fishing at Mottisfont improved in 1906. Pike were declining, and the stock had a better chance of surviving. On 28 April Halford and Coxon took delivery of seventy two-year-olds. He got his fish from various sources, but mainly from Corrie's fish farm at Chilland or from Hungerford. The stew at Mottisfont, fifty-five yards long and four yards wide, had been made by selecting a clean healthy carrier in the meadow and fencing it off with two screens. These screens needed clearing twice a day, or more often during times of heavy weed cutting. Yearlings were kept in the stew for up to a year on a moderate diet, while two-year-olds were generally put straight into the Oakley Stream or the Main. In an article in

Journal of the Fly Fishers' Club in 1915 Martin Mosely wrote that Halford restocked with fish of about a pound or a little under, in a fishery with a size limit of 1lb 4oz. This was usually but not always so, for Halford's records show that in some years a proportion of the two-year-olds were kept in the stew for a further year. However he was always emphatic that stocking with large, overfed and frequently unhealthy fish was a bad idea – he calls it 'a pernicious practice' – and responsible for the widespread degeneration of chalk-stream trout. For him a two-year-old weighing 1lb 8oz to 2lb or a three-year-old weighing 3lb was overfed. General O'Callaghan, a fairly frequent guest at Mottisfont, who despised heavy, forced stew trout (which he called 'Leadenhall fish'), was loud in his praise of the fine appearance of the fish there. All the evidence is that, although Halford was and always had been in favour of stocking, he wished to have his fishery as wild as possible and was proud of his experiments. Early in 1906 he planted out 5,000 alevins, well on in their development, on to a shallow on the Oakley Stream, and was later heartened by the increase in the number of small trout in the area.

So entranced was Halford with his new fishery that he spent 108 days there during the season of 1906. He now fished exclusively with the New Patterns. So, for the most part, did his friends. It is quite likely that in his anxiety to give them as complete a trial as possible he requested his guests to use the New Patterns exclusively, and perhaps even supplied a suitable selection as part of the hospitality of the visit. In a period of nine seasons only a handful of guests broke away and used their own cherished patterns – generally experienced men with their own ideas, such as Senior, Sheringham, Humbert and A. Clement Poole.

In 1906 there were twenty-two guests, including Corrie and his daughter, William Senior, Arthur Humbert, J.J. Bolding and C. Ernest Pain, later the author of *Fifty Years on the Test*. Pain came twice, caught a fish of 2lb 6oz on his first visit, but could only catch a number of barely sizeable fish on the second. It is not clear if he attempted to retain these, but small fish became known thereafter in the journal as 'Pains'.

By the end of the season Halford had caught fifty-nine trout weighing over 116lb, and his guests had caught seventeen weighing over 33lb; thirty grayling had also been caught weighing nearly 53lb.

The largest trout of the year, whose capture is described in *Modern Development* (pp.211–13), was caught on a Medium Sedge with a new rod made for him by J.J. Hardy, and weighed 3lb 14oz. He must have felt that his system was working well.

Everything in this ideal place must have seemed settled for a programme of agreeable fishing that would carry Halford into a tranquil and happy old age. But 1907 was to bring tragedy into his life. There seems to have been no warning of its approach, the even tenor of his life proceeding as in former years. On 3 April Corrie sent 200 twelve-inch fish, which were placed in the Oakley Stream – 'The best I have ever seen & a credit to Chilland' – and he began his season. On 15 April a hatch of olives produced a good rise, and Halford caught four trout weighing 7lb 10oz. After this satisfactory day he returned all unawares to his lodgings at Dunbridge, where he received a shock telegram from a close family friend Bertie Browne. Mrs Halford had been staying at Crowborough in Sussex, and had fallen from a window of the Beacon Hotel. Halford arrived in London too late that night to go down to Sussex, and Ernest arrived at Pembridge Place at 1.30 in the morning with the news that she was dead. A few days later an inquest returned a verdict of 'Suicide during temporary insanity.'

No adequate explanation has survived of this appalling event, although the facts that emerged at the inquest were clear enough, as far as they went. Mrs Halford had recently suffered a nervous breakdown. In 1907 the treatment of such cases did not amount to much, and the specialist, Dr Russell, gave the conventional advice of that date that she should go away for rest and a change of scene. She had been staying at Crowborough in the care of a professional nurse when the death occurred.

Florence Halford appears to have been a talented woman, frustrated as so many intelligent middle-class women of that era were for lack of a worthwhile occupation. Her only son had left the family home in 1895 to get married, and the daily round of running the house and the servants, the afternoon in the carriage leaving cards, perhaps even some charity work, may not have been enough for her. There is a tradition in the family that she had always been 'a bit of a hysteric'. Equally she must have felt rather neglected at times, with her husband absent from home for long periods. In 1893 William Senior had included an article written by her, 'The Dry Fly Fisherman's Wife', in the Christmas edition of *The Field* along with a number of other light-hearted articles of the type that were usually published at that time of the year. It describes her predicament as an angling wife in social gatherings when questioned by other wives about the appeal of fishing, and at first it appears to be a mildly amusing item in a well-worn genre (see Appendix 6). But it is signed 'Victim Wife', and there is an unmistakable undercurrent of bitterness in it. Marriage to a man who focused all his attention on fishing, and who on holiday with his wife in the Austrian Tyrol would spend time searching the streams for stoneflies, may not have been altogether ideal. By 1907 they appear to have been living separate lives in the same house in London. But there is no hard evidence here, and no way of accounting for such a tragedy. As the philosopher said, whereof we cannot speak, thereof we must remain silent.

The blow fell heavily on Halford, and his state of mind can only be guessed. He stayed away from the river for a fortnight, then returned at the end of April, fishing and planting grannom eggs from the Kennet. Going mechanically through these well-loved procedures was perhaps his only way of carrying on, and the familiar place became a refuge. His series of articles in *The Field* describing his fishing at Mottisfont, entitled 'The Log of a Dry Fly Man', of which sixteen had appeared since April 1905, ceased abruptly. In fact he wrote very little until April 1909, no doubt to the astonishment of his readers. He felt unable to appear at the annual dinner of the Fly Fishers' Club for two years, generally shunned social occasions, and descended into a state of depression that caused alarm to his friends. Gradually his family eased him through this sad stage of his life, Ernest's wife Connie being the main influence. His fondness for his two grandchildren Cecil and Nora was also important, as was his relationship with his relative Martin Mosely. The journal several times records 'Martin arriving by the 6.37 train'. Friends and family made an effort in 1907 to come down to Mottisfont, knowing of his misery, and feeling that he should not be left alone. Arthur Manville (another relative), Bertie Browne and Senior all came to stay.

There was excellent sedge fly fishing in early July, later described by him at some length in *Modern Development*. The fall of spinner had become very sparse by the end of June, and he considered packing up for the season, but he discovered that the sedge, which he had always thought of as a fly of the late evening, was just as effective in the afternoon. In four days he killed seventeen trout weighing just under 37lb. Four of these, weighing 9lb 14oz, were caught on 6 July, and the journal records: 'All four fish killed just opposite hut in afternoon. A perfect sample of two brace of Test trout. Ernest & Connie arrived at 7.30.' The family were continuing to rally round.

Halford's health was still shaky the following year. He came down to Hampshire early in April but was unwell and withdrew to London almost at once. He did not come back until 5 May. During the summer things began to improve, and 1908 turned out to be an excellent season as well as being the year of Halford's physical and mental recovery.

It was also the year when he began to experiment with nymphs. This rather startling development was instigated by Martin Mosely, and Halford never mentioned them in his articles in *The Field* or indeed anywhere else. Neither did anyone else make them public during his lifetime or afterwards. As we have seen, sunk flies cast upstream had never been entirely banished from chalk streams in spite of Halford's best efforts, and they were being brought back to public notice by the efforts of Skues, who had been thinking about nymphs since 1889, and writing about them since 1891. He was not the only angler interested in the idea. Sheringham provided a good description of a subaqueous technique in *The Field* in June 1907, in an article in a series called 'Hints to Young Anglers'. He suggested that, if a fish that is apparently smutting refuses the angler's smallest black hackle when floating, it should be thoroughly soaked and cast upsteam just under the water in front of the fish – 'Possibly he will see the fish move a little to one side and then return to its place; possibly he will even see it open and close its mouth; in either case he should tighten.' Three years before the publication of Skues' first book, here was an excellent description of the wet fly on the chalk stream.

The first mention of nymph fishing at Mottisfont occurs in the journal on 9 May 1908, when Halford caught a trout of 1lb 9oz and also 'returned 1 with Martin's nymph. A fine day with little fly & no rise after 1.30.' Earlier, on 22 April he had broken his usual rule of sticking to the New Patterns and went back to a fly he had not used for years, the Grannom Pupa. With this he caught a fish of 1lb 4oz: 'Tried this fly as fish were flooping. Autopsy showed nothing but olive nymphs.' An educated guesser might infer that, aware of the published articles by Skues, Sheringham and others, Halford and Mosely were – somewhat furtively – giving sunk flies another testing. On 12 June Halford records: 'Killed a breakfast fish in Norman Court with Martin's nymph.' Other nymph experiments continue in 1909. On 7 April he caught a grayling of 1lb 3oz in Oakley Hole on the Main, and on 27 April a trout of 1lb 9oz: 'Rough day with occasional heavy showers – saw first iron blues – fish all fighting & bulging on both shallows.' After the season of 1909 these trials cease. As well as the public silence on the subject there is no further explanation in his private papers, and we are left to wonder exactly what 'Martin's nymph' looked like, and what Halford's technique of fishing it might have been.

Other departures from the strict Halford line occurred from time to time at Mottisfont. Bobby Coxon, who was now 14 and had left school to help his father, remembered Halford using bait from time to time – though this was not fishing as such, merely a quick way of obtaining trout to send to friends in London. The bait used was Spratt's Grains, a pheasant food, and only fish of 1lb 8oz and above would be sent to London. Bobby's role was to sew up the fish in frails of Norfolk reed, using needle and pack thread, and by late morning they would be in the train bound for Waterloo. Getting trout in this way was a common enough device in private fisheries – although probably not a matter to introduce into conversation at the Fly Fishers' Club. John Halford recorded a taped interview with Bobby in 1987, from which this and other memories emerged. Bobby was by then ninety-three and quite blind, but his memory was excellent, and in a fine example of the old Hampshire accent, now seldom heard, he recollected scenes of days at Mottisfont before the Great War. One of his early encounters with Halford, when he was about eleven years old, did not go well. Wearing a hat of staring whiteness (on his mother's instructions), he rambled absent-mindedly down the bank on a bright day for some distance before meeting the master; he was speedily dispatched home with instructions not to appear again in such headgear. In spite of this unpromising start Halford came to appreciate Bobby, in particular his deft handling of the landing net, and paid him a warm compliment in *Modern Development*: 'I venture to predict that there is every likelihood of his becoming as good a keeper as his father, who, to my mind, is one of the best I have ever seen.' Most of Bobby's memories were of the endless round of work of those days, keeping the banks in good order, driving piles, cleaning the screens, and hardest of all, the weed cutting. 'Don't cut your weeds like a turnpike road!' Dick would say to the boy. But he also remembered the horse dragging the harrow over the shallows to clean up the gravel for the spawning, and the ancient hollow oak near the hut, still to be seen today, which was a useful vantage-point for keeping watch for poachers. And he praised the skill of the master and his guests: the long period of watching, the stealthy approach, and the deadly delicate presentation. He also admired their restraint, happy with a brace for a whole day on the water, at a time when stocking policies were less aggressive, both in terms of size and numbers, so that a three-pounder was a prize, and the combined bag for all rods was never more than 150 fish in a year. 'They aren't fishermen today,' he said scornfully. 'They just want to catch fish. I didn't ought to say it, but things is altered.'

In 1910 Halford's sixth book, *Modern Development of the Dry Fly*, was published. The title might appear at first glance to indicate a book ranging over the latest inventions of the fly-dressers, amateur and professional, of the day. In fact 'the Dry Fly' meant Halford's dry fly, and referred to his New Patterns only. The work on the series had been done some time before, and the book might have appeared earlier had it not been for Halford's slow recovery from the trauma of his wife's death. Here at last was presented in one place the thoughts previously scattered amongst a number of articles in *The Field*. It was a much better-organized book than *Dry-Fly Entomology* and in order of excellence comes third to *Dry-fly Fishing* and *Floating Flies*. In fact by 1910 Halford probably looked back on *Floating Flies* as an incomplete stage of his early thinking, almost a piece of juvenilia. It is true that he and Marryat had laboured long to describe the best methods and materials, but to what end? To assemble a vast jumble of ninety different and inconsistent flies, with a number of patterns to imitate the same insect, and some originating far back in some benighted pre-dry fly era. This new tidy and rational system would change all that. One suspects that, had Halford had chosen a *nom de plume* in 1910 instead of 1885, it would not have been 'Detached Badger', a fly he never used after 1902; a more likely choice might have been its nearest analogue in the natural world, 'Olive Spinner ♀'.

Modern Development had a good logical structure. The tying of the New Patterns was described, then there was a section on fly-tying methods in general, and the final part was anecdotal and described the efficacy of the new flies on the river. The core of the book was the first section, and its list of flies has been much discussed and criticized ever since. At the time some readers at least felt able to breathe a sigh of relief that one hundred patterns had become thirty-three. Their nomenclature and its significance has already been discussed in Chapter 8. As to types, the first twenty-five were ephemeropterans, with duns and spinners represented in male and female forms: six Mayflies (including Spent Gnats), seven Olives, four Pale Wateries, four Iron Blues and four Blue-Winged Olives. Then follow two Black Gnats, a Brown Ant, two Welshman's Buttons and three Sedges (Small Dark, Medium and Cinnamon). Alone in the list the Brown Ant and the Sedges are not differentiated by sex.

The most obviously striking thing about the New Patterns is the minute attention to detail of colour and form. The whole question of colour in flies preoccupied Halford for years, and at times his mind hunted around between several positions. When he first arrived on the Test he was influenced by Francis Francis, who returned frequently to the question in his articles, and who thought that using a fly of the wrong tint accounted for false and short rises. By 1889, having performed many autopsies and observed the enormous range of colours in creatures eaten by trout Halford was not so sure: 'Above all, the study of autopsy should teach one lesson, viz., that the precise shade or tint of the artificial and the exact imitation of the natural fly most plentiful on the water are not so all-important as many fly-fishermen seem to imagine.' He was still repeating this opinion ten years later.

However, if not vital, colour was important for him, and he was seriously alarmed by Herbert Maxwell's article in *The Field* in June 1897, with its suggestion that fish could not distinguish colours at all. Maxwell had experimented on the River Gade in Hertfordshire, using Mayflies with bright scarlet or blue hackles, and had killed a good many trout. Two days later he repeated the experiment on the nearby River Beane, with similar results. Writers who have since commented on this trial have not thought that any real conclusions could be drawn from it: the Gade and the Beane were grossly overstocked, it was during the mayfly season, and conditions of light and background were not discussed or revealed by Maxwell. Writing some years later, Dr Mottram considered it a worthless experiment that proved nothing. Sidney Buxton was on the same water the day after one of Maxwell's experiments and found that the fish were very foolish: he caught over fifty fish of a pound or more. But Maxwell had succeeded in worrying Halford, and he could not get the threat to colourism out of his mind for years. He included a discussion of it in the revised editions of *Dry-fly Fishing*, in the *Autobiography*, and in *Modern Development*. It appears several times in articles in *The Field*, and makes its appearance yet again in his last book *The Dry-Fly Man's Handbook*. On the eve of his collaboration with Edgar Williamson his position was that colour was of some importance but that it could be exaggerated. Within a year or so, under Williamson's influence, he was matching colour as tightly as possible. He went out of his way to include in *Modern Development* eighteen extracts from the colour chart of the French Chrysanthemum Society, thus providing an even more exact and scientific standard than had been included in *Floating Flies*. His statement of his own view however seemed to hedge the bets. There are occasions, he wrote, when 'one is almost tempted to believe that the colour perception of the Salmonidae is developed to the highest degree'. He did not say what these occasions are, and retreated back to the position that all fishermen must naturally wish to tie the best-looking imitations of nature, and that such flies are more likely to give us confidence in use – which is as much as to say that the aesthetic sense of the angler is more important than the ability of the fish to discriminate.

If colour was carefully attended to in the New Patterns, translucency was not, and this has always been the chief charge laid against them. When laid out for inspection, especially on a white background, they have a pleasing appearance. But somehow there is a lack of a sense of life about them, beautiful artefacts that they are. This is even more so if they are held up against diffused light. The body materials of the artificials make no concession to transparency:

of the thirty-three flies, nineteen have bodies of condor quill, which in most cases was to be stripped (thus losing any possible benefit in terms of broken light from the condor flue). Other opaque material included hen quill, peacock quill and raffia. Three of the spinners had bodies of horsehair, which can be partially translucent. Otherwise the bodies of the flies presented an appearance of impenetrable solidity. Wings for the duns were traditional and opaque, being of starling or coot, although the hackle point wings of the spinners were an improvement. And once again gallina is used for whisks, not just for Mayflies but also for small flies. However the gnats and the sedges were more successful and can still be useful today. It was the diaphanous ephemeropteran flies that were not well served in Halford's fly system.

It is interesting to note that in 1910, as that system was congealing and coming to a halt, others were beginning to work on different lines. A. Clement Poole and even the faithful Mosely were experimenting at Mottisfont in that year with long-flued hackles to produce the Variant, an invention which however effective it may be in practice, is scarcely in the direct line of exact imitation. Two years later Leonard West was advocating the use of sharp glassy hackles to produce a sparkling prismatic effect. In the inter-war years J.W. Dunne was to make his ingenious transparent patterns on white hooks, although they turned out to have problems in use. And from there stretches a long line of experiments, taking us into our own age where the quick impression in a dry fly has often been thought more important than the copy that is photographically correct.

Translucency for Skues meant the broken-edged image of a seal-fur body. But such a solution did not produce the tidy appearance that Halford increasingly valued as he got older. Truly, as Hills acutely remarked, Halford in his enthusiasm seemed to be forgetting the fish. In several of his earlier writings Halford had shown an awareness of the problem of translucency, but he never pursued it to any practical conclusion, and with the New Patterns he put all his effort into getting form and colour correct, even to the extent of including in several of the flies three turns of brown or maroon horse hair to imitate the eyes of the insect. Exact imitation could go no further.

Having referred to the defects of the New Patterns it is only fair to say that these flies were marketed by the trade for nearly half a century and only fell out of favour some years after the Second World War. Later experts like E.W. Harding (1931) and C.F. Walker (1957) said somewhat disdainfully that they never used them and did not know anyone who did, but many beginners, or anglers at a less rarefied level, were happy to have a sort of kit that would carry them through most chalk-stream situations. (There has always been a distinct dividing line between those who like to be told what to do by an authority and those who, having mastered the basic rules, derive their pleasure from making their own experiments.) And these flies undoubtedly caught thousands of fish over the years. Partly this was because so many people used them. Also, as post-Halfordian writers were fond of pointing out, it might have been because chalk-stream trout are often not very difficult to catch anyway.

The public reception of the book was mixed, but there were a large number of reviews (Halford was always good for copy). *The Times Literary Supplement* and *The Athenaeum* were pleased not to have to carry so many flies; *The Spectator* worried about the need for flies of both sexes, and suggested that hermaphrodite flies would save a lot of space; and the *New York Times* wondered why 'so pretty and effective a form of fishing should be so popular in England and so little known in this country'. There was a slight undercurrent of grumbling in some reviews. Even in *The Field* Senior denied that this was the last word on fly-making, as if history might now stop, and referred to the creative work of other seekers ('signs of an independent movement, which might perhaps be summed up as impressionism'). 'John Bickerdyke' in the *Daily Telegraph* distinguished between the select and scientific purists of the dry-fly school and the school of nymph-imitators, 'of which Mr G.E.M. Skues is the distinguished leader', and pointed out that the sub-surface technique presented if anything greater difficulties. *The Academy*, referring to 'the Autocrat at the Waterside', went further: 'Such fishing almost ceases to be a recreation; it becomes in his hands almost a sacred ritual.' Marston had been one of the first to mention this aspect of Halford's work nearly a quarter of a century earlier, when reviewing *Floating Flies* – even at that date he had sensed the terrible earnestness of the new school. Surely fishing was supposed to be fun? The most searching review was from the pen of Skues in *The Fishing Gazette*. He referred to the 'malign influence which has always dogged Mr Halford', preventing him from designing the coloured plates so as to place natural and artificial flies side by side, noted the lack of translucency in the spinners, pointed out that the testing of the effectiveness of the patterns at Mottisfont must have necessarily been inconclusive if only Halford's patterns were used, and proceeded to take issue on a number of fly-tying points. The relationship between the two men, deteriorating for a decade, was now beyond repair, even though at the end of his review Skues rather forlornly expressed the hope that Halford would not take his remarks amiss.

Although he was not likely to admit it in public, Halford did pay heed to Skues' criticism about the need for something more accessible about natural flies. But although he had studied the work of the leading professional entomologists he knew he was not one himself. Martin Mosely came to the rescue and in 1913 began to prepare a book on water flies for the use of anglers as a supplement to Halford's last book, *The Dry Fly Man's Handbook*. Mosely's work was interrupted by the Great War, and *The Dry-Fly Fisherman's Entomology* did not appear until 1921. He went to some trouble to get a skilled artist to colour the plates but is said to have been disappointed with the results. However, the book remained the best thing of its kind until J.R. Harris (1952) and John Goddard (1966).

Some writers about this time were even becoming a little irreverent about Halford and his doctrine. Sheringham had occasionally poked gentle fun at the purists. Halford was probably much more nettled by the writings of William Caine, the angling humourist, whose book *Angler at Large* appeared in 1911, although most of the chapters had already appeared as articles over his *nom de plume* 'W. Quilliam' in *The Field* and elsewhere. Several of them are lampoons on the purists, with provocative titles such as 'The Great Dry Fly Myth'.

Caine, who fished the Salisbury Avon, described the members of an imaginary syndicate: Blennerhassett, a noisy man who marches down the bank and gets in everyone's way, Slattery, described as Fortune's pet, and Chavender, an amiable visitor who catches vast drafts of fishes. There is also a purist, called Purfling. He is first encountered on the bridge:

> I asked if there was any fly showing yet. He replied that he had seen one female *Baetis rhodani*. A suspicion entered my mind. I thanked him for the information, and said that it sounded a rather difficult

> insect to imitate. 'For myself,' I added, 'I generally stick on an Olive Dun here at this time of the morning in May.' He smiled indulgently. 'I see,' he said, 'that I ought to have said Olive Dun.' 'It would have been better,' said I. 'I am no scholar.' . . . My suspicion grew. To make quite sure, I asked, 'Have you done anything yet?' He stiffened. 'There has been no fly,' he replied. . . . Then he went away.

Caine realizes that he has encountered a purist. Later he meets him again. Purfling has been sitting over a trout for an hour. He has made no attempt to fish for it: it has not been rising. A motor coming to collect him is heard in the distance, and he begins to retreat slowly backwards from the area. 'This was not human, but it was Purfling. "My dear man," I cried, "try an alder over your fish before you go." He sighed and went away from me without a single backward look at the water.'

After witnessing this astonishing feat of self-denial Caine is moved to write a dramatized colloquy on the model of Walton called 'Isaac on a Chalk Stream'. In this piece Piscator represents the dry-fly purist and Venator the eager learner. A successful angler on the water at the same time is called Raptor (otherwise a Pot-hunter) and, following the Virgilian style of Walton's dialogue, the keeper is called Corydon. Piscator at first cannot be prised away from the ale-house, assuring Venator that 'the fly will not show before seven minutes after eleven of the clock, at soonest', and calls for another draught of ale (his fourth) from the hostess. When they do arrive the rise is over, and Raptor is leaving the water with his three brace. After a good deal of bungling Piscator hooks a fish. What follows is a direct parody of Halford's advice in such cases (see above, p.187), first published in 1889 and repeated and extended by him several times in print:

> VEN: Have a care, sir; he is for the weeds.
>
> PISC: . . . .
>
> VEN: Oh, sir. What is to be done now?
>
> PISC: Marry, a strong fish; no man alive could have held him; but I have not done with him, scholar. Mark now, how I shall play him with the hand. See, a gentle pull and draw; a steady sawing motion of the arm, and ——
>
> COR: Haw! Haw!
>
> PISC: Corydon, we do not desire your company.

At the end of the day Venator has caught fish; Piscator, after numerous mishaps, has not. From what we know of Halford it seems doubtful that he felt able to appreciate the humour of this and other similar sketches.

On 30 August 1910 Halford left Martin Mosely, who was helping Coxon to cut the weeds, and drove in the trap to Linhay Meads to see his neighbour Mr Walden. Agreement was soon reached, and Halford left having arranged to take another piece of bank for £50 a year. In the last years of his time at Mottisfont he acquired several other small parcels of adjacent water, and there was space and to spare for him and his numerous guests. The quality of the fishing remained high but the nature of it altered a little, with rainbow trout now recorded. There was already an enthusiasm for rainbows in Britain by this date, and the species had become established in many waters – in 1903 a consignment had been put into the lakes at Buckingham Palace. Halford came late to the rainbow but soon appreciated their sporting qualities. Grayling at Mottisfont had declined almost to vanishing point, and in 1913 the grayling column in the journal becomes the rainbow column. In the earlier years twenty or thirty grayling would be caught there, often of good size. In 1907 twelve over two pounds had been recorded, the largest one weighing 3lb 6oz, caught by Arthur Humbert. On 5 April 1910 Halford caught his biggest-ever grayling, weighing 3lb 9oz, but it was not put into a glass case and he never made reference to it in his writings; it may safely be inferred that it was in poor shape. In 1912 only one grayling was caught, and in the autumn of that year the first rainbows were caught. On 26 August 1913 Cecil caught a pretty brace of rainbows. They were not large, but the proud grandfather immediately arranged for them to be set up by Cooper in a case, which still exists. In the same month he presented Cecil with a three-piece rod, made and inscribed by Hardy.

On the morning of 28 May 1913 Halford was on the Main. In earlier years this would have been the height of the mayfly season, but the decline had continued year by year, and by the time of Halford's reign at Mottisfont only a few mayflies would appear, usually ignored by the trout. The best fish at this time were generally taken by the Welshman's Button, and this was the fly he selected to put over a large trout. After a long fight he landed an old male weighing 4lb 3oz. It was twenty-three inches long, and therefore rather past its best. But it was the biggest trout from the fishery during his tenure of it. It was not a record he was going to be able to beat – 1913 was his last season.

10 Halford, Skues and History

The angling careers of Halford and Skues touched at many points, and as time passed the contacts brought little joy to either of them. They have not chosen to tell us much about their relationship, and a good deal has to be guessed. Halford said very little about his attitude to Skues, and in any case was the first to leave the scene. And Skues, although he outlived Halford for decades, made his references within the old-fashioned framework of good form and social convention, and never quite said what he really felt. His unpublished memoir, which exists in typescript at the Fly Fishers' Club, disappointingly fails to enlighten us at all about the two great questions of Skues' life – his relationship with Halford, and the circumstances of his withdrawal in 1938 from the Abbots Barton syndicate.

Skues attitude to Halford has often been discussed as if it was an unvarying thing. In fact his feelings underwent a considerable alteration during their joint lives, and continued to change considerably after Halford's death. At first, like most of his contemporaries, he was a bemused and uncritical admirer of what he felt was an enormous achievement by a great man. *Dry-Fly Fishing*, he thought, contained all that anyone needed to know on the subject, and one's fishing life would be a process of learning and applying on the river all Halford's advice and hints. By the time Halford died, though, the relationship between the two men had deteriorated badly, although there is no sign that the polite veneer of social intercourse was ever breached. With Halford in his grave Skues probably felt freer to pursue his nymph experiments, and his second book, *The Way of a Trout with a Fly* (1921), was received with acclaim. Some years later in 1929 he felt secure enough to write in *The Salmon and Trout Magazine* a magnanimous tribute to Halford (although its beginning was somewhat marred by the erroneous reference to Frederic *Maurice* Halford, a mistake copied by several subsequent writers). In this he made it clear that he thought that Halford's influence was now in the past, and that some at least of his doctrine was being questioned. However, it would be a pity to go too far, wrote Skues, and to reject all of his teaching. At the time Halford was working on fishing problems he was performing an essential service, and his second book was still up-to-date and relevant. The fact that he did not attempt to give the law about other forms of fly fishing was perhaps an advantage: all his energy was thereby focused on the dry fly alone. Towards the end of the piece Skues does, however, remark, with apparent innocence, that Halford would still be famous even if he had written nothing after 1889 – as if he privately thought that it might have been better if he had in fact stopped then. But, read as a whole, the piece was a generous tribute to a man who had caused Skues a good deal of irritation in the past.

Soon after this piece was published things began to change on the chalk streams. Skues had imagined that Halford and his influence had been laid to rest, but, as with Mark Twain, news of the demise turned out to be exaggerated. The 1930s saw a considerable resurgence of Halfordism, as I discuss later, and by the end of the decade Skues was beginning to lose his temper. He would not have written the article of 1929, or anything like it, in 1939. In *Nymph Fishing for Chalk Stream Trout* (1939) he devotes a long passage to what he considered to be the unsightly parts of the Halford edifice. But perhaps the most revealing evidence can be found in Skues' last work *Itchen Memories* (1951), describing his first meeting with Halford in September 1891. Historically interesting, it also deserves close reading as a text, for there is a good deal of quiet fury perceptible not far beneath the surface. Skues hears that the 'great man' – a scornful phrase repeated for emphasis more than once in the piece – is to fish at Abbots Barton and will be staying at the George Hotel. He goes there in the evening to join the group of 'humble listeners'. On the fishery the following day Skues encounters the 'great man' again, who crosses the meadow and accosts Skues and his friend from the other bank 'to advise us kindly' on the fly to put up, casting his own across to them to look at. Skues not only rejects in his mind (though without saying anything) Halford's choice, but is 'shocked' at the coarse gut, and even more shocked on every day throughout the week to have caught more fish than Halford. An earlier reference to this encounter appeared in *Journal of the Fly Fishers' Club* in 1917, and its rather different flavour provides an index of Skues' changing view of Halford: 'We met at the hut about lunch time, and "Detached Badger" asked what I had made of it, and I shall never forget his generous and cordial "Well done!" when I answered "Two and a half brace." 'Whatever may subsequently have happened, the warm afterglow of Halford worship had still been with Skues in 1917.

Some clues as to how the change in the relationship might have come about may, I hope, have already emerged from what I have suggested about Halford's personality. Something more needs to be said now about his adversary.

Skues' formative years at Winchester College may have been important. It was an experience of very striking contrasts. On the one hand, it was a privileged situation unavailable to the vast majority of boys in Great Britain. Winchester was an ancient and famous foundation, housed in venerable buildings in a fair town lying athwart one of the world's great trout streams. It had high scholarly aims, and the teaching programme was thorough and rigorous; the ideal Wykehamist mind was intended to be highly trained and the character reasonable and restrained. In the nineteenth century the College turned out a stream of able administrators, diplomats, soldiers, sailors and churchmen. But the atmosphere, as at many public schools of that era, was rigid and hierarchical. Winchester was described in 1908 as the most conservative institution in the world. For those prepared to go along with the system, who after all may have been the majority, things worked well; but there was always a much smaller group of boys who were not prepared to conform, and Skues fell into this category. In his unpublished memoir he wrote: 'All through my five years at Winchester I was dimly conscious of a pressure to mould me to a pattern, and though I count these five years as the happiest of my life . . . my instinct was to resist the pressure and to retain my individuality.' But there were also other influences. During Skues' time at Winchester the headmaster was the terrific reformer George Ridding, who had fallen on the place like a typhoon, had banished a good deal of the medieval clutter and customs of Winchester life, had pulled down a range of unsuitable and insanitary buildings where fever had flourished, and whose favourite words at a meeting were 'Let's be real!' So Skues had the odd experience of spending his formative years in a traditional school against which he kicked, with a volcanic reformer in charge, whom he may have observed with interest.

There was also another, darker, side to Winchester. Like most public schools, out of schooling hours the place was mainly run by the prefects, who had unchecked powers of corporal punishment. Great reformer as he was, Ridding had left this aspect of the College life undisturbed, and the unfortunate Skues happened to arrive there at a time when this had turned into what can only be called an orgy of sadism, which has been recorded in several other memoirs of Old Wykehamists of the time (see, for example, Sir Charles Oman, *Memories of Victorian Oxford*). Skues relates in his memoir that he was flogged eleven times in his first eight weeks, and in later life was convinced that this had actually affected his growth. Luckily the situation was so completely out of hand that it got into the correspondence columns of *The Times*, where it ran for weeks, and Macpherson – the boy at the centre of the scandal – for a brief season became known all over the British Empire. The headmaster was forced to intervene, and the regime of punishment became more reasonable. Skues, though, remembered Macpherson less as a victim than as a hero, because the following year he caught a trout weighing over 5lb on a Red Quill in nearby Logie Stream. Another lad called Mitchell caught a six-pounder in the Warden's garden. But such triumphs were not for Skues. A scholarship boy with parents far away in India, and with a small allowance of pocket money compared to some of his more fortunate fellows, he flailed his appalling rod and tackle over the world-weary trout of the Old Barge and College Meadow with little effect.

He was to do little with Itchen trout until 1883, some years after he left school, when he was given standing leave to fish above

Winchester at Abbots Barton. The fishing was leased by Irwin Cox, one of the proprietors of *The Field*, and here Skues was to fish for over half a century and develop his forward-thinking ideas. The tale of his early fishing has been told more than once, and I will not repeat it here. An important point is that Skues learnt first to be effective with the dry fly, and only later began to develop an acceptable way of reintroducing the wet fly to the chalk streams. Abbots Barton was a particularly suitable place for sunk-fly experiments. Much of the upper Itchen was of brisk flow, as was the Test, and it was easy for hatching fly to escape from the nymphal envelope and sit on the surface. But the long, impounded length of the main branch at Abbots Barton, with its slow flow and smooth surface, presented a problem of surface tension for the ascending nymph, which would drift down for many yards attempting to break through. On some days trout would be nymphing all morning here – condemning a Halfordian purist to hours of inactivity – whereas at Worthy a few miles upstream a rise to hatched duns of the same species would be in progress.

In these early years Skues, a quiet modest man, seems to have been a little nervous of the great anglers with whom he sometimes shared the fishery. He exchanged a few words with Francis Francis, but regretted all his life not having had the courage to accost George Selwyn Marryat. At times, when Winchester were playing Eton at cricket, he would see the tall familiar figure in the distance, wearing the Tam o' Shanter stuck with flies, but would avoid a meeting.

Irwin Cox had also given Halford leave to fish at Abbots Barton, and Skues was bound to run into him sooner or later. In the late summer of 1889 Halford fished there for six days, one of which was blank, and caught the respectable total of twenty trout weighing 24lb 8oz. He fished there for another five days in 1890 but did not encounter Skues until 1891. As mentioned above, Skues tells us that this meeting was in September, but Halford's journal reveals that on 18 May 1891 he and Skues and Percy Gye the barrister had all been on the water at the same time. (Skues may not have known this.) Halford was always very aware of other anglers on the water, and would record their exploits: on that day the journal says: 'Wet – good hatch from 3 to 4. Gye 2 trout, Skues 2 trout. Fish bulging – iron blue, olive & pale watery.' Halford returned to Abbots

Barton to fish on 4 and 5 September, went the next day to fish the famous salmon pool at Woodmill on the lower Itchen that belonged to Samuel Montagu, then returned to fish at Abbots Barton on 7 and 8 September. His four days fishing produced ten trout weighing 12lb 12oz. The first meeting between Halford and Skues therefore took place on the evening of 4 September. It is a pity not to know more about this curious encounter. Skues has told us enough to enable us to sketch the scene, the rest we have to imagine: the circle of anglers, the whisky and tobacco, Halford, serene and Delphic, handing down small tablets of the law from time to time, and young Skues, a possible ally, perhaps a little deficient in the docility to be expected from junior colleagues but swiftly suppressed ('With some trepidation I ventured to chip in and was duly, but good humouredly, corrected and put in my place'). But Halford was impressed with Skues and offered to put him up for the Fly Fishers' Club. (Skues had only just emerged from a dangerous attack of influenza and was not sure of living much longer and so declined this offer, but when he did join, in 1893, Halford and William Senior were his sponsors.) Thereafter they saw a good deal of each other. Skues' contributions to the angling press at this period show that he was very much under the Halford spell. It would in fact be fair to call him a disciple until the mid-1890s. As his brother C.A.M. Skues wrote in 1950, 'It took him many years to develop that keen power of observation that made him such a master.' He was no doubt delighted to secure one of the much-coveted invitations to Ramsbury, but could only record a series of breakages and lost fish.

In 1897 Skues became a member of the committee of the Fly Fishers' Club (see Appendix 7), which means that he and Halford were even more in each other's company. He took an increasing part in the affairs of the Club, eventually becoming curator of the fly-tying collection. But in that same year Skues began to show his independence by penning the review mentioned in Chapter 8. This review was intended to be even-handed, but it gave out a certain signal. He had been thinking about nymphs since 1889, and in later years he liked to indicate that he had fought a single-handed battle against the doctrine of the dry fly, but the truth was that he was in good company: as I have shown, a number of anglers kept an open mind about wet-fly fishing on the chalk stream. In October 1891

William Senior, feeling perhaps that the dry-fly code was becoming more rigid by the year, wrote a long article in *The Field* called 'Wet Fly on a Chalk Stream', describing success on the Driffield Beck with the method, and quoting the opinion of Lock, the keeper at Abbots Barton, that when there was a strong downstream wind 'your only chance now is to put on a couple of big flies'. This piece produced a response a week later from Skues, at that date a little-known contributor, describing a day of failure turned into success by the use of a half sunk Dark Olive (see Appendix 5). He mentions it at the beginning of *Minor Tactics of the Chalk Stream* (1910) as being an important event, the full significance of which he took some years to appreciate. Skues continued to bombard the journals with ideas about wet flies, so by 1910 *Minor Tactics* did not come as thunder out of a clear sky: readers of *The Field* and *The Fishing Gazette* had known about these ideas for years. In April 1906 Halford published an article in *The Field* once again attacking the wet fly in strong terms, but he set up a straw target: the practice of marching downstream terrorizing the fishery with clumsy across-and-down tactics. He must frequently have read that this was precisely what Skues was *not* advocating; indeed a week later on 21 April Skues wrote once more to praise the technique of casting upstream with a sunk fly. He points out that on days of bright sun and jumpy trout it was in fact *less* likely to scare fish than a dry fly. This was a particularly shrewd stroke, because Halford had been insisting for years that one of the main advantages of the dry fly was that it was more subtle and discreet, whereas the wet fly was intrusive and, by frightening fish, was likely to spoil the fishing for everyone. A year later Sheringham, in a series of articles for beginners in *The Field*, actually recommends the use of wet flies for bulgers. It is not difficult to imagine that Halford must have become alarmed. The purity of his once-revolutionary doctrine was being tinkered with by people whom he must have regarded as unauthorized revisionists. He repeated that he was well aware that trout took underwater food most of the time, but this had no bearing on the question: such food could not be successfully imitated. Let the supporters of the wet fly prove their case on chalk streams. It might work occasionally, he conceded, but only on what he called 'happening days'; in normal conditions such attempts were 'foredoomed'.

By this date, if there had ever been a master and disciple relationship between the two it was long over. There had never been any chance of Skues being asked to fish at Mottisfont. A correspondent called 'Catherlough' wrote in *Journal of the Fly Fishers' Club* in 1937 that on his second visit there he was unwise enough to begin a discussion with his host about Skues and the nymph. After this there was no third invitation, 'and Mottisfont knew me no more'.

Skues differed publicly from Halford on other topics as well. In 1908, in a letter to *The Field* and an article in *The Fishing Gazette*, he took issue over the naming of the Welshman's Button. This had become one of Halford's favourite flies over the years, and was particularly useful in late May and June on waters where the mayfly had declined. By the end of his life (see *The Dry-Fly Man's Handbook*, p.261) he was calling it 'the fly-fisherman's sheet-anchor', a term that in earlier times he had applied to the Red Quill). It was certainly very successful at Mottisfont. Martin Mosely, fishing at the Oakley Hole, a noted place for big fish, captured a trout of 3lb 11oz on a female version of the Welshman's Button, on 11 June 1910. Two days later, using the male version, he caught three more trout of over three pounds in the same place, and lost another heavy fish. It must have been all the more irritating for Halford to read in the press that this cherished pattern was wrongly named, and that, according to Skues, who quoted an alarming weight of historical evidence, the name was more properly applied to a beetle. Halford's response was to insist that all chalk-stream fishermen agreed that the sedge fly *Sericostoma personatum* was called the Welshman's Button. This seems to have been true as far as it went, and years later Martin Mosely (*Journal of the Fly Fisher's Club*, Spring 1939) accepted that it might have originally been a beetle, and that perhaps some visiting fisherman had brought the name from Wales to Hampshire in the middle of the nineteenth century and misapplied it to this sedge fly. As it was now an established and clear identification in Hampshire, whereas the opposition were chaotically unable to agree about which beetle was meant, Mosely suggested leaving things as they were. Anglers elsewhere in Britain must have felt, not for the first time, that undue weight was being given to rulings coming from the chalk stream. And from Halford's point of view, once he had pronounced on a matter, it was settled. By 1908 he was getting impatient with hecklers in the crowd.

Fly nomenclature was far less important to Skues than the wet-fly question. As time passed Halford's plan for the correct tactics on chalk streams was if anything becoming more austere and rigid. The usual reason suggested for this is simply that he was getting older and more set in his ways. As I have suggested in Chapter 6, there could be another explanation, and one that can be seen as more creditable to Halford than has been allowed. The changes in the angling world in the previous two decades, for many of which he had been largely responsible, had been a source of alarm to him for some time. The delight and fascination of the new art of the dry fly had drawn in numbers of anglers, and the Halford–Marryat method – patrolling carefully and quietly, or merely sitting at a vantage point until the rise began, the unobtrusive but deadly attack when conditions became just right, and the sportsmanlike withdrawal after catching a brace or two – did not commend itself to everyone. Club and subscription waters were becoming crowded places, with half-trained newcomers restlessly pacing the banks casting continuously at likely-looking fish or just likely-looking places, using up a great deal of bank space, disturbing the tranquillity of the fishery, catching some fish and educating many more. There were also complaints in the angling press that the new technique could be too effective. On days when there was a long-lasting and general rise, it was suggested, far too many fish could be taken out of the river. Halford must have felt at least partly responsible for things getting out of control. These arguments were to surface again in the nymph debate in 1938.

It is against this background that the appearance in 1910 of *Minor Tactics of the Chalk Stream* needs to be seen. The useful term 'Minor Tactics' had been used by Skues as far back as 1900 as a title for several articles in *The Field*. (These did not deal with sunk flies, but one of them disagreed with Halford's rough method of playing fish: Skues argued that hard-held fish would go to weeds, and that it was sometimes better to master fish by playing them lightly and confusing them.) The book was written at Sheringham's suggestion and had been assembled in part out of previously published material. It was probably the most remarkable book of the twentieth century for the chalk-stream angler, and has been so much discussed that I shall not attempt any detailed dissection of it here. Skues was careful to begin with a respectful tribute to Halford and to *Dry-Fly*

Fishing, calling it the last word on the subject, and proceeded to suggest the sunk-fly alternative merely as an extra skill for the angler when conditions were appropriate. Wet flies were for supplementing, not supplanting, the major tactics of the dry fly. For the most part Skues was proposing the use of small, sparsely dressed wet flies with upright wings in the Scottish style. The coloured frontispiece showed eight examples of these, and only one nymph and several near-nymphs (the Dotterel Hackle and versions of the Tup's Indispensable). But almost as soon as the book had been published Skues began to move away from the winged wet fly to the nymph form, and in December 1911 he published in *The Field* an article on the dressing of nymphs, with the well-known pictures by Captain St Barbe Goldsmith that were afterwards included in *The Way of a Trout with a Fly* (1921). If, therefore, *Minor Tactics* had been delayed a year or two the patterns based on traditional wet-fly forms would have disappeared from the book, and a team of nymphs would have taken their place.

The book's reception was encouraging. In a note to the second edition in 1914 Skues wrote with some astonishment that, in the fifty or so press notices and reviews of the book, no harsh word could be found; indeed some critics had urged him to be more aggressive with the dry-fly purist. Yet it has constantly been stated by later writers that the book caused a storm of protest. *The Field* was friendly and wrote of 'Suggestive trains of thought . . . followed with logical clearness . . . in which the saving grace of humour has a prominent place' and praised the author for avoiding a tone of 'ultra-solemnity'. Marston in *The Fishing Gazette* was cordial but doubted if the dry-fly lobby was capable of being converted; he handed over to E.M. Tod to write a full-length notice, which duly appeared on 2 April 1910. Tod was delighted with the book. He had long been irritable over what he considered the unreasonable pretensions of some south-country fishermen, and now their battle line was breached. His review was long, detailed and favourable – a strong contrast to the review he was to write three years later for Halford's last book.

Halford wrote no review of the book, nor did he make any overt public response. This has led some writers to wonder if he ever saw a copy: an odd, and inherently very unlikely, idea. In any case Halford's own copy of *Minor Tactics* has survived, with Skues' respectful inscription inside: 'F.M. Halford, ex dono G.E.M. Skues, 31st March 1910', and he must have had more than an inkling of its contents from Skues' previously-published articles. Pencil marks are placed against a number of passages, as if he were planning to do a review of it, but generally without any comments. This is in strong contrast to some of the other books in his collection, such as David Foster's *Scientific Angler*, which contain trenchant and peppery comments ('Bosh,' etc.). The impression left of Halford's reading of *Minor Tactics* is one of bemused concentration. The occasional remark is to be found here and there, but only on points of detail. For example, on p.35, against Skues' mention of the freshwater shrimp – a rather risky step in 1910 – Halford wrote: 'Marryat used Gutta Percha tissue for bodies of shrimps.' The only underlining of a passage of any substance was on p.127, where Skues mentions casting a wet fly not only to individual fish but also 'to places where it is reasonable to expect that a fish of suitable proportions may be found'. This again was perhaps a little unwise of him, for to his enemies this would appear to be verging on 'fishing the water'. But in all Halford's annotations there was no attempt at rebutting any of the main arguments of the book.

Halford must have pondered this attack – for however politely expressed, attack it was. The authority who had dominated his constituency for over twenty years and who had been preaching the inutility of the nymph in Hampshire was being addressed by name in a book and informed, in effect, that he was labouring under a delusion. It was probably for this reason that Halford decided to produce another book himself. The angling world was rather surprised. He had made his last bow at the end of *Modern Development*, writing: 'At my age it is scarcely possible that I shall write another book.' Like his fictional contemporary Sherlock Holmes, he was back before his public again three years after his announced withdrawal; and, like Holmes, he was never quite the same again. It is hard to see how *The Dry-Fly Man's Handbook* (1913) can be said to contain much that had not been said before. It purported to squeeze between the covers of one book all that the chalk-stream angler needed to know, including all the latest advances in tackle: a sort of omnium gatherum of all things Halfordian. But, although he does not acknowledge this, its main purpose may well have been to make clear and to shore up his position about the wet fly. Heresy had appeared and there was need for another reproving encyclical to be issued. However misconceived the plan may have been, there is little doubt that Halford thought it important. In July 1912 he wrote to the American author Emlyn Gill apologizing for being remiss in answering his letter, because 'I have been in the throes of arranging, correcting &c all kinds and sorts of matter connected with my new book – which is my *maximum opus*.'

His oblique purpose emerged in the chapter entitled 'The Ethics of the Dry-Fly', an important though oddly-expressed part of the book. He conceded that in the hands of a past master the wet fly is scientific and deadly, and assures his readers, as he had many times before, that 'There is room amongst true sportsmen for the votaries of either style of fly-fishing.' But that did not mean room on the same river; as in his previous writings, the context made it clear that wet-fly fishing was not for chalk streams. And he repeated his opinion that of course fish can be caught from time to time on a sunk fly on what he called 'happening days': in other words, such an event would be a fluke, and not something upon which one could build a new system, as Skues was claiming to do. Tolerance was extended to the wet fly – but only in what he considered to be its proper place. Then followed the famous definition of the ultra-purist, who will never cast except at a rising fish, and the purist, who might occasionally cast at a fish in position though not rising. He then proceeded to attack the same straw target as before: the guest arriving at a fishery where no fish are rising who 'will proceed to the upper limit of the fishery and flog it steadily down with wet-fly'. As Skues and the new school had been careful to explain that they had no intention of advocating such a crude and boring procedure, it is hard to see why this pointless attack was made again – but then the name of Skues never actually appeared in this or any other part of *The Dry-Fly Man's Handbook*. He then turned to the practice of fishing a wet fly blind upstream. Less harmful, admitted Halford, but it still frightened fish, and its exercise required the use of too much water. Finally came the most curious passage of all, which refers to the Skues method and needs to be quoted in full:

> I am told, however, that there is a school of fly fishermen who only fish the sunk fly over a feeding fish or one in position if it will not take

> a floating fly. This, they urge, is a third method of wet-fly fishing, the other two being the more ordinary of *fishing the water* with sunk fly either upstream or downstream. Candidly I have never seen this method in practice, and I have grave doubts as to its efficacy.

'I am told' would suggest to the reader that a vague rumour of the practice had reached his ears, whereas it is clear that he really knew all about it, had read *Minor Tactics* and indeed everything else on the subject in his own journal *The Field* and elsewhere – and, furthermore, had been trying some surreptitious experiments of his own with nymphs. He perhaps gave himself away in the *Handbook* (p.66) when he said that the presence of wings in sunk flies puzzled him – an obvious reference to the Scottish patterns in *Minor Tactics* – because he had never seen winged insects drowned by the action of the stream. (In retrospect, Skues may have felt stung by this, and wished that he had waited until he had developed the more logical nymphal forms before publishing his book.) Somewhat inconsistently, Halford insists on p.126 that he and Marryat had priority in the matter of nymphs, having made 'most effective patterns' years ago: they discontinued their use because 'they were essentially wet-flies' and because they pricked and frightened a number of fish.

The response of the critics was much less friendly on this occasion. Even *The Field*, which called it 'masterly', thought that the passage beginning 'I am told' ought to be expunged from any future edition, adding 'The school of fly fishermen, of which Mr Halford is "told", has had its doctrine admirably expressed by Mr G.E.M. Skues in *Minor Tactics of the Chalk Stream*, a book so familiar to all serious students of the sport that Mr Halford does ill to ignore it so loftily.' Marston, reviewing the book in *The Fishing Gazette*, remarked that 'Mr Halford is rather too much inclined to make a business of what should after all be a recreation'. And he also took exception to the same passage, reminding Halford that he could hardly pretend not to know all about the new and effective methods of Skues. Across the Atlantic, Theodore Gordon wrote to Skues: 'I have been reading Mr Halford's book at night. He is certainly becoming more and more set in his ideas and is so entirely without experience of certain kinds of fly-fishing.' The most savage review of all, and indeed of Halford's entire career, was contained in *The Salmon and Trout Magazine*. It acknowledged the 'sheer supremacy of knowledge and experience', but regretted 'the strange and even embittered intolerance shown in several passages', reminded the author that angling was sport not polemics, and that within reason there should be room for other theories that have stood the test of experience. It also singled out the offending passage, insisting that 'Mr Halford, in that comprehensive knowledge that none deny, must surely have acquainted himself more fully than it would seem with the literature of the subject, and the efficacy of the sunk fly for a rising but reluctant fish in a chalk stream has a host of witnesses, including the angling editor of *The Field*.' A correspondent in *Journal of the Fly Fishers' Club* in January 1913 suggested a public debate: 'I think it might be a good plan if you could work up a really hot discussion on the ethics of dry-fly fishing. A good start could, I think, be made if two such antagonists as D- B- and S- and S-* could be induced to start on Purism *versus* Nymphism.' Nothing came of this idea for another quarter of a century.

It is fair to add that all reviewers praised the main parts of the work, the encyclopaedic coverage of topics, the excellent photographs, many of which Halford had taken himself, and the sections on Blagdon by Sheringham, on sea trout lochs by A.C. Poole and on Loch Arrow by John Henderson. The book was scarcely with the public before *The Fishing Gazette* was able to announce that a translation into French, *Précis de la Pêche à la Mouche Sèche*, had been completed by J.L. Wauthier, which would fill a gap, Albert Petit's book *La Truite de Rivière* being long out of print.

The blots on an otherwise sound book are difficult to understand, and the 'I am told' passage is a strange piece of sophistry for a man usually as intellectually honest as Halford. The only explanation can be that he was seriously shaken by *Minor Tactics* into an uncharacteristic piece of shuffling. In the same year that he was writing this passage his letter to Emlyn Gill quoted earlier contained sentiments that could only be called broadminded and understanding, and in strong contrast to the tone of Chapter III of the *Dry-Fly Man's Handbook*. Gill had suggested that the chalk-stream waiting game might not work well in America. Halford responded:

> It is almost impossible for any one to judge of the methods you recommend to your dry fly men, but where insect life on the surface is scarce

* I.e. 'Detached Badger' and 'Seaforth and Soforth' (Skues' pseudonym for his articles in *The Field*).

> & trout are not often seen *in position* I can quite sympathize with the notion of searching for the feeding fish. Here on the Test we are exceptionally placed. On a favourable day or evening there are clouds of flies on the water & the biggest fish are on the rise. A friend fishing my water killed one on a male Welshman's button dressed on a 2 hook weighing 3lb 14oz.*

As we have seen, Halford's approach was to consider a problem, conduct a series of experiments, sometimes at inordinate length, and then arrive at an immovable conclusion, as if fly-fishing was a branch of Euclidean geometry. The attitude of Skues was as different as could be imagined, so it is not surprising that their separate programmes were irreconcilable. For him the problems of angling were for discussion as much as solution; the possibility of the final answer was an illusion (and, if attainable, would make fishing boring), and the concept of knowledge as a moving frontier was much more interesting. But he was thorough as well. Being law-trained he was accustomed to master the detail of a case, and, if attacked, to be tenacious of points. Lawyers are also used to looking for precedents from past cases, and a solicitor who dealt in real property would spend much of his time in investigating title to land.

His training therefore gave Skues a sense of the importance of the past. His encyclopaedic articles on the history of fly patterns and other aspects of tackle and practice began in 1900 and were to continue to the end of his life. He spent long hours in the Reading Room of the British Museum burrowing back into the old-time authors to establish profitable lines of thought. He also had a much wider experience of other rivers than Halford – who, as we have seen, made only brief and discouraging experiments on traditional wet-fly streams and only once fished outside the British Isles. Skues knew the same chalk streams as Halford and one or two that he did not, such as the Wey, the Tillingbourne, the Pang and the Darenth. He had also fished the Teme, the Okement, the Lyme, the Derbyshire Wye, the Manifold, the Ure, the Coquet, the South Esk and the Tweed. And he had fished in France, Germany, Bosnia, Norway and Sweden. He was thus much more conscious both of historical development and of geographical variation.

Halford, by contrast, was only interested in the here and now: the

* Caught by Dr Wallis Jonas on 12 June 1912 (journal).

chalk stream in his own time. He seems to have had little curiosity about the past, and almost never quotes from the old angling authors, except Ronalds and Francis Francis. In some respects he resembled the men of the Renaissance, who were carried away by the achievement of their own age and despised their medieval predecessors, doubting if anything valuable could have been achieved by them. The absence of literary allusion in Halford's work has led some later authors to imagine that he knew little of earlier workers in the field. J.W. Hills (without any evidence to show) says airily, 'I do not imagine that he read many books on fishing.' In fact, as Max Walbran had been able to observe in 1893, Halford had an excellent library of books: he just did not rely on them in the same way. As a revolutionary, he wished to break with the past, not study it. He was too busy establishing his own system – or perhaps he wished it to appear to be *sui generis* – to be interested in history. Some small part of his library survives with his great-grandson, John Halford; the rest was dispersed many years ago, and no doubt individual volumes still exist in private hands. A complete list would be interesting.

In some respects there were resemblances between the two men. Halford has been accused of excessive attention to detail and of being too much in love with the complexity of the subject. But Skues was hardly less so. Donald Overfield has identified eighty-two patterns, dry and wet, of his invention. The nymphs, in particular the 1939 series, follow the Halfordian principle of being as precise as possible. 'Exact imitation' lives on!

In the years after Halford's death Skues' work made slow progress. It is not quite true, as James Robb suggested, that *Minor Tactics* 'put an end to the dry fly purist and brought the angling world back to sanity'. Not all at once, anyhow – the reality is much more complex. Skues' first book was not a *coup de grâce*: it is better seen as an entering wedge that only took effect with time. Some open-minded anglers responded quickly to it. J.W. Hills was giving nymphs a trial at Ramsbury in 1914, and by the 1920s there were more owners and clubs on chalk streams prepared to give a cautious welcome to the nymph. The atmosphere of the period was favourable to a new idea. A distaste for authoritarian pre-1914 systems and dogmas was evident in art-forms, music and literature; it was the age of Lytton Strachey, of mocking eminent Victorians and of the new term 'debunking'. In 1926 Sir George Aston in *Letters to Young Fly Fishers* wrote that nymph fishing was 'an art now practised by most dry-fly anglers'. In 1927 the Piscatorial Society allowed nymphs and other clubs followed suit, often restricting their use to the period after 1 July. In 1929, in *Trout Fishing from All Angles*, an authoritative book in the Lonsdale Library of Sport, Eric Taverner wrote of his experience of sunk-fly fishing on the Wylye – and, moreover, of casting across and down, which would not meet with approval there today.

But Halfordism was not dead, and it had a surprisingly vigorous revival in the 1930s, for some anglers had never been quite happy about Skues and his nymphs. Dr A.C. Kent, the editor of the *Journal of the Fly Fishers' Club* and once a frequent guest at Mottisfont, commented warningly on Sir George Aston's passage quoted above: 'This is interesting, but we fancy there are many fishing the Test who do not yet practice the subaqueous art.' If Skues thought that his doctrine was now safely established, the events of the next decade must have undeceived him. In the early 1930s members of the Fly Fishers' Club found their *Journal* increasingly occupied with contributions on the subject. Many of these were by Skues himself, either under his own name or under some newly-coined pseudonym to add to his already extensive repertoire, and were intended to prepare the ground for the conflict he knew was approaching. The counter-attack developed from the winter of 1936. The skirmishing continued up to the date of the famous nymph debate of February 1938 at the Fly Fishers' Club, where a number of papers were presented and addresses made. One of the Halford camp, Sir Joseph Ball, came forward to present the case for the now long-dead leader of the purists. Ball was a barrister and a frequent contributor of angling articles to the *Daily Mail*; at that date he had a fishery at Kimbridge, though he later he moved to the Town Mill at Ramsbury, once the headquarters of the Halford partnership. He was determined to traverse all the recent points made by Skues in articles in the *Journal* and elsewhere, and to uphold the exclusive use of the dry fly on chalk streams. The debate was extensively (but unfortunately not completely) reported in the Spring number of the *Journal* and reprinted by Donald Overfield in *G.E.M. Skues: The Way of a Man with a Trout* (1977). It is of considerable length and I can only comment upon it here.

Twenty-four years after his death, Halford's influence was strongly present at the meeting, but the arguments of some of his followers deserve perhaps a little better than the wholesale condemnation they have subsequently received. And it is worthwhile to wonder sympathetically what it was that the anti-nymph lobby were so alarmed about.

The chief protagonists, Skues and Sir Joseph Ball, engaged in a long contest on points, some of them rather pettifogging. At times it resembled a dispute between two medieval schoolmen over how many angels could dance on a pinhead. The question of whether nymphs swim actively up to the surface, as Halford and Marryat thought, or whether they floated up in an inert condition, perhaps buoyed up by some form of integumental gas, must appear to us now as of minuscule importance. It may be true, as Marryat once remarked, that you could imitate the nymph but not the wriggle, but, after all, trout are still prepared to take artificial nymphs, wriggling or not.

More important was the argument that, if all anglers could be trusted to fish the nymph in the Skues manner, all would be well. However, the practice, it was suggested, lent itself to abuse, and anglers less well-informed (or less well-disposed) would soon be fishing across and down, perhaps with large silver-bodied flies, scaring fish and spoiling fisheries; hammering of every fish in sight would be a temptation, and rivers would become decimated. Dr J.C. Mottram – who had described a series of nymphs of his own invention in *Fly-fishing: Some New Arts and Mysteries* (1913), and who as recently as 1935 had published an article advocating the use of nymphs (including leaded patterns) – had suddenly changed sides and appeared against Skues at the debate. Nymph fishing, he now believed, resulted in catching undersized fish. There was a distinct feeling at the meeting in favour of Halfordian restraint, that one need not be fishing continuously throughout a day on the river, and that if fish declined to rise it would be better to leave them alone. The rules on the chalk stream, it was argued, were there to make a fair contest between angler and fish, and also to avoid spoiling things for one's fellow anglers. As Major T.T. Phelps put it: 'What was best for the other man?' Perhaps it was easier for men like Tommy Phelps and Joseph Ball, who had their own fisheries and could choose their own times, to advocate such self-denial. (In his charming book *Fishing Dreams* (1950) Phelps mentions allowing serving members of the armed forces to fish on his water on the lower Itchen during the Second World War, but not to use nymphs. Some, he thought, might be trusted to use the nymph legitimately, but many of his visitors were beginners or knew nothing of chalk streams.)

Of the two men who might have given vigorous support to Skues one, J.W. Hills, does not appear to have intervened very decisively (unless he was inadequately reported), and of the other, Dr E.A. Barton, there was no sign at all. Skues must have left the meeting feeling very bruised. Just as Halford had once subsided deeper into ultra-purism in an attempt to put a brake on the pelting and harrying with the dry fly that he realized had become so common, so Skues felt he had to deal with a similar trend in his own day. He therefore set to work to write a guide book that would leave anglers no excuse for ignorance about legitimate nymph techniques and patterns. A year later *Nymph Fishing for Chalk Stream Trout* (1939) was published.

In other ways, too, 1938 was a bad year for Skues. The ghost of Halford, which had been present at the debate at the Club, still seemed to pursue him. The other members of the syndicate at Abbots Barton were probably a little jealous of such a consistently successful angler in their midst. His chief opponent was the barrister Gavin Simonds, a Wykehamist of a younger vintage, later Viscount Simonds and Lord Chancellor from 1951 to 1954. Simonds objected to what he considered an excessive use of the nymph by Skues. And it was Simonds who established a stew at Abbots Barton in 1937. Neville Bostock, another member at Abbots Barton, defended the stocking of this once-wild fishery: 'Skues was dead against stocking, as the wild fish were so fine in quality. But the water was hard fished and gradually and surely there were less and less fish to be seen in the stretch, until at last it was hard to find a rising fish.'

At the end of 1938 Skues, no doubt with a heavy heart, withdrew from the syndicate and from the water he had fished since 1883. He went to live at Barford St Martin in Wiltshire, where he could fish the river Nadder, an interesting stream of its type, but not to be compared with the Itchen. In July 1940 he went to Winchester to watch the annual cricket match against Eton, and afterwards walked over to talk to the keeper and see the scene of his former triumphs. He wrote sadly to his friend C.A.N. Wauton: 'It was a lovely day and a beautiful lot of trout were lying out, mostly under the far bank and sucking in nymphs voluptuously. It made me realize what I had given up.' It may be that the Simonds family felt a little conscience-stricken at the old man's withdrawal, for they made a great fuss of him when he returned as a guest for a day in June 1942. He lived on until 1949, but he was never to find comparable fishing again.

Epilogue

The golden glow of the Edwardian summer afternoon still persisted. To some it may have seemed that it would go on for ever. In fact the shadows were lengthening over the stream, though perhaps mercifully men did not know it. The season of 1913 was a success, and Halford and his friends did well. He spent his days receiving and helping guests, without fishing much himself. The note 'I only fished evening' becomes frequent in the journal. In August he developed an abscess caused by an uncut wisdom tooth and returned to London ('Had to lay up and consult Bartlett'). He was away for a fortnight for treatment and recovery, returning on 23 August. Fishing for brown trout had gone very quiet, but he stayed on until the autumn to fish for the smallish rainbow trout that were now to be found all over the Oakley Stream. His last fish of the season, indeed of his career, was a rainbow trout of 1lb 2oz. He handed over the fishery to the faithful Coxon and returned to London.

Early in the New Year he withdrew abroad. It had been his habit for some years to escape the English winter and to stay in resorts on the Riviera, or in Andalucia or North Africa. Here he would take a number of photographs, a hobby he had taken up in the late 1890s and, with his usual energy, thoroughly mastered. More recently he had begun to experiment with the new 'Autochrome' colour process. This was expensive and therefore suitable for the wealthy amateur, but the results were good, better in fact than many later processes. Halford's Autochrome glass plates survive, stored in handsome mahogany boxes. Many of his black-and-white pictures also still exist, in a series of albums finely bound in plum or green morocco.

These show that he went to Spain in 1908, to Pontresina in 1909, to Egypt in 1910, to Biskra in 1911, and to Spain again in 1912 with Bertie Browne. They capture life on shipboard, entering harbours, street scenes and the palm-shaded gardens of comfortable hotels in the usual resorts of the Edwardian well-to-do. Europeans on decorous outings are formally dressed, and the women wear improbable hats. Halford appears to have been more casual in his dress than the others – one photograph shows him on a camel at the Pyramids wearing his customary fishing hat. One album includes a caricature, the work of a local artist, that depicts him scurrying by at great speed with his camera. Clearly relaxing in a shady place with a novel was not to Halford's taste: holidays were for active pursuits.

In 1914* he stayed at the Hotel Majestic in Tunis (the capital of what was then a French protectorate), accompanied by Ernest. Connie, who usually came on these trips, stayed in England. Halford spent the time in photography, while Ernest improved his tennis game. They left Tunis on 24 February on the *Duc de Bragance* bound for Marseilles, described later by Senior as a 'wretched boat'. The two-day trip was stormy, and most of the passengers retired unhappily to their cabins. Halford, however, had always been a good sailor and was the only passenger aboard capable of appearing at meal times. At Marseilles Ernest left to go to Paris on a business trip, and Halford boarded the P&O liner *Morea*, which sailed at 10 a.m. on 28 February; he took his last photographs at Marseilles that morning. Soon after the ship passed Gibraltar he fell ill. At first it seemed no more than a feverish cold, but it turned to pneumonia, and his condition rapidly became serious. As the boat neared the English Channel a wireless telegram was sent ahead to alert the family. Ernest, by then back in London, with Connie, Bertie Browne and the family doctor hastened down to Plymouth by the midnight train and were able to get on board a tender going out to meet the ship. They had been planning to take him ashore to a nursing home near Plymouth, but on seeing him they realized that there was no chance of that. As the *Morea* steamed along the Channel Halford's condition worsened, and he died in the afternoon of 5 March 1914, as the ship came up the Thames into Tilbury Docks.

* The following is in part based on William Senior's account in *The Field*, reprinted in *Lines in Pleasant Places* (1920), pp.143–45.

The funeral followed rapidly afterwards, in accordance with Jewish custom, and few of his friends could be assembled in time. The family were there, and William Senior. Dick Coxon, who only a few days before had been getting the fishery ready for his employer, also stood by the graveside.

The suddenness of Halford's death astonished the angling world. *The Fishing Gazette* and the Fly Fishers' Club only knew of it the day after the funeral – to the regret of Marston, who would otherwise have represented both at the service. The tributes began to pour in. The family 'In Memoriam' book, which included as many published notices as could be found, runs to twenty-one pages, and includes contributions from every conceivable paper. Even the *Jewish Chronicle*, not normally known for its coverage of fly-fishing topics, did its best. Senior, in *The Field* mourned the death of a friend as well as a colleague. Halford, he wrote, had been an uncommon type, the sort of man 'you can respect, admire, and trust; and should you know him well enough, you can add your love without being foolish.' Perhaps of his surviving friends Senior had been closer to him than anyone. He continued:

> He was a delightful companion – generous, big-hearted, amusing, a sayer of good things in a human way, and finely opinionated, which, of course, was not a serious matter when he expected and liked you to be opinionated also. He was a dangerous man to tackle in an argument if your knowledge of the subject was rickety. He was emphatically what is termed a well-informed man, for that thoroughness of his stamped his knowledge and ruled his memory. You could not always agree with him, but could seldom floor him, the ground he stood upon being rock-solid. As both a giver and taker of chaff he was an adept. He had the courage of his opinions, and none wiser than he when it was best to keep his opinions an unknown quantity. In travelling or by the waterside he was wonderfully helpful if help was good for you – perhaps, if anything, too helpful, though I cannot conceive a more pardonable fault than that.

Dr A.C. Kent, in the *Journal of the Fly Fishers' Club*, wrote: 'By what is really a life's work, Halford has raised fly fishing for trout, both as a sport and as a scientific pursuit, to a higher level than it has ever before attained, and by so doing has made fly fishing a better and more absorbing recreation for us all.' In *The Fishing Gazette* Marston wrote a little more soberly and judiciously. He had known Halford since the 1880s but was not a close friend. He had, as we have seen, disagreed with him on a major issue and had always thought it his duty as an even-handed editor to tell his readers so; this frankness may not have been to Halford's taste (at any rate Marston, who had fished a good deal with Halford in earlier days, had never been invited to Mottisfont). He paid tribute to Halford's committee work at the Fly Fishers' Club and to his 'pleasant, courteous, tactful and able manner', and regretted that he had been 'obliged to criticize one or two things in the last book he published – in which he, as I think, and said, unfairly condemned the work of another writer, Mr G.E.M. Skues, author of "Minor Tactics on Chalk Streams" [sic]. My criticism was not nearly so severe as other papers on this point.' His reference of course was to the damaging review of 1913 in *The Salmon and Trout Magazine*, which journal's obituary of Halford added at this inappropriate time several more unkind comments on his intolerance and inflexibility, though it concluded by saying that 'what he did for angling is almost beyond computation'. The local paper in Hampshire, the *Romsey Advertiser*, dwelt on his generous support of local organizations and his acts of charity, including the establishing of a soup kitchen in the village during the hard winter of 1912. At Mottisfont church the following Sunday the vicar remembered Halford's popularity in the village, adding: 'Though not belonging to our communion he never let his opinions separate him from close intercourse with his neighbours, but he always treated their convictions with the same respect as his own.'

The family decided to carry on with Mottisfont and continued to fish it well into the 1920s. The journal shows that 1914 was a good season, producing 114 trout weighing 180lb. Cecil, still at school at Clifton College in Bristol, did well in the holidays, catching a number of fish including several rainbow trout, which were now getting much larger. One of his rainbows, a grown-on fish that had been some time in the river, weighed 4lb 2oz and was caught on a Coachman. Ernest, now in charge of the journal, wrote: 'Cecil killed the big fish, a rainbow in perfect condition, in the rough above the bunny* & took it down to Broad's farm where Bobby landed it.'

* A Hampshire term for a small culvert.

Senior and John Henderson came to stay with Ernest for three days in early May. Olives and iron blues hatched, and the party did well – their combined bag included four two-pounders – but their evening conversations must have been full of sad regrets.

During the Great War and for long afterwards the fine fair summer of 1914 remained as a poignant memory, at least for those who survived. Perhaps Halford was fortunate to die when he did, so being spared from living on to witness that great human tragedy, and into an era afterwards which he would not have sympathized with or understood.

One by one the chief actors in the piece made their exits. Marryat, Day and Leech had died years before, and T.J. Mann had died on his steam yacht in 1898. T.P. Hawksley, Basil Field and Walter Pope all died in 1908, and Major Turle in January 1909. One February day in 1909, in spite of the warnings of a friend standing by, Max Walbran waded into the swollen river Ure and was swept to his death – a curious as well as a sad accident, some commented, for no one knew northern spate rivers better than Walbran, and he was always warning others of their power in winter. The same river had nearly killed him in 1886.

Samuel Montagu the banker, 'the fastest calculator in the City', was made Lord Swaythling in 1907 and died four years later, at the age of seventy-nine, at his house in Kensington Palace Gardens. Although at one time a member of the Houghton Fly Fishing Club and a close friend of Marryat, he had really been more interested in salmon fishing. A year later, in September 1912, Dr Wickham died at the age of eighty. His later fishing had mainly been on the upper Test.

Major Carlisle had left the Test valley in 1898 to live on the other side of Winchester at Chandler's Ford, though still within reach of the Itchen. He seems to have fished less and less, though; his last day of trout fishing was at West Drayton on the Middlesex Colne in 1910. His means did not allow him to make a seasonal migration southwards each year, as Halford was able to do, and he found the countryside dull in winter and would make excuses to slip away to his London club from time to time. In 1913 and 1914 he published several pieces of reminiscence in *The Field* on chalk-stream fishing in what he humorously referred to as the barbarous and unregenerate days before the dry-fly revolution, and in the *Journal of the Fly Fishers' Club* about his voyages under canvas to and from the East. But he was now in his eighties, and the impressive physique that had carried him through the fatigues and horrors of campaigning in India was beginning to break down. At times he had to apologize to correspondents for being slow in responding to their letters, the pain of bending over his writing desk being too acute. He died in December 1915, within a week of his eighty-sixth birthday. William Senior, by now one of the few who could remember the fishing world of the 1860s and 1870s, wrote Carlisle's obituary with a heavy heart, calling him 'a universal favourite' and remembering again the fishing at Houghton and the good talk on long-ago evenings. Carlisle was not a purist, wrote Senior, nor was he one of your over-eager fishermen: he had a relaxed and sauntering style, and his chief pleasure was to put a friend on to a likely fish.

Senior himself survived the Great War, dying in 1921 shortly after the publication of his last book, *Lines in Pleasant Places*. Sheringham died too soon in 1930, at the age of 54, followed a year later by Dr Tom Sanctuary at Kirby Misperton on the River Costa, where he had been fishing since 1893. His extraordinary fishing diary spans the years 1875 to 1930, although a number of years are not recorded. He did not maintain the remarkable catch levels of the earlier years – in 1875 he had caught 833 trout – but in forty-eight seasons he accounted for 4,752 trout and 2,921 grayling. Nathaniel Lloyd died in 1933, after a distinguished career as an author and practitioner in the field of architecture. Once regarded as one of the most skilful dry-fly fishermen in England, he had abandoned fishing in favour of golf, at which he also became adept. In 1905, twelve years after first meeting her in May 1893, he had married Daisy Field. Daisy retained her love of gardening all her life and lived to a great age, dying in 1972. H.S. Hall, the odd card in the pack, who might have been the dominant influence in the early days of the dry fly, died in 1934. He had retired in 1900, having made substantial money from writing text books for schools, in particular the standard algebra. Latterly he succumbed to the lure of Blagdon Lake and was seldom seen on the chalk streams.

Although some of the Halfordian followers, such as Arthur Gilbey, lived on for a few more years, with Hall died the last main link with the revolution of the dry fly. G.E.M. Skues, an entirely different sort of innovator, survived into a lonely old age in a Wiltshire hotel, dying in 1949.

Appendix 1

Halford's Annual Catches: 1879–1913

Year	Trout			Grayling			Largest Trout		Largest Grayling		Rivers
	No.	lb	oz	No.	lb	oz	lb	oz	lb	oz	
1879	50	41	10	38	32	5	2	12	1	14	Test, Itchen, Wandle, Misbourne, Kennet, Wharfe, Nidd, Rye, Laver
1880	33	50	11	62	91	0	3	7	3	2	Test, Anton, Wick, Wandle
1881	48	80	1	44	58	1	3	12	2	12	Test, Anton, Wick, Wandle, Newchurch (I.O.W)
1882	64	103	5	42	49	7	3	8	2	6	Test, Wick
1883	42	52	4	59	78	11	2	8	2	12	Test, Wick, Evan (Moffat), Annan
1884	77	127	7	83	104	2	4	4	3	5	Test, Anton, Wick, Wylye
1885	35	60	5	123	168	8	3	6	2	12	Test, Wylye, Hampshire Avon
1886	80	150	8	50	77	3	4	9	2	12	Test, Kennet, Hampshire Avon, Wylye
1887	34	69	4	27	48	11	4	2	2	14	Test
1888	20	38	13	38	46	0	3	4	2	13	Test
1889	89	111	15	3	4	5	4	2	2	0	Itchen, Test
1890	52	63	6	5	6	10	2	15	2	12	Itchen, Test
1891	105	123	5	10	11	14	2	10	3	0	Itchen, Test, Anton, Wey (Surrey), Colne, Wharfe, Driffield Beck, Costa
1892	39	64	1	12	21	2	4	3	3	3	Test, Anton, Wey (Surrey), Wylye, Kennet
1893	115	172	14	–	–	–	2	11	–	–	Kennet, Anton
1894	61	95	4	–	–	–	3	6	–	–	Kennet, Misbourne
1895	84	121	14	7	7	12	2	8	1	11	Kennet, Ilm (Weimar), Anton, Colne, Wylye, Itchen
1896	48	67	8	2	5	4	2	5	2	12	Kennet, Test
1897	40	48	4	14	13	4	2	9	2	7	Test, Itchen, Derwent (Derbyshire)
1898*	46*	69	2	3	1	15	2	6	Not stated		Test, Itchen, Frome (Dorset), Wylye
1899	32	52	7	3	6	10	2	13	2	15	Test, Itchen, Frome (Dorset)
1900	19	34	5	–	–	–	2	14	–	–	Test
1901	14	23	10	–	–	–	2	2	–	–	Test, Itchen
1902†	100†	121	15	8	13	4	2	1	2	0	Itchen, Test, Candover Brook, Dever, Grange Lake (rainbows)
1903	62	87	4	3	6	0	2	6	2	4	Itchen, Test, Candover Brook

APPENDIX 1

Year	Trout			Grayling			Largest Trout		Largest Grayling		Rivers
	No.	lb	oz	No.	lb	oz	lb	oz	lb	oz	
1904	180	221	5	1	1	5	3	7	1	5	Itchen, Test
1905	52	105	10	13	22	14	3	7	2	4	Test, Itchen
1906	59	116	3	25	45	9	3	14	2	14	Test
1907	88	168	3	16	27	9	3	10	2	8	Test
1908	92	160	15	26	37	4	3	1	2	7	Test
1909	89	148	5	17	27	0	3	3	2	13	Test
1910	102	179	10	3	5	11	3	10	3	9	Test
1911	97	156	6	–	–	–	3	0	–	–	Test
1912	79	127	3	1	1	8	3	0	1	8	Test
1913‡	81‡	167	3	–	–	–	4	3	–	–	Test

* Includes 3 seatrout, largest 5lb 4oz, † includes 35 rainbow trout, ‡ includes 26 rainbow trout.

Appendix 2

An early contribution by Halford in *The Field*, 20 December 1879 (he did not adopt the pseudonym of 'Detached Badger' until 1885). 'South-West' had reported catching forty-one trout weighing 77lb 3oz.

THE TEST

SIR, – Your able correspondent 'South West' has given a very full description of the result of his season's sport on the Houghton Club water, and, being anxious to compare the bag of a non-resident member with his, I have just made up my diary.

I find from it that I fished on twenty-eight days, or parts of days, and killed sixteen trout weighing 23lb. 15oz., and twenty-four grayling weighing 27lb. 12 oz.

Of the trout, six were killed with Grannum [sic]; five with Drake's Extractor, three with Blue Quill Gnat, one with Little Tempter, and one with Silver Sedge.

Of the grayling, eleven were killed with Blue Quill Gnat, seven with Silver Sedge, four with Drake's Extractor, one with Red Quill Gnat, and one with Wickham's Fancy.

In addition to the above, fifteen trout were returned as under the prescribed limit of size, and forty-two grayling; of the latter, at least twenty were above 11in. in length.

The water has certainly been wonderfully improved, and the increase in the number of fish should be a source of gratification to the proprietor, and an inducement to continue his efforts in turning in young fry. As regards the limits of size, the 12in. for trout should be retained; but with respect to the grayling, it is, in my opinion, very questionable whether it should not be reduced from the present standard of 13in. to one of 11in.

So large a proportion as forty-two grayling returned out of a total of sixty-six indicates that two thirds of the rising fish are unsizeable. If the grayling are allowed to increase so rapidly, the result must infallibly be that the trout will be gradually driven out of the lower part of the water.

F.M.H.

Appendix 3

From *The Fishing Gazette*, 28 June 1884:

WHO INVENTED DRY-FLY FISHING?

SIR, – I believe the late James Ogden, of Cheltenham, claimed to have been the inventor of the dry-fly system, but I expect it is a case of evolution, and that the first man who threw a dry fly is lost to fame, *caret quia vate sacro*.* I see your correspondent, 'Hampshire', saw me cast twenty-eight yards of line with a single-handed rod; it was not measured, and if I were you I should reel in about six yards two feet eleven inches and three quarters, or you will raise 'Merry Nell' at the forthcoming FISHING GAZETTE Tournament on July 26, unless I come and do it, or burst a little gut trying to do it. I have just been staying at Houghton Mill. I fished one evening at Piddlesworth,† and got a brace of fish and two great silly dace that hadn't as much judgement as not to rise like grayling, and so met a dry death. I don't hanker after fishing a single blank in hay fields; docks is cusses, and thistles is blisphemy, and all fishermen's recording angels have to be double-baulked in hay time. Who might 'Hampshire' be, if it is not a breach of etiquette to say?

– I am, &c.,

GEO. I. MARRYAT‡

[We must leave 'Hampshire' to make himself known to Mr. Marryat, if he cares to do so. We can fully sympathise with Mr. Marryat and the exasperating state casting from a hay field induces in all but angels. Last Monday we had a fair dose of this form of hay fever. You can see a fish rise just on the edge of the weeds, say within an easy cast up stream, fifteen yards perhaps. You kneel down and creep as near the water as possible to get free of over-hanging green things. Two or three flutters of the fly to dry it, then a nice back cast, and with your eye intent on the feeding place, you make the forward cast. Everything goes nicely until you have got full steam up, and then – bang – your fly has got round a slender but tough bit of rye grass, or the red scale-like flowers of the dock. On such an occasion the best thing to do is to set your teeth well into the screw of your whisky flask and take a solar observation, remember the 'World's' advice as to what to say, and repeat 'Godfrey Daniel's blast and furnace works' until relieved. Repeat it to the farmer if he asks you why you don't walk 'all over the field.' – ED.]

* The Latin quotation is not absolutely correct (viz *carent* for *caret*). The passage is from *Horace Odes* IV, 9, line 25 *et seq*. In full it runs:

> Vixere fortes ante Agamemnona
> Multi: sed omnes illacrimabiles
> Urgentur ignotique longa
> Nocte, carent quia vate sacro.

['Many heroes lived before Agamemnon, but they are unmourned and unknown, lost in darkness because they lack a dedicated poet.' The sense is that the early hero of the dry fly is lost to us for want of a written description.]

† Piddlesworth = Pittleworth, near Mottisfont.
‡ This should, of course, be Geo. S. Marryat, a mistake due to his handwriting.

Appendix 4

From *The Field*, 5 August 1882:

FLY-TYING ON EYED HOOKS

SIR, – In reply to a request by Mr Hobbs in last week's *Field*, I send a few hints about fly-making on eyed hooks. As there are still many different opinions in vogue as to what an artificial fly should represent – whether it is to be a monstrosity of the angler's invention, or a close imitation of a natural insect – I may as well state at once that I have very little faith in what Kingsley calls 'casualty flies', and for trout fishing in southern streams I depend almost entirely on a knowledge of entomology, and the use of the most life-like and skilful imitations that I can get. This being premised, it follows that I do not pretend to have reduced fly-tying to a uniform system, which will suit under all circumstances for every fly alike. Duns and spinners, alders and sedges, black gnats and midges, bumbles and palmers, all present little peculiarities of their own, about which no definite rules can be laid down, and a method of tying which suits one kind of fly in every detail, requires judicious modification when it is applied to the imitation of an insect of a totally different species. But if a man has thoroughly mastered the dressing of one class of flies, his own common sense and ingenuity will do the rest, and will be more valuable than any written instructions. My present remarks, therefore, will be limited to an attempt to describe a method which makes a good floating fly of the ephemeral class – one which shall be very durable, and at the same time fairly neat in appearance, and which, if properly thrown, will alight with wings erect, and float down attractively over the rising fish.

Take a No. 0 hook, and three or four turns of well-waxed silk up to the eye, and two turns back again; this is merely a substratum on which to tie the wings without danger of their slipping round the shank of the hook. Place the hook in the vice, and, to keep the tying silk taut, twirl it two or three times round the screw-head. This is a useful dodge, which I use constantly, to avoid unnecessary half hitches. Then pick out a starling's feather, and strip off all the fluffy part at the quill end up to where the fibres of the feather are pretty nearly of one length. Mark off with the dubbing needle a nice even strip of about half an inch in width, pull the fibre gently back with the forefinger and thumb of the right hand, till they all stand even and at right angles to the quill; then, with a smart twitch, pull the slip off. Go through this process again, and put the second slip evenly on top of the former. Fold the double slip down the middle, and you then have a compact quadruple slip, about a quarter of an inch wide, or rather less when the stray and errant fibres have been discarded. Take the wings in the finger and thumb of the left hand and apply them to the hook, with the butt end towards the bend of the hook, and the soft fibrous extremities projecting over the eye, while the silk is fastened tightly round once or twice with the right hand. Then the wings are pulled back into the natural position, and three or four turns of silk made in front between the feather and the eye. The wings are then divided with a needle, and the silk passed between them once, then round the hook, and through again to the front. The silk thus forms a cross between the wings on top of the thorax. Then take the hackle, and tie it in by the butt between the wings and the eye; leave it there to finish off with. Snip away the greater part of the refuse at the butt end of the wing feather, leaving enough to tie down and slightly taper the body. Put in the whisks, body silk, quill, or dubbing, and carry the tying silk up to the wings, and take a half hitch. This, it will be noticed, is the first knot which is necessary. Follow up with the body and finish it off. Lastly, with the tip of the hackle in the tweezers, take one whole turn in front of the wings, then between, round, and back, making a figure of eight knot with the hackle, just as before with the silk. Fasten off behind the wings with a couple of half hitches, trim off stray fibres and hackle points, and the fly is finished.

If the fly is wanted for fishing wet, I should put only half as much feather on, and omit the figure of eight between the wings.

Perhaps Mr Hobbs will say my method is very elaborate, but it is really extremely simple, and rapid in execution; and, of all the methods I have tried, this makes the most killing fly, though not perhaps the neatest. Anyone who considers excessive neatness the first desideratum will have to pick his two wings separately from right and left feathers' and indulge in all sorts of niceties, which may result in a very pretty fly-book, but the flies will not float so well, and will not kill so well – that, at least, is my experience.

I puzzled out fly-making for myself, without any hints from anyone. After making two or three hundred flies, I made the acquaintance of two other amateur fly dressers, with whom I compared notes frequently during the last two or three years, and to whom I am indebted for several wrinkles. Beyond this, I never had a lesson in fly-making in my life; and I have never so much as seen a professional fly-dresser at work, so that I must ask Mr Hobbs and any other readers of this letter to take it for what it is worth, and be indulgent in their criticism. Still, I have proved beyond a doubt that for duns and spinners the method I have described makes an admirable fly. So well satisfied am I with the results this year, that I think it is extremely improbable that I shall ever adopt any other style.

If Mr Hobbs will send me his address through *The Field* office, I shall be glad some day to send him a few pattern flies; though, as I am away from home, I cannot promise them for the next fortnight or so.

H.S. Hall

Appendix 5

From *The Field*, 10 October 1891:

WET FLY ON CHALK STREAMS

SIR, – I read the article on this subject with great interest. I tried the wet fly this year on the Itchen, on a blazing day, under the following circumstances. The river was covered with smuts, and there was a small pale watery dun coming down. The fish, however, were only taking a smut here and there. There was scarcely a breath of wind. In a corner, however, where many dead carcases of flies drifted, I saw a single half-hatched, big dark olive. I tried the fish first with pale watery dun, then with small pink Wickham, then with smuts, and then with blue quill, but all in vain. Then, about one o'clock, it occurred to me to try a half-sunk big dark olive. The fish had almost ceased rising, but the smut was still on in myriads. I picked out a fish, soaked my fly well, and put it to him without drying. He sucked it down and I killed him. Between one and three o'clock I landed four and a half brace, but had to return three of them; they were all taken on the half-sunk big dark olive. There was no hatch of the fly till next day. I coaxed up the contents of the stomachs of some of the fish, and found they consisted of nothing but a mass of smuts, not a trace of an olive of any sort.

I have tried old Lock's advice on a windy day on a chalk stream, with the wind down stream, but seldom did any good. I generally found it better to do my best to cut across under the wind and fish the rises. I have, however, seen a brace of small coch-y-bondhus, mounted and fished wet on the 'chuck-and-chance-it' principle, account for six brace on such a day when the dry fly was hopelessly out of it. Old Lock usually recommended a big hare's ear and a Wickham's Fancy in

> the spring for this kind of fishing. I never tried a north country hackled fly on a chalk stream, but see no reason why such a fly should not succeed at times when the natural insect is either knocked down by wind or rain, or when the fish are taking larvae.
>
> VAL CONSEN

This is the occasion referred to by Skues in *Minor Tactics of the Chalk Stream* (1910), p.2, as being his first experience of the effectiveness of a sunk fly on the Itchen. He mistakenly thought that the occasion was in 1892.

It is curious that he calls himself 'Val Conson' (misread as 'Val Consen' by the Editor). That pseudonym was normally used for his contribution to *The Fishing Gazette*. (It is an example of the shorthand of the lawyers' office for 'Valuable Consideration', a term normally used in writing out abstracts of title in conveyancing.) The pseudonym usually used by Skues for his writings in *The Field* was 'Seaforth and Soforth'.

Appendix 6

From *The Field*, 30 December 1893:

THE DRY FLY FISHERMAN'S WIFE

SIR, – Not that I wish to be thought otherwise than very proud of being the wife of a dry fly fisherman, but, as in all great positions, there is something of disadvantage to regret in mine. It is one with which some lady readers of the *Field* will, I think thoroughly sympathise. At the approach of Christmas especially, I thank heaven, I have a large circle of friends and acquaintances, and, of course, have to return the visits they are kind enough to pay me; yet I wish I could go to their houses like any ordinary individual, and talk on the subjects ladies are usually considered to be fond of – servants, children, dress, scandal, and so forth. But alas, no! There is little chance of any of this for me. The moment I appear I become the cynosure of much curiosity, and all the ordinary subjects of conversation are at once tabooed for the extraordinary love of discussing my husband and his fishing. Sometimes I cunningly determine not to make my appearance till rather late, so that tea may be in high flood, and that then, perhaps, I shall not excite so much attention. But my manoeuvre is quite ineffectual. In truth, I am becoming so resigned to my fate that I meditate astonishing some fashionable physician by consulting him on an absolutely new disease – nothing short of exhaustion, caused by cross-examination on my husband's fishing.

The reader does not quite realise what kind of cross-questioning I mean. Let me, therefore, present a couple of reminiscences of afternoon visiting. I start, say at three, and make up my mind for an interview without the distraction of tea. I find several visitors already assembled, and after enquiries as to my health, the regulation formula commences with:

'How is your husband?' 'Quite well, thanks.'

'Fishing?' 'No.'

'Why not?' 'He does not fish in the winter.' (Chorus of 'Oh!' varied by 'Why not?')

'There is no trout fishing,' I calmly respond. 'No! and when does it commence again?' 'About the beginning of April.'

'I suppose you fish?' 'No, I am not clever enough.' (With great scorn): 'Not clever enough? well, I do not think it requires much cleverness to fish; what do you say?'

The visitors reply in a breath: 'Of course not; we all fish, and it's such fun seeing a float bob up and down, and pulling out nice big fish.'

'Oh,' I answer, with an air of lofty superiority, 'that is not at all the fishing my husband goes in for; he does not sit in a boat.' (Chorus of 'Oh!' and ejaculations of 'Not sit in a boat?') 'No he walks about and wades.'

'What does that mean?' 'It means wearing indiarubber stockings and walking in the water through difficult places.' (Chorus of giggles): 'We should not like that.'

Mistress of the house: 'Well, there is one comfort attaching to it, in the out-of-the-way places your husband goes to; you always have fish to eat.' 'Oh, no, we don't.'

'Why not?' 'We don't like trout.' (Chorus of 'Oh, really now.')

Hostess: 'Well, all I can say is, that I do not think it is worth the trouble of wading through the water, getting your death of cold, and probably laying up a stock of gout and rheumatism for the future, to catch fish you do not like. What do you all say?'

Loud chorus of 'No' from the congregation.

I rise now and say, 'Well, I shall send my husband round to defend himself,' and put an end to this pleasing interview.

Let it now be remarked, *en parenthèse*, that I am often bitterly reproached at home for never hearing any news, or knowing anything that is going on. Ye gods! How can I know anything? My whole time is taken up in defending dry fly fishing and its votaries. The day comes, however, when I feel in rather better spirits, for there is a new engagement to discuss, and there is influenza about again, prolific no doubt of some interesting cases of suffering amongst mutual friends. For once my fishing husband and I may surely retire to the background. But the fates, as usual, are against me, and my hostess is alone and ready for the fray. The old, old questions are propounded, and then Mr Lockwood (I mean the lady of the house), begins quite a new line of cross-examination. I have just answered the question 'Why don't you fish?' and am rapidly approaching a state of hypnotism which would have been greatly appreciated by Mr Kennedy, when she said 'Does your husband fish in London?' I revive somewhat, and, checking a desire to say 'Yes, in the bath-room,' manage to collect my thoughts and answer gravely, 'He cannot very well do so anywhere near home, as unfortunately they do not allow fishing in the Serpentine.'

She receives this piece of news quite seriously, and then I feel glad to fly to tea; for, in truth, I am getting rather hysterical.

These are only samples of my visiting life, and I am writing, Mr Editor, to ask you to help me. Could you not give me a printed form of questions and answer (such as specialists use); then on entering a house I would present it to the lady, and say, 'all information respecting fishing is contained here.' This would, to some extent, meet my case, and I could happily retire into insignificance, and have no borrowed greatness thrust upon me. As it is, I often ask myself, 'Shall I ever be compensated, even in a future state, for what I undergo here?'

And it seems to me that if I could persuade one of those dear genii of olden times to transform me into a trout, I would try to make my brethren even more difficult to catch than they are at present; and, whilst discussing on their days at home the bright chalk-stream water and Mayfly sandwiches, I would tell them of all I have suffered in civilised circles on land. When we heard one of our old friends crawling about, and trying to throw the dry fly in the latest and most scientific fashion, I would say, 'Lo, let us disappoint him; we will rise and, exciting his wildest hopes, refuse with scorn his tempting lure.' Gracefully disappearing, we could leave him to the, to him, by no means novel reflection that the education of trout is quite up to date, and far superior to his own.

VICTIM WIFE

Appendix 7

Fly Fishers' Club: Committee in 1897

President of the Club and Chairman of Committee for the Year,
R.B. Marston

R.C. Blundell
Reg. E. Booker
John Brunton MA MD
M. Burnett
C.H. Cook
Henry Ffennell
Basil Field (ex-President)
Arthur N. Gilbey
Frederic M. Halford
T.P. Hawksley
T.J. Hodson
W. Pingo Horton
N. Lloyd
R.B. Marston (*The Fishing Gazette*)
Lieut.-Col H. Murray
Hedley F. Norris
G.H. Orton MB
J.T.P. Pechey
Arthur Price
Wm. Senior
G.E.M. Skues
W. Thomas

Hon. Treasurer: R.B. Marston
Hon. Secretary: D. Wilson
Bankers: Messrs Coutts & Co., 59 Strand

Bibliography and Sources

As I have mentioned earlier Halford was not in the habit of keeping correspondence. In June 1932 when Otto Kienbusch, President of the Angler's Club of New York, enquired of the Halford family about the survival of family letters, he was told there was almost nothing. Halford seems to have had no intention of revealing himself to posterity if he could help it, save through his published writings. This sort of thing is fairly common with certain types of cautious and self-protecting people; Freud boasted that he had destroyed all his earlier papers in order to throw future biographers off the track. The main Halford items still extant are accounts of his income and expenditure, his book of press cuttings, the family In Memoriam book of his obituary notices, and, most important of all, his angling records. These exist in three volumes covering the period 1879 to 1913, and are described in this book as the journal. There is also a separate log recording the catches of all rods and guests on the Ramsbury fishery, and a book detailing its management. Apart from these scant literary remains, some of Halford's rods and tackle still survive, also several glass-cased fish and a number of photographs.

The fishing journal of Dr Sanctuary, covering the period 1875 to 1931, is a valuable supplementary source. Diaries and letters from the families of Field and Lloyd, including several Marryat letters, have helped to broaden the general picture in the 1890s. Papers relating to Williamson's negotiation for a new lease at St Cross are in the Hampshire Record Office, and for the Ramsbury tenancy in the Wiltshire Record Office. Otherwise materials in local record offices appear not to be numerous. No doubt items exist in private hands which I have not discovered. The unpublished memoir of G.E.M. Skues, 'Trivialities of a Long Life', contains much that is interesting.

The old volumes of *The Field*, *The Fishing Gazette*, *The Journal of the Fly Fishers' Club*, *The Transactions of the Fly Fishers' Club 1885–1910* and *Baily's Magazine of Sports and Pastimes* are essential reading for anyone investigating the angling world before the First World War.

Printed Works

(Place of publication London unless otherwise stated)

Aldam, W.H., *A Quaint Treatise on 'Flees, and the Art a Artyfichall Flee Making'* (1876)

Angler's Notebook and Naturalist's Record (1880)

Aston, Sir George, *Letters to Young Fly Fishers* (1926)

Bainbridge, G.C., *The Fly Fisher's Guide* (4th ed., 1840)

Barrington, C.G., *Seventy Years' Fishing* (1906)

Beazley, David, 'The Saga of the "Snecky Limerick"', *The Journal of the Fly Fishers' Club* (Summer and Winter 1995)

Bergman, Ray, *Just Fishing* (1933)

Bingham, Charles, *Chalk Stream Salmon and Trout Fishing* (1993)

——*The River Test* (1990)

Blacker, William, *The Art of Fly Making* (1855)

Bucknall, Geoffrey, *The Bright Stream of Memory* (1997)

Buxton, Sidney, *Fishing and Shooting* (1902)

Cadman, Henry, *Harry Druidale, Fisherman from Manxland to England* (1898)

Caine, William, *An Angler at Large* (1911)

Chapman, S., 'The Innovating Entrepreneurs in the British Ready-Made Clothing Industry', *Textile History* 24, no. 1 (1993)

Cholmondeley-Pennell, H.C., *The Modern Practical Angler* (1870)

—— (ed.), *Fishing: Salmon and Trout* (5th edn, 1889)

Cook, C.H. ('John Bickerdyke'), *The Book of the All-Round Angler* (1888)

Dewar, G.A.B., *The Book of the Dry Fly* (1897)

—— *The South Country Trout Streams* (1898)

Durnford, Richard, *The Diary of a Test Fisherman 1809–1819* (1911)

Eaton, A.E., *Revisional Monograph of Recent Ephemeridae or Mayflies* (1883)

Englefield, James ('Red Quill'), *Dry-Fly Fishing for Trout and Grayling* (1908)

Fisher, A.T., *Rod and River or Fly Fishing for Salmon, Trout and Grayling* (1892)

Foster, David, *The Scientific Angler* (1882)

Francis, Francis, *Angling Reminiscences* (1887)

—— *A Book on Angling* (1867)

—— *The Practical Management of Fisheries* (1883)
—— *Sporting Sketches* (1878)
Gill, Emlyn M., *Practical Dry-fly Fishing* (New York, 1912)
Gingrich, Arnold, *The Fishing in Print* (New York, 1974)
Goddard, John, *Trout Fly Recognition* (1966)
Granby, Marquess of, *The Trout* (1898)
Gray, Hilda Orchardson, *The Life of Sir William Quiller Orchardson R.A.* (1931)
Greene, Harry Plunket, *Where the Bright Waters Meet* (1924)
Grey, Edward, *Fly Fishing* (1899)
Haggard, H. Rider, *Rural England* (1903)
Halford, F.M., *An Angler's Autobiography* (1903)
—— *Dry-Fly Entomology* (1897)
—— *Dry-Fly Fishing in Theory and Practice* (1889)
—— *The Dry-Fly Man's Handbook* (1913)
—— *Floating Flies and How to Dress Them* (1886)
—— *Making a Fishery* (1895)
—— *Modern Development of the Dry Fly* (1910)
Hamilton, Edward, *The Riverside Naturalist* (1890)
Harding, E.W. *The Flyfisher and the Trout's Point of View* (1931)
Harris, J.R., *An Angler's Entomology* (1952)
Highley, Samuel, *Where to Fish Round London* (1880)
Hills, John Waller, *A History of Fly Fishing for Trout* (1921)
—— *My Sporting Life* (1936)
—— *River Keeper* (1934)
—— *A Summer on the Test* (2nd edn, 1930)
Horsley, Terence, *Fishing for Salmon and Trout* (1944)
Hutchinson, Horace, *A Fellowship of Anglers* (1925)
—— (ed.), *Fishing* (1904) 2 vols
Jackson, J., *The Practical Fly-Fisher* (1854)
Jacques, D., *Fisherman's Fly and Other Studies* (1965)
Jones, E.L., *Seasons and Prices* (1964)
Keene, J. Harrington, *Fishing Tackle: Its Materials and Manufacture* (1886)
Lawrie, W.H., *A Reference Book of English Trout Flies* (1967)
Lipman, V.D., *A History of the Jews in Britain since 1858* (1961)
Maas, Jeremy, *Victorian Painters* (1969)
Macdonald, John (ed.), *The Complete Fly Fisherman: The Notes and Letters of T. Gordon* (1949)
McLachlan, R., *A Monographic Revision and Synopsis of the Trichoptera of the European Fauna* (1884)

Marinaro, Vincent, *A Modern Dry-Fly Code* (New York, 1950)
Maxwell, Sir Herbert (ed.), *Chronicles of the Houghton Club, 1822–1908* (1908)
Migel, Michael, *The Masters on the Dry Fly* (Philadelphia, 1977)
Mingay, G.E., *The Victorian Countryside* (1981)
Mosely, Martin E., *The Dry-Fly Fisherman's Entomology* (1921)
Mottram, J.C. *Fly Fishing: Some New Arts and Mysteries* (1913)
—— *Thoughts on Angling* (n.d.)
Ogden, James, *Ogden on Fly Tying* (Cheltenham, 1879)
Oman, Charles, *Memories of Victorian Oxford* (1941)
Orwin, C.S. and Whetham, E.H., *History of British Agriculture 1846–1914* (1964)
Overfield, T. Donald, *Famous Flies and Their Originators* (1972)
—— *G.E.M. Skues: The Way of a Man with a Trout* (1977)
Page, R.B. (ed.), *Further Chronicles of the Houghton Club 1908–1932* (1932)
Pain, C. Ernest, *Fifty Years on the Test* (1934)
Petit, G.-Albert, *La Truite de Rivière* (Paris, 1897)
Phelps, T.T., *Fishing Dreams* (1949)
Pictet, F.J., *Histoire Naturelle des Insectes Neuroptéres* (Geneva, 1843)
The Book of the Piscatorial Society 1836–1936 (1936)
Pollins, Harold, *Economic History of the Jews in England* (1982)
Powell, T.A., *Here and There a Lusty Trout* (1947)
Pritt, T.E., *Yorkshire Trout Flies* (Leeds, 1885)
Reynolds, W.F.R., *Angling Conclusions* (1947)
Robb, James, *Notable Angling Literature* (n.d.)
Roberts, John, *The Collins Illustrated Dictionary of Trout Flies* (1995)
Robson, Kenneth (ed.), *The Essential G.E.M. Skues* (1998)
Ronalds, Alfred, *The Fly-Fisher's Entomology* (1836)
Rose, R.N., *The Field, 1853–1953* (1953)
Roth, Cecil, *The Rise of Provincial Jewry* (1950)
Schullery, Paul, *American Fly Fishing: A History* (New York, 1987)
Senior, William, *Lines in Pleasant Places* (1920)
Shaw, Fred G., *The Science of Dry Fly Fishing and Spinning* (1907)
Skues, G.E.M., *Itchen Memories* (1951)
—— *Minor Tactics of the Chalk Stream* (1910)
—— *Nymph Fishing for Chalk Stream Trout* (1939)
—— *Side-Lines, Side-Lights and Reflections* (1932)
—— *Silk, Fur and Feather* (1950)
—— *The Way of a Trout with a Fly* (1921)
Smythe, P.M., *The Diary of an All-Round Angler* (1956)

Stewart, W.C., *The Practical Angler* (1857)

Taverner, Eric, *Trout Fishing from all Angles* (1929)

Thomas, Terry, *Casting* (1960)

Thompson, F.M.L., *English Landed Society in the Nineteenth Century* (1963)

Tod, E.M., *Wet-Fly Fishing Treated Methodically* (1903)

Usher, H.J.K. *et al.*, *An Angel without Wings: The History of University College School 1830–1980* (1981)

Venables, Bernard, *Fishing* (1953)

Verrall, G.H., *A List of British Diptera* (1888)

Walbran, F.M., *Grayling and how to Catch Them* (Scarborough, 1895)

Walker, C.E., *Old Flies in New Dresses* (1898)

Walker, C.F. (ed.), *The Angling Letters of G.E.M. Skues* (1956)

—— *Chalk Stream Flies* (1953)

—— *Fly-Tying as an Art* (1957)

West, Leonard, *The Natural Trout Fly and its Imitation* (1912)

Williams, A. Courtney, *A Dictionary of Trout Flies* (1949)

—— *Angling Diversions* (n.d.)

Wolf, Lucien, *Essays in Jewish History* (1934)

Index

INDEX